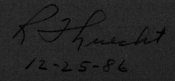

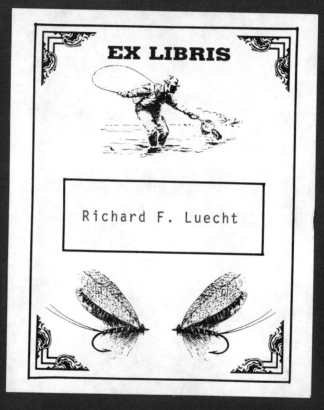

EX LIBRIS

Richard F. Luecht

Imitations of the Trout's World

Imitations of the Trout's World

Bob Church &
Peter Gathercole

THE CROWOOD PRESS

First published in 1985 by
THE CROWOOD PRESS
Crowood House, Ramsbury
Marlborough
Wiltshire SN8 2HE, UK

British Library Cataloguing in Publication Data

Church, Bob
   Imitations of the trout's world.
   1. Trout fishing   2. Flies
   I. Title   II. Gathercole, Peter
   799.1′755   SH448

ISBN 0–946284–75–X

Acknowledgements

To Jeanette Taylor for typing the final manuscript. Also to John
Wilshaw, Editor of *Trout Fisherman Magazine* for editing the
finished manuscript and allowing us to use ideas and line
drawings originally used in our articles. To the Irish Tourist
Board for the picture of the massive brown trout from Mask.
To John Goddard for the Caenis pictures. To Oxford
Scientific Films for the Daphnia picture. To Dr Nick Giles for
advice and help in collecting specimens.

We dedicate this book to all trout fly fishers.

Photoset by Kelly Typesetting Ltd, Bradford-on-Avon, Wiltshire
Printed in Hungary

Contents

Preface

Twenty years or so ago I looked to experienced fly fishers such as Cyril Inwood, Norman Bryan and Dick Shrive for guidance. Mind you, they didn't always tell me a lot. Sometimes as a joke they even misled me as to what fly, line or area was the best to try.

Norman brought me through those early days but it soon became clear to me that the men to study were Cyril and Dick. They caught more trout than the rest and each fished and favoured different styles of approach.

Gradually things fell into place and I started to catch a good number of trout, leading up to my best year in 1982 with a total of 747. To be honest there is no substitute for experience. You may get older and slow down but this is offset by knowing just what to do at the right time.

If you are one of those anglers who still holds a post-mortem with your fishing pal on the way home about lack of success then this book is for you.

I met Peter Gathercole some seven years ago and was impressed by his fly tying skills and detailed neatness. A few years on Peter was matching results with the best of them, and had become established as one of our leading professional fly dressers. Peter started to study ento-mology and has mastered the art of photographing these tiny creatures.

Whilst fishing I asked Peter if he would like to join me in a new book. I soon realised that between us we had all the knowledge to produce something of great interest to beginner and skilled fly fisher alike.

Our aims are to teach fly dressing to beginners and to improve the technique for average fly tyers by showing a number of advanced methods. Then comes the message of the book, studying links between the natural creatures which trout feed on, then matching them with artificials. To make the actual fishing techniques more interesting we relate factual instances experienced at top waters all over Great Britain and Ireland.

For the fly fisher competent at catching trout on his own creations, there is nothing better than trying out the ideas of another successful angler. We cover some unusual patterns and developments, describing them in detail so you can try them out for yourself. All of these patterns have been well proved by their inventors and ourselves.

Finally, I am sure you are now all in the mood to perhaps visit some of the famous waters we have fished. We give a detailed insight into them, showing maps, hotspots, methods and tackle. I began by saying that there is nothing like experience and I stand by that. If you study this book carefully and digest it well, it could be worth up to twenty years' experience and that can't be bad.

Bob Church

Foreword

Combine the undoubted skills of our best known fly fisher and that of master insect photographer and fly dresser and we have a book that's been long overdue.

Angling books of calibre are scarce, most new volumes, with notable exceptions, being little more than a going over of old ground offering little of any significance to the knowledge hungry modern fly fisher.

This book, thankfully, does not follow this well beaten path, taking as it does anglers with relatively scant experience a good way down the road to success.

After dealing simply yet comprehensively with most of the most common fly dressing materials it then uses the patterns described through a series of fishing situations staged at a large number of stillwaters in England, Scotland and Ireland. This section will provide hope for all of us who are stumped with what Bob and Peter have cogently dealt with as situations of cause and solution.

Peter's work on the chapters detailing the links between the natural insect and the choosing of the correct artificial pattern are no less than we have come to expect.

John Wilshaw
Editor, *Trout Fisherman Magazine*

FLY TYING INSTRUCTION

1 Tools

In the past the only aids to the fly dresser were his own fingers plus perhaps a pair of scissors and a dubbing needle. Now the list is by no means so restricted, as a glimpse through the pages of any popular material catalogues illustrates.

This profusion of tools can be a bugbear. For this reason we are only going to mention those which we feel as professional fly dressers are absolutely necessary. This does not mean that we shall be sticking to the traditional tools, on the contrary as there are many modern gadgets which prove of immense value. Unfortunately there are many which have been manufactured simply to provide the inexperienced with something new to buy.

There are many types of vice on the market, of which most are adequate for the task they are asked to perform. For instance, for tying small flies up to about a Size 10, a simple collet chuck type vice is quite sufficient. If on the other hand you hope to tie large flies and lures, then a more robust model will be required to hold the hook firm and to prevent it from moving about unduly. Models to cope with these larger hooks include the collet type, but this time incorporating a large knurled wheel at the rear to enable the jaws to be tightened adequately, and the lever operated vices. This last type is best for tying all types of fly except perhaps very large salmon flies. These lever operated vices work on a double cam lever principle and will grip even large lure hooks, something that the top quality collet types sometimes fail to do.

Scissors are perhaps the next most important item. Although it is possible to cope with just one pair, it is an advantage to have at least a couple of pairs. There are quite a few different types although we have never really been able to see the point of having both curved and bent types. If you do decide on two pairs then you will find that it pays to keep one pair with fine sharp points for all the delicate work such as cutting silk and hackles, and a more robust pair for cutting quills and wire. One thing we must add is that as you become more proficient you will find that many materials can be pulled or twisted off rather than trimmed with scissors.

Next, to hackle pliers. All we can ask from a pair is that the jaws actually meet properly and don't cut the hackle, and that they have a hole large enough to insert the index finger for winding. A great deal of anguish can be caused by a bad pair. Either they slip just as you have completed the winding of a tricky hackle or worse still, snip through the hackle stalk so that you either have to use less hackle or even select a new one. We prefer two types, the traditional short nose model for general work, and a modern type, called the Ezee which is superb for all the tiny hackles used on the minute dry flies which are becoming more and more popular.

Although some traditionalists may say they are not really a necessity, we would never be without a bobbin holder, in particular a spigot bobbin holder. For those who don't know, a spigot bobbin holder consists of two sprung metal arms which grip the bobbin between them and a tube through which the silk is fed. With bobbin holders silk waste is kept to a minimum, and the weight of the holder keeps a good tension on the silk ensuring that the materials already tied in do not unwind. As with most other tools it is false economy to buy a cheap one because these usually wear out rather quickly. You will also find that a holder with flared ends is the best because their smooth trumpet shape prevents the tying silk cutting at awkward moments.

We are including the whip finish tool because some tyers find it an absolute necessity. We prefer to whip finish by hand and after some experience we are sure you will too. The tool is a simple affair, consisting of a thin

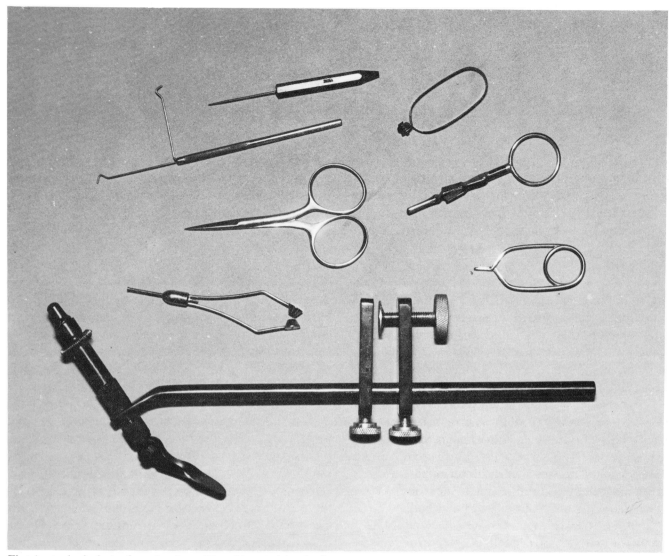

Fly tying tools clockwise from vice; Lever Vice with material spring in place. Spigot Bobbin Holder. Scissors. Whip Finish Tool. Dubbing Needle. Soft Jawed Hackle Pliers. Spring Loaded Hackle Pliers. Serrated Jawed Hackle Pliers.

tapered metal rod with a hook on the end, with a short length of wire with another hook coming off at an angle of between 45 and 90 degrees a third of the way down the rod.

One small item well worth buying is a material spring. It is only a simple little device which fits around the collar of the vice and holds any spare materials out of the way prior to winding on. It really is a great help as it prevents tinsel, silk and such from twisting together as they invariably do the moment they touch.

Lastly a set of three differing size wing cutters can be a help for preparing synthetic wings. You can do without

hackle guards, dubbing teasers, dubbing twisters, hair stackers and such. They tend to waste more time than they save. A dubbing needle is of course a great necessity but a pack of large sewing needles is cheaper and better. We find it pays to be practical about fly tying and if any job can be done better with the fingers then do it. Rather than being the relatively simple craft it is, fly tying is becoming more like brain surgery with the myriad of tools and materials now available. It is only our opinion of course but we believe that the better the fly tyer the fewer tools he uses rather than the reverse.

2 Modern materials

For the greater part, the materials we use in dressing our artificials are procured from various animals and birds, usually as a by-product from the fashion and fur trades.

Typical materials include hair from the squirrel and deer and feathers from such birds as pheasants and domestic poultry, the latter being mainly the neck feathers known to the fly dresser as hackles. Wool in various colours and the fur from seals are also essential parts of the fly dresser's stocks. These natural fibres have been joined in recent times by a host of artificial materials with many of the characteristics of natural fibres such as hair and wool.

During the past decade or so we have even seen some of our more inventive tyers employing some of the more modern plastics in a never-ending effort to produce even more life-like imitations. Of these materials perhaps the most talked about has been latex, though being rubber it is not in the strictest sense a man-made product. Latex has the great advantage of being soft yet tough, perfect for forming wonderfully life-like segmented bodies. It is particularly good for forming fairly bulky bodies such as those of the sedges. It also has the added advantage of being easily coloured with a felt tip pen providing the fly dresser with infinite colour variations in his patterns.

A further spin-off on the quest for the perfect segmented body is a material known under the trade name of Swannundaze. Unlike latex this was designed specifically with the fly dresser in mind. It is though a rather hard material, too hard in our opinion to be used on its own and it is far more effective when used as a ribbing over a softer substance such as seal's fur.

On the artificial hair side, much experimentation has been done to achieve the translucent properties once provided by polar bear hair which is now no longer available. Tyers have even used the hair from a child's dolls and very successful the flies were too. A stranded material called Fishair is available and, although it will never replace squirrel hair and bucktail, it does have certain advantages over natural hair, the main one being that because it is man-made, it can be produced easily and cheaply in a tremendous variety of colours and in fluorescent shades, something not too easy to obtain in natural hair.

Although not really now a modern material, it is probably the nylon threads that have been the greatest boon to the fly dresser in general. They are much stronger for their diameter than silk. This allows many more turns to be used creating a stronger better dressed fly. For our own fly tying we now use these threads almost exclusively in both pre-waxed and unwaxed forms. They give all the strength and durability required of a tying thread. Fine nylon threads have been especially made for tying tiny flies right down to Size 26s.

Of all the modern man-made fibres, the most versatile has to be polypropylene. Its most common use has been that of a dubbing material blended to imitate the translucent properties of seal fur, although there does seem to have been a degree of overkill to this end. When it comes to the new modern dubbing materials, there are a vast array of them all performing virtually the same function.

Polypropylene has also been used to a fair extent in the creation of new forms of winging, particularly in the case of the dry fly. The main benefit of polypropylene is that it is relatively buoyant and so is ideal for the dressing of dry flies and especially the spinner patterns which have no hackle and wings to support the weight of the hook. For winging, it is available in both a yarn and a sheet form, the yarn being used in much the same way as is a bunch of hackle fibres when tying a spent wing. The sheet is cut with wing cutters to form a life-like copy of the natural wing.

Another modern advance available to the fly dresser is the range of waterproof marker pens. These come in a dazzling variety of colours and are an immense help especially to the amateur who finds it a bind to mix a dye bath when he wants an unusual colour. The pens are particularly good when used in conjunction with latex which is never an easy material to colour with conventional dyes at the best of times.

Some materials, though not exactly new, are being used in new and exciting ways. One in this category is marabou. Although used as a winging material, the fluffy feather has been with us for quite a while now (Appetizer Lure 1972), it is only over the last two or three years that it has been put to new uses. One of these is as a body material, dubbed on in a similar way to seal's fur, the effect giving the appearance of moving gill filaments when picked out a little on a nymph imitation. Another material that falls into this same group is chenille, again although not exactly a new material, it has been developed in both texture and design, so that the latest kinds have tinsel wound through them or have mixed colours to give them a more natural effect. Some are very fine both in diameter and texture, the best of these being the sueded chenilles which have a much tighter and finer texture than the conventional type. This enables them to be used for tying even very fine patterns such as nymphs and buzzers which were totally out of the question with ordinary chenille.

3 Personal techniques

When the budding fly dresser first becomes proficient in his new art he strives not only to improve the quality and neatness of his flies but also tends to copy the efforts of his more masterful contemporaries in the hope of emulating them. This is a path followed by anyone learning a craft or skill for we all need a target to aim for if we are ever to improve. It is only when the fly dresser has fully mastered the basic fly tying techniques that he can form his own personal style or technique.

Every really good fly tyer has his own style. It only needs a glance at the flies tied by different people to realise that no one ties a fly exactly identical to the next man. After a while it is quite easily possible to identify a certain tyer's flies simply by the distinctive style. Even though most fly dressers stick to a basic set of proportions when they tie a fly, there is still room to experiment when it comes to deciding where and under what circumstances the fly is to be used. Take for instance a typical wet fly such as a Peter Ross. Not only is this a good reservoir pattern, but it is also a top class sea trout fly. Although in each case the basic materials and tying techniques are identical, the way in which those materials are employed is altered to suit the conditions under which the flies are ultimately going to be tested.

In the case of the fly to be used on the reservoir, the dressing should be quite sleek and relatively sparse. The wing should not be too bulky and should be tied to lie low along the hook shank. In all, the general appearance should be of something quite light with the ability to sink quickly below the surface even in calm conditions. On the other hand, the sea trout version will be used on a river where the strong current will force the wing back along the shank of the hook and the flow of the river acting on the line will easily pull the fly below the surface. For these reasons the pattern needs to be a good deal more bulky than the reservoir dressing, with the wing using a fair bit more teal flank feather and set at a greater angle to the hook shank. Likewise the hackle should be a good deal heavier and tied in at a less acute angle than that on the reservoir pattern.

So you can see that technique, although a personal thing, does have a practical use, but at the same time it should not be made a scapegoat for sloppy tying. We like to tie our flies as neatly as possible and use little wrinkles picked up over the years to help us to do this with the minimum of fuss.

Using scissors too often as some sort of cure-all is a particularly bad habit which should be avoided if at all possible. It is far easier and a lot less time consuming to apply the materials properly in the first place than to mess about trying to remedy the problem by heavy pruning. If a dubbed body sticks out all over the place, simply remove it and try again; you will be the better fly tyer for it in the long run. Likewise if a hackle is too long, remove it and use one of the correct length. After the whip finish if you snap the silk off with a smart tug you will find that the end springs back out of sight beneath the whip finish rather than leaving an unsightly cut end.

It always seems such a pity that whilst many dressers can tie neat tidy flies they complete the heads of their creations with just a simple coat of varnish which does little to enhance the fly's overall appearance. A few seconds extra spent on each fly can make flies stand out above the rest. Lures especially can be improved with the addition of a perfect smooth shiny head which not only improves the appearance of the lure but enhances its durability. To obtain that neat shiny effect takes three separate coats of varnish. We say varnish but what we actually use is Vycoat, a plastic based liquid which doesn't dry brittle to crack and peel off but sets to a tough yet pliable coat. Vycoat is used for the first coat applied directly to the bare whipping turns of the head. Although we usually use black tying silk for the heads of our lures,

the next coat to be applied is of black Cellire. This serves a dual purpose giving a smooth black appearance and prevents the Vycoat from turning a cloudy white on contact with water. After the coat of black Cellire has dried, the final coat to be applied is a second of Vycoat. The Cellire underneath prevents it from turning milky white and the Vycoat helps to prevent the Cellire from cracking as it would invariably do. Leave the fly to dry, a process that now takes a little longer than if just Cellire were used.

So there you have it, a brief idea of what technique actually means together with a few tips that we hope will go some way towards a better and neater fly.

4 Tying a wet fly: the Invicta

To illustrate the procedure for dressing a typical wet fly, we have chosen the Invicta, not because it is particularly easy for the novice to tie but because being a fairly complex pattern, it embodies many of the different techniques needed to dress many of the patterns we use. The Invicta mastered, the tying of nearly every other pattern of wet fly will offer few problems.

Not only is the Invicta a very good pattern for illustrating a number of techniques, but it is also an extremely effective catcher of trout since it is a good imitation of various species of sedge on the point of hatching from the pupal form into the adult winged insect (a state known as eclosion). The translucent body of dubbed yellow seal's fur, brown wing and palmered hackle, form a startlingly good imitation of the general confusion of the hatching sedge.

To tie the Invicta, or any other wet fly for that matter, the first step is to fix an appropriately sized hook in the vice, this one being an ordinary down eyed wet fly hook with a standard length shank. Sizes vary, but for an Invicta the most popular are 10s, 12s and 14s. When fixing the hook in the vice the usual advice is to place it in, in such a way that the jaws of the vice totally mask the point of the hook. We don't particularly like this method

preferring instead just to catch the bend in the jaws so allowing more working space between the hook and the vice. The theory behind the masking of the hook point with the jaws is that it prevents the tying silk from being snagged or broken on the sharp hook. With our method, extra caution is needed if the problem is to be avoided but it is well justified by the increased working space.

After fixing the hook securely in the vice, the next step is to catch in the tying silk. This is done by simply holding the loose end of the silk in one hand and the bobbin in the other, looping them both around the hook shank towards the eye of the hook and then winding the bobbin end a few times over the loose end. Remember to keep the loose end held firmly to prevent it slipping. When this procedure has been completed, the loose end can be removed with a pair of scissors. The silk you are actually going to use for tying the fly is now wound down the hook shank towards the bend in tight touching turns. Winding the silk in such a way forms a strong bed on which to tie the rest of the materials and helps the finished fly to stay in one piece.

After forming this bed of silk, it is now time to catch in the tail, which in the case of the Invicta is a small topping feather taken from the crest of the Golden Pheasant.

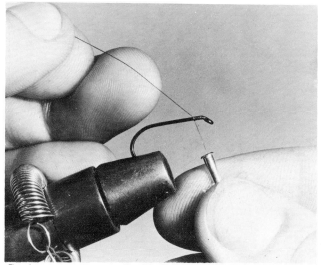

Catch on a length of brown pre-waxed tying silk and run onto bend.

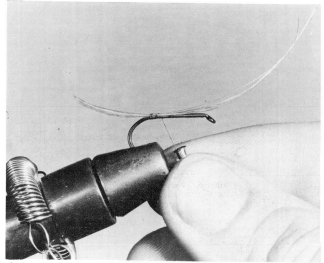

At bend catch in a golden pheasant crest or topping feather.

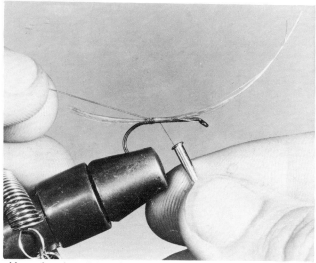

Also at bend catch in a three-inch length of fine round gold tinsel.

Trim off excess topping and tinsel and run silk over waste ends. Then take a pinch of yellow seal's fur and dub it onto pre-waxed silk.

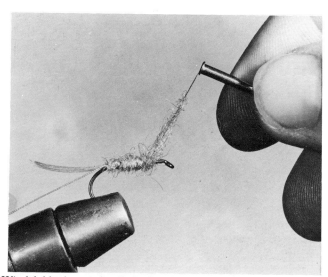

Wind dubbed rope of seal's fur from bend up to a point just short of the eye.

Catch in a soft natural red cock hackle.

Take a pair of hackle pliers and taking the tip of the hackle, wind it in a neat open spiral to the hook end.

Bind hackle to body with a neat spiral of tinsel wound in opposite direction to the hackle.

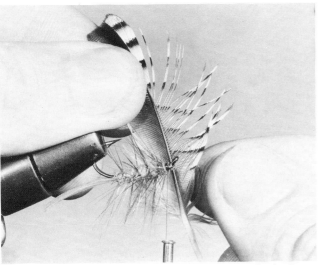

Invert the hook in the vice and prepare a blue jay feather for the throat hackle.

Prepare the fibres of blue jay, trim them to length and tie in the bunch.

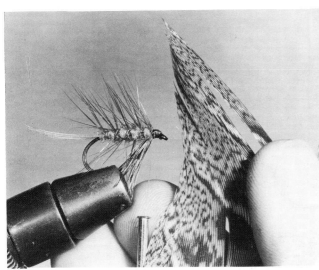

Prepare a slip of hen pheasant centre tail for the wing.

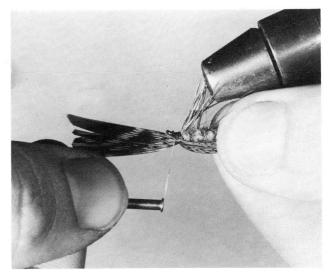

Catch the folded slip of hen pheasant using a winging loop, then trim off the excess. Finally, build up a neat head, give a whip finish and a couple of coats of Vycoat to the head.

The finished fly.

Unfortunately during the time taken between when the bird is killed to when its feathers appear on your tying bench these tend to become twisted. If a neat tail is to be achieved then they need to be straightened again. This is a quite simple procedure. All you need to complete it is a sheet of clean glass and a small amount of water. Immerse the feathers in the water and after a few moments remove them and place them onto the sheet of glass. Each feather can be positioned with the required degree of curve, as it does alter slightly depending on the size of fly for which they are intended. Allow the feather to dry completely and it will retain the curve and flatness.

Now prepare the topping for tying in, making sure that the curve of the feather is right for the size of the hook. Next, take the prepared feather and catch it in with three or four turns of tying silk. To prevent the feather from twisting around the hook shank, the first couple of turns should not be made too tightly. At the same point, that is just before the bend of the hook, catch in 3in (7.6cm) of fine round gold tinsel. The ends of the tinsel and feather projecting towards the eye can then be bound down firmly and any waste trimmed off.

The next step is to form the body which consists of yellow seal's fur applied in a procedure known as dubbing. This is done by first twisting the loose strands of seal's fur onto a silk made tacky with wax and then winding the resulting yarn onto the hook shank. If you are not using pre-waxed silk then you must wax your silk to make it slightly adhesive. If you don't you will find it rather difficult to make the springy seal's fur bind to the silk.

After you have waxed the tying silk, take a pinch of the correctly coloured seal's fur, place it in the palm of your hand and rub it with your index finger. This mixes the direction in which the fibres lie and helps them to twist evenly around the silk. Offer the seal's fur up to the silk and then twist the two together making sure to keep twisting in the same direction all the time; if you don't they won't bind together firmly. Try to make the resulting rope taper at both ends as this will help to give the finished body the slim carrot shape we are aiming for. Next, simply start to wind the seal's fur rope up the hook shank stopping just short of the eye. Don't go too close as it will make the tying in of the wing difficult. About 2mm or perhaps just a little less from the eye should be about right.

The body hackle is the next item to be caught in and a suitable feather to use is a softish cock hackle which has a length of fibre slightly greater than the gape of the hook. After you have chosen the feather it needs to be prepared by stripping the soft flue from the base of the feather. The feather can then be caught in at the eye with two or three turns of silk. Next, grasp the end of the hackle with a pair of hackle pliers and wind it down the hook shank towards the tail in neat open turns. When the correct point is reached, the hackle can then be bound down to the body with the round gold tinsel. The tinsel, which traps down the hackle and strengthens the seal's fur body, should be wound through the hackle in a neatly spaced spiral in the opposite direction to the hackle. If it isn't, it will simply lie alongside the hackle instead of binding it down.

Clip the waste end of the hackle off and then invert the hook in the vice, this is to enable the false hackle of blue jay to be tied in. By false we actually mean a hackle formed from a bunch of fibres clipped from a hackle rather than simply wound on. So after the hook has been inverted in the vice, the next step is to take a blue jay feather and from it tear a bunch of the fibres making sure to keep the tips perfectly level. The bunch must now be trimmed to length before it is tied in, the correct length being just greater than the distance between the eye and the point of the hook. The reason that the hackle should be trimmed before tying in, is that it will help to prevent any pieces of material from sticking out and obstructing the eye, something that will invariably happen if the trimming is attempted after the bunch of fibres has been tied in.

After the tying in of the false throat hackle, the hook can then be reverted to its original position in the vice ready for tying in the wing. In the case of the Invicta, the wing consists of sections taken from a hen pheasant centre tail. This is a difficult leather to work with at the best of times and requires a good deal of care. To prepare the wing first take a good quality hen pheasant centre tail. The main qualities to look for are softness, flexibility and good markings. From each side tear a slip about a quarter of an inch wide. Making sure that the points are even, lay one slip perfectly on top of the other. Fold the resulting pair in half, and the wing is ready to be tied in.

With a material as prone to splitting as hen pheasant tail try not to touch it too much and when you do, hold it gently but firmly. Hold the slip between forefinger and thumb and offer it up to the hook to be tied in by using what is known as winging loops. These loops are not pulled tight right away like normal turns of silk but are thrown loosely around the wing and are then drawn secure from below the hook eye. This has the effect of pulling the wing straight down onto the hook shank instead of twisting it. Before everything is pulled tight the wing should be judged for length, the correct length being just greater than the length of the hook. After the wing has been bound in securely the waste end of the slip can then be trimmed away and the fly finished off by building up a nice neat head, a whip finish and treated to a couple of coats of Vycoat.

5 Tying a nymph: the Spring Favourite

The general idea of a nymph is either to imitate or suggest the various forms of sub-surface aquatic life on which the trout feed. With this in mind most employ the more sombre coloured materials as well as those which give the impression of the legs and gills. The marabou Spring Favourite is one of the more modern nymph patterns that has been used to good effect on both the large and smaller still waters combining as it does many of the properties that make nymph patterns so successful. Its inventor Bob Church first intended it to be a general pattern to suggest the greenish coloured creepy crawlies that trout always seem to have in them, but as events turned out, it proved much better than this.

During the months of May and June it proves particularly effective, hence its name of Spring Favourite, and by coincidence, almost perfectly imitates a small species of green midge pupa which is a dark green and has white tail breathers and a bright yellow patch on its thorax. At the right time of year it can prove absolutely deadly and is the only pattern we have ever used that during a rise can be taken by almost every fish it is cast to. The use of marabou as a body material further adds to the pattern's effectiveness giving as it does a wonderful impression of the moving gills of the natural nymph. Being a nymph that suggests some of the smaller aquatic life forms, it will be found that a smaller hook such as a Size 12 or 14 is most useful, though a Size 10 can prove effective if conditions are a little rough.

To dress the Spring Favourite, fix in the vice the hook size of your choice in the manner described for the dressing of the Invicta, and run onto the hook shank a length of black tying silk. We say silk, but what we use

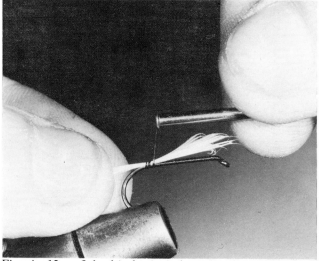

Fix a size 12 wet fly hook in the vice and run a length of black tying silk down to the bend. Then catch in a bunch of white hackle fibres and two inches of gold wire. Next, run the silk back up to the eye.

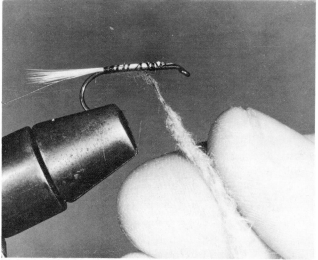

Take a pinch of dyed olive marabou feather and dub it onto waxed silk as you would seal's fur.

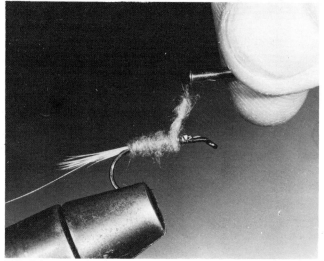

Wind the rope of dubbed feather up the shank for two-thirds of its length and wind the gold wire up through it as a rib.

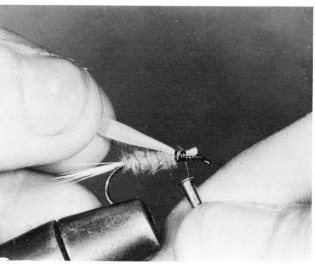

Next catch in a slip of grey feather fibre for the wing cases.

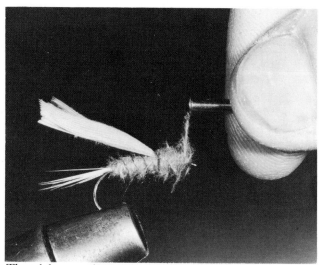

Then dub on another pinch of marabou as the thorax.

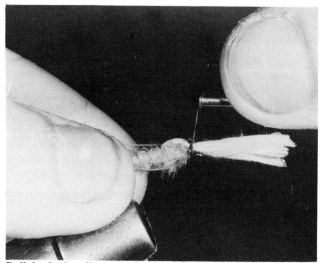

Pull the feather fibre over the back of the thorax and bind it down.

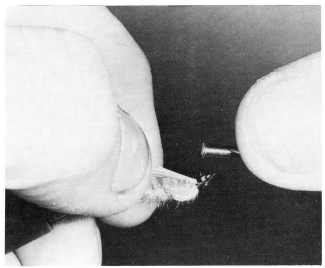

Reverse the hook in the vice and tie in a bunch of dyed yellow cock hackle fibres.

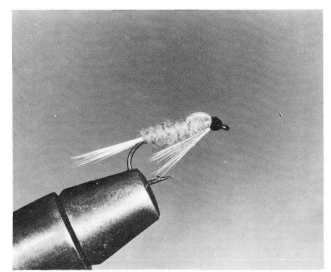

The completed Spring Favourite.

these days is a fine strong pre-waxed nylon thread. Run the tying thread down the hook shank in tight touching turns to the bend and at this point catch in the tail formed from a bunch of white cock hackle fibres. The tail should be about the same length or perhaps just a little longer than the gape of the hook. The next step is to catch in the ribbing material which in this case is three inches of fine gold wire.

After catching in the tail and the ribbing material form the abdomen from olive marabou dubbed on in a similar way to seal's fur. To prepare the marabou for dubbing it is best to use the very fluffy fibres found at the base of each feather. This very fluffy part is too short to be used for winging and so would usually go to waste. Tear off the marabou trying not to include any of the stiff ends which will only mar the marvellous soft effect that the marabou gives. Place the marabou along the length of the silk and twist the two together, again remembering to keep twisting in the same direction forming the required spindle which should be tapered at both ends. After this has been completed, the dubbed spindle can be wound onto the hook shank starting at the tail and progressing up the shank to a point about a third of the total length of the hook shank from the eye. The abdomen is completed by winding the fine gold wire rib over the marabou in the opposite spiral.

A slip of grey mallard primary feather is the next material to be tied in. This will represent the top of the thorax and the developing wings of the nymph. So, from a mallard primary feather remove a slip about ½in (13mm), fold it in half and then in half again, before catching the pointed end in with a couple of turns of silk. The thorax itself is formed from a small amount of the same material as that used for the abdomen and should also be dubbed on, but unlike the abdomen, it should not be wound into a tapered carrot shape but into a small ball. After the thorax has been wound on, the slip of grey mallard feather can then be pulled tight over the back and bound down securely at the eye. With sharp scissors, clip off the waste ends of the mallard feather before inverting the hook in the vice ready for the tying in of the false hackle of dyed yellow cock hackle fibres.

To form the false hackle, take a dyed yellow cock, or, if you want extra movement, a hen hackle and from it tear a small bunch of the fibres making sure that the points are kept even. Clip the butts of the bunch to the required length so that when the hackle has been tied in the hackle points just cover the point of the hook. To complete the nymph replace the hook in its original position, build up a neat tapered head, make a five turn whip finish and a couple of coats of Vycoat. If the finished pattern is still a little smoother than you would like take a dubbing needle and pick out a few of the marabou fibres from the body to give extra movement.

6 Tying a lure: the Goldie

Precious few new patterns stand the test of time, most being destined to become just another of the multitude of forgotten patterns. But every now and again one stays the course to become an essential part of the stillwater trout fisher's armoury. One of the patterns that falls into this category is the Goldie, a lure that has proved its worth time and time again especially where the catching of good-sized brown trout is concerned. When dressed in its standard single and tandem forms it has accounted for countless numbers of fish for both of us and our friends, the combination of black, yellow and gold proving to be a particularly killing one.

After selecting the hook size of your choice fix it firmly in the vice and then run on a length of black nylon, which is somewhat stronger than the silk used to dress an ordinary wet fly. We prefer Monocord, which is very strong for its diameter and, being pre-waxed, grips slippery materials such as hair very well indeed, exactly the properties demanded of a large hair wing lure such as the Goldie. Once the tying thread has been run on, continue winding it in tight touching turns down the hook shank towards the bend. The forming of a neat even bed of silk is particularly important when tying tinsel bodies as any bumps will be easily seen on the finished body. The

next step is to tie in the tail, formed from a bunch of dyed yellow cock hackle fibres. The tail has to be quite long, so try to get the fibres as long as possible. The butts can be laid along the hook shank helping to form the smooth underbody essential when laying on a tinsel body. The next step is to catch in a 4in (10cm) length of gold wire ribbing. Now wind the silk back down towards the eye in tight touching turns forming an even bed on which to lay the tinsel body.

Once the silk has been wound to a point about 2mm from the eye, the gold tinsel, which will form the body, can be caught in. We prefer to use the plastic materials which do not tarnish and are much easier to work with than the older metal tinsels which have a nasty habit of cutting through the silk. Take about 8in (20cm) and trim one of the ends to a sharp point which is tied in near the eye of the hook. Wind the tinsel down the body towards the tail in close touching turns with no unsightly gaps. The tail reached, continue the process back up the hook stopping just short of the eye.

After the tinsel body has been completed and the waste removed, the next task is to wind the wire rib over the body in neat open turns in the opposite spiral to that in which the tinsel itself was wound. The body complete,

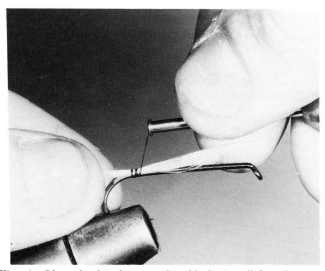

Fix a size 8 long shank in the vice and run black tying silk from the eye to the bend. At this point catch in a bunch of dyed yellow cock hackle fibres for the tail and a few inches of gold wire.

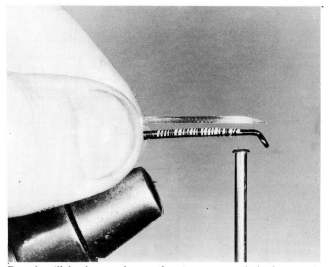

Run the silk back up to the eye, forming a neat underbody.
Take a five-inch length of gold lurex or flat tinsel and cut one end to a point. Catch the tinsel in by the pointed end.

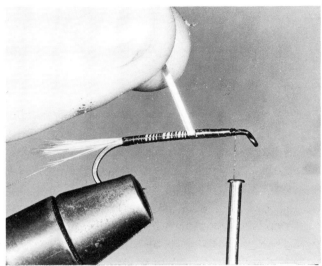

Wind the tinsel down to the bend and then back up to the eye in neat touching turns.

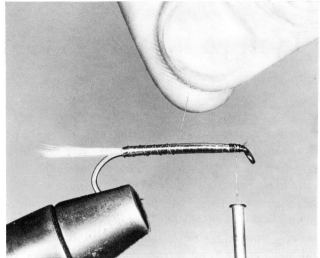

Next wind the gold wire over the tinsel in a neat open spiral in the opposite direction to the tinsel.

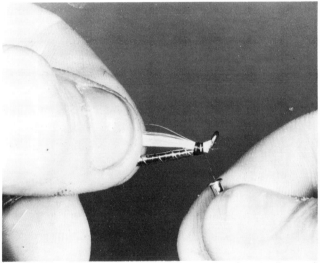

Reverse the hook in the vice and catch in a bunch of dyed yellow cock hackle fibres as a hackle.

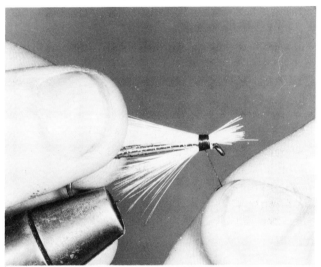

Replace the hook in its original position and tie in a bunch of dyed yellow hair.

Finish the wing off with a few fibres of black squirrel hair as an overwing and give a drop of Vycoat to the head to hold the hair in place.

The completed Goldie.

13

the hook should be inverted in the vice ready to accept a false hackle of dyed yellow cock hackle fibres. The bunch of fibres should be clipped to length before they are tied in to prevent any unsightly stragglers from blocking the eye. The actual length of the hackle should be judged so the tips of the fibres fall just short of the hook point. If the hackle is too long it will unbalance the lure and if too short will not have that little flash of sparkling life we are looking for.

When the hackle has been tied in, revert the hook to its original position ready for the hair wing to be tied in. Unlike most hair wing lures, the Goldie has a bi-coloured wing. The first step in tying this wing is to tie the under-wing which consists of a bunch of any dyed yellow hair with skunk, goat or plain coloured squirrel the better choices. Make sure that the tips of the hair are even before binding the bunch down with five or six very tight turns of tying thread. The correct length for the wing on a Goldie is about one and a half times the length of the hook. After binding down the underwing and trimming off the excess, it is now time to tie in the overwing of black squirrel tail. This bunch of hair should only be of half the amount used for the underwing and is tied in exactly the same way. To finish off the Goldie, trim off the excess black squirrel tail, build up a nice neat tapered head, give a five turn whip finish and form the smooth shiny head in the way described in the chapter on personal techniques.

7 Tying a dry fly: the Grey Duster

Although the dry fly as a technique has a somewhat limited application on our lakes and reservoirs, there are times when it will either beat every other method hands down, or at least prove to be the most enjoyable method of catching trout. One particular time when a dry fly can prove more effective than other methods is during a rise to Caenis, or as it is often known, the Angler's Curse. When these tiny creatures are hatching off in quantity, the trout often become preoccupied with them and can be rather difficult to catch, though a pattern such as the Grey Duster dressed on a Size 14 or 16 hook gives a good imitation which does work at times.

To dress the Grey Duster, fix in the vice a Size 14 or 16 fine wire hook. This can be either of the traditional up eyed dry fly type or one of the newer fine wired down eyed sort. A fine wire hook is needed to keep the weight of the fly as low as possible. After fixing the hook in the vice, run on a length of fine brown pre-waxed tying silk down to a point just before the hook bend. At this point catch in the tail, which consists of a few fairly long fibres taken from a well marked badger hackle. The actual length of the tail should be around one and a half times the length of the hook shank.

The next step is to form the body from the blue under-fur of a wild rabbit. Take care to remove any of the guard hairs which will only ruin the effect. The fur can then be dubbed onto the tying silk in the method described for the Invicta, so that it forms a neat tapered carrot shape. The body should end just over 1mm from the eye to leave room for the winding of the hackle.

When selecting the right hackle for the Grey Duster, care should be taken to choose a well marked badger hackle that has a good black mid rib, white outer and black edge. The actual length of the hackle fibres is also rather important as it is these that help the fly itself to float. The correct length of the hackle fibres should be around twice that of the hook gape. After the correct hackle has been chosen, the fluffy material at its base should be removed in preparation for catching the hackle in. The next step is to grasp the very end of the hackle with a pair of hackle pliers and wind into the portion of bare silk next to the eye, four or five turns of the hackle. The hackle point can then be tied in with a few tight, well placed turns of silk and the excess stalk and hackle tip removed. All that is needed now to finish off the fly is for a neat small head to be built up before a final whip finish

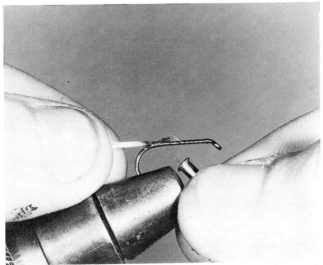

Fix a fine wire size 14 in the vice and run brown tying silk down to the bend. Catch in a few fibres of badger hackle tied long as the tail.

Take a pinch or more of grey rabbit fur and dub it onto the silk, which should be waxed to help the fur adhere.

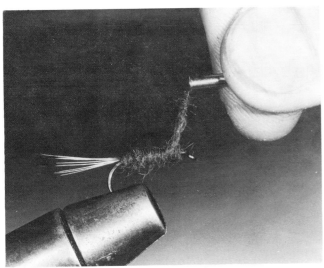

Then wind the fur rope from the tail up to the eye.

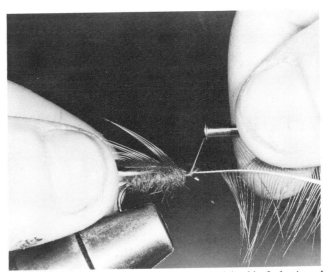

At the eye, catch in a well marked badger cock hackle. Judge it so that the fibres are slightly longer than the hook's gape.

With a pair of hackle pliers, grasp the hackle tip and wind on three turns. Then catch the hackle tip in a few turns of silk and trim off the excess.

The Grey Duster.

15

and a couple of coats of Vycoat.

A variation well worth tying is the parachute hackled Grey Duster. This has its hackle wound horizontally to the hook shank rather than vertically. The beauty of this type of hackling is that it uses larger hackles than could be used normally for the same size of dry fly, thereby saving on waste.

To tie the parachute hackled Grey Duster the silk is run on and the tail tied in is exactly the same as for the ordinary pattern, but instead of the body material being wound up to just short of the eye, it should only be taken to a point halfway along the hook shank, which is where the hackle is tied in. Choose a well marked badger hackle with fibres just a bit longer than one normally used for the normal pattern and from its base pull away the fluff and the hackle fibres from about 1in (25mm) of the stalk.

Catch the hackle in at the point where the actual hackle fibres begin, leaving a long portion of bare stalk projecting over the eye and then after forming a loop in this stalk, catch the loop in next to the first catch in point. With a pair of hackle pliers wind on three or four turns of hackle around the base of the loop and pull the loose end, slowly pulling the loop closed. As the loop decreases in size, insert the tip of the hackle through it keeping tension on the hackle at all times. When it has been inserted properly pull the loop closed tight. To complete the fly the loose end of hackle stalk is tied in, the excess hackle tip is removed and the rest of the body covered with dubbed rabbit underfur. The fly is completed in the usual way.

8 Tying a leaded nymph

Although it is often better to use a sinking line to fish your flies below the first foot or two of water, there are times when a floating line is a better proposition. At such times some other method is needed to help get your flies down to the bottom feeding trout the best being to weight the fly. These can be fished at depth in conjunction with a floating line and leaded patterns work well on either river or lakes watching the movement of the line as an indication of a take.

Although the addition of lead in a fly dressing is by no means a new thing, it is during the last ten years or so that the technique has been fully developed. It comes as no surprise to know that it is Dick Walker who has been instrumental in developing the idea of leading a fly to get the fly down quickly to deeply cruising trout.

Many patterns can be weighted, but nymphs are the most usual candidates for being mainly suggestive patterns they work particularly well when trundled along the bottom where most of the natural creepy crawlies live. Creatures which by nature of their habitat are best imitated by leaded patterns include the shrimp, the hog louse, damsel fly larvae and the mayfly nymph. As can be

expected, it is to these creatures that most attention has been paid. Dick Walker crops up in the credits for those who have had a large influence in the design of many of our more modern leaded nymph patterns. His most famous pattern is his Mayfly Nymph, followed by his shrimp imitation. The leaded Mayfly Nymph in particular has been a pattern instrumental in revolutionising the style of fishing on many of our rivers and small stillwaters particularly where the fish are visible and can be stalked and cast to individually.

It was at Avington and similar clear small stillwaters where the tactic of using a heavily leaded nymph cast to individually stalked large rainbows has been really developed. Because these large fish were often to be seen cruising at a relatively high speed at depths of up to ten feet or so, what was needed was a pattern which would sink very quickly. The leaded Mayfly Nymph designed by Dick Walker must be the most singularly effective pattern used to tempt these large cruising rainbows and has accounted for many double figure rainbows. It has the beauty of being a highly visible pattern which works well both from the angler's and the fish's point of view. It is easy for the angler to see where the fly is sinking in relation to the fish and also to observe if the fish actually takes the nymph. Other patterns which fall into the group include Alan Pearson's Green Beast and Bob Church's Westward Bug, both of which have accounted for a great many large fish since their inception. The Green Beast is, as its name implies, a green coloured nymph dressed on a longshank Size 8 hook. As far as its imitative properties go, it does represent a damsel fly nymph quite well though it works just as well when there are few if any of the naturals about, so it is almost certainly best to class the Green Beast more as a suggestive than an imitative

pattern. The same goes for the Westward Bug which is most certainly not an imitative dressing but, being a very buggy sort of fly, works very well indeed on trout feeding on nothing in particular. The pattern itself is actually dressed with a body of brown marabou dubbed on and ribbed with orange floss, finished off with a shell back of grey feather fibre and a natural red or honey coloured hackle at the throat.

Apart from these rather large leaded nymphs there are a whole range of patterns which, although weighted in some fashion, are much smaller and more on the lines of imitative rather than suggestive types. These include

After running on a length of brown tying silk, cut a thin strip from a section of lead foil.

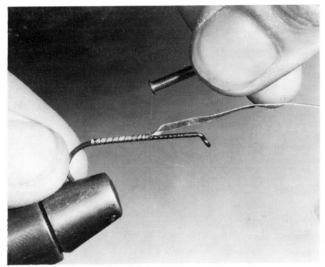

Bind on the length of lead foil.

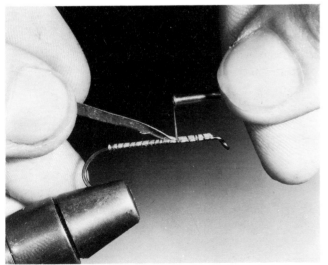

Continue adding strips of lead foil building up the underbody.

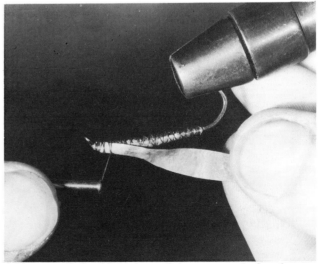

Add progressively wider strips until six or seven strips have been used to give the correct weight.

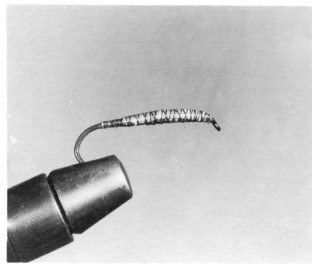

The finished lead underbody.

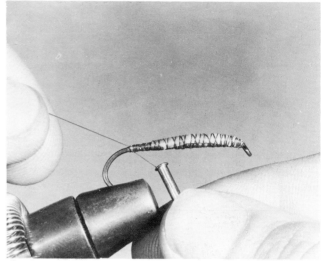

Catch in a length of brown tying silk leaving waste end which will act as the ribbing.

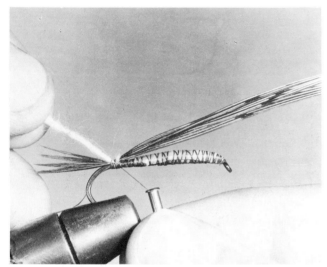

At the bend catch in a bunch of cock pheasant centre tail fibres and a length of angora wool dyed ivory.

Take the wool and wind it for five turns.

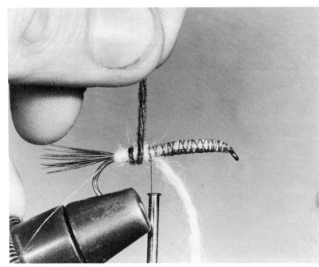

Take the butts of the pheasant tail fibres, twist them together to form a rope and wind it over the angora wool for two turns.

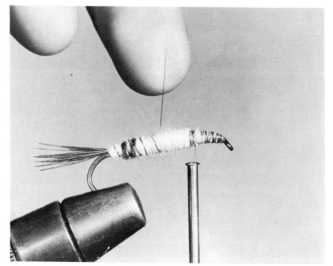

Continue winding the angora wool up to a point two-thirds along the hook shank and then rib the abdomen with the tying silk.

18

Catch in a bunch of cock pheasant centre tail fibres, which will form both the wing cases and the legs.

Next catch in a short length of angora wool and wind it to form the thorax.

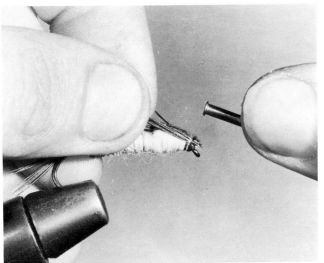

Then stretch the pheasant tail fibres over the thorax. Divide the bunch into two sections and double them back as the legs.

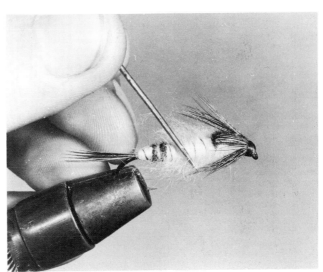

Pick out the fibres of angora as the gills and trim them to length.

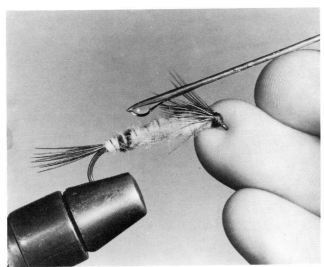

Run a few drops of Vycoat onto the back and underside as well as the fly's head.

The finished Walker's Mayfly Nymph.

John Goddard's P.V.C. Nymph which is a very good imitation of an olive nymph, and his shrimp imitation The Shrimper. Both are dressed on much smaller hooks than those previously mentioned. It is quite possible to dress almost any of your most popular imitative patterns as leaded versions if you want them to get down those extra few feet. This goes for all your chironomid pupae and larval imitations, and those representing the various species of ephemeropteran nymphs. The only proviso to this being that care must be taken not to make your imitations too bulky by over-use of the weighting material. This ruins its intended shape and therefore its imitative properties. At this point it would be a good idea to mention colour coding of leaded patterns. This is particularly important when you have patterns which are identical save for the fact that one is leaded therefore possessing different fishing properties. For this reason it is a good idea to use some sort of code such as a different coloured silk for the head of the leaded pattern, to that usually used. Although it is only a minor point, it is a rather important one and can save a great deal of frustration when it comes to choosing the correct version.

There are a number of ways of adding additional weight, the most popular being to use either copper or lead wire or foil. When only a small amount of extra weight is needed you may well find that the copper wire is quite adequate, but for our own use we tend to stick to either lead wire or foil as lead has greater weight for its bulk than copper and helps prevent the problem of over bulky bodies. For those though who would prefer to use copper wire remember to use wire that is not too thick and inflexible as this only makes it that much more difficult to apply neatly. Most of the wire sold actually for fly dressing is perfect and can be used with confidence. You will find it best to form a bed of silk on the hook shank before you proceed to wind the wire as this will help it to grip and prevent it from turning and slipping. After forming the bed of silk, tie in 4in (10cm) of your copper wire in at the tail and wind your silk back up the hook shank to a point just short of the eye. From this point on, you must decide what type of nymph you are going to dress as this has a direct effect on the profile of the underbody you must create. An example of this is a shrimp which has a rather hump-backed appearance and so the wire underbody must follow the same contours. Just as when tying an olive nymph or such like, the underbody must be thin under the abdomen becoming more bulky and pronounced at the thorax to mirror the shape of a natural nymph. The extra bulk is created by winding the wire back and forth over itself. Take care not to overdo the bulk as it will ruin the effect of the completed fly. The underbody is then completed by tying in the loose end with tying silk and then removing the excess wire with either a pair of scissors, or if the wire is thin enough, by simply snapping it off with your fingers.

When it comes to using lead wire, much the same applies as when tying a copper underbody. The only problem with lead wire being that it can be a trifle thick for the very smallest patterns. This is the reason why we prefer lead foil. Because it is such a versatile way of adding weight it is the one most commonly used on many of the large leaded nymphs. This does not mean that it is unsuitable for the smaller patterns; nothing could be further from the truth. It is easy just to add a small amount of weight by binding a couple of fine strips of foil along the hook shank rather than by adding the bulk of lead wire. With lead foil it is also possible to add weight to just one side of the hook shank to make the fly swim upside down. If extra weight is added to the bottom of the hook, the nymph always swims on an even keel.

As an example of dressing a leaded nymph we will use Dick Walker's mayfly nymph, because not only is it an exceptionally good pattern but it is a good example of his style of tying a lead underbody. To dress his nymph, the first step is to fix a Size 8 longshank hook in the vice and to run on a length of brown tying silk at the eye. Next, take a piece of lead foil and from it cut a strip about 2mm wide, binding it down to the top of the hook shank with the tying silk. The foil by the way comes from the tops of wine bottles. You do get some strange looks scavenging for the empties after a party, but it's all in a good cause!

After you have bound down the first thin strip of lead, continue the process building up the underbody. This is done by binding on further strips of lead, each a little wider but slightly shorter than the one before creating a tapered body. On a Size 8 longshank hook you will find that about six or seven such strips are sufficient. You will have to use correspondingly larger or smaller numbers of strips depending on the size of the hook. Once you have completed the lead underbody, now to the task of actually tying in the materials that go to make a Walker's mayfly nymph. These include cock pheasant tail fibres, angora wool dyed a pale ivory and brown tying silk.

Run on the brown tying silk, winding it down to the bend at which point five or six fibres of well coloured cock pheasant tail should be caught in as a tail. Remember not to remove the waste ends of the pheasant tail fibres or the brown tying silk which will be used at a later time to rib the abdomen. After you have completed the tail, catch in a few inches of the angora wool, winding it down towards the eye for three turns going over the butts of pheasant tail fibres. Now take hold of the ends of the pheasant tail and then wind another three turns of wool this time simply over the lead underbody and not over the pheasant tail. That done take hold of the ends of pheasant tail twisting them into a rope and then wind on two turns over the previous three turns of angora to represent the dark bands seen on the natural nymph's abdomen. Now catch in the pheasant tail rope and trim off the waste before winding the angora wool up the hook to a point no more than ¼in (6mm) from the eye. Rib the whole body with neat open turns of the brown tying silk remembering to wind it in the opposite direction to that in which you wound the wool. After completing the abdomen we need to form the thorax which is done by taking another bunch of pheasant tail fibres this time though numbering some twenty or so fibres. This bunch is caught in by the butts rather than the tips to form both the wing pads and legs, and for this reason you must be careful in judging the correct length to use. As a general guide you will find it best to cut the bunch of fibres so that it is approximately twice the length of the actual abdomen. After trimming the bunch to the correct length, catch it in along with a couple of inches of the same colour of angora wool as you used for the abdomen. Next, wind on the wool to form the thorax and then stretch the bunch of pheasant tail over it to form the wing pads, catching the points in with the tying silk.

To form the legs, divide the bunch of pheasant tail into two equal segments and then bind each back on separate sides of the hook. From then on, the only thing you need to do to complete the pattern is to simply build up a nice neat head and give a five turn whip finish. Then with a dubbing needle pick out the fibres of wool along the sides of the abdomen to represent the gills of the natural trimming the excess tufts to length. The last detail is to run on a few drops of Vycoat along the top and underside of the abdomen, and the head and you have a completed Mayfly Nymph.

Apart from the more usual types of leaded patterns, a new type of fly has been gaining increasing popularity on all types of water. If you haven't already guessed, the lure is the Dog Nobbler made popular by Trevor Housby. Love them or hate them, you simply cannot ignore the fish catching properties of the Dog Nobbler which is based on the small American lead headed jigs.

The Dog Nobbler is not really a pattern at all, but is rather a style of tying which can incorporate a whole host of different coloured dressings. For this reason we will forget about colours and simply give instructions for dressing the basic style, leaving the choice of colour to you. Although there are hooks on the market designed specifically for dressing Dog Nobblers, a Size 8 long-shank is as good a hook as any.

To dress the Dog Nobbler, fix the hook in the vice and run a length of black tying silk onto the bend. At this point tie in a good bunch of marabou feather dyed to the colour of your choice. It is particularly important that you get this tail right as it is this that gives the pattern its sensual movement. The tail should be double the length of the hook shank. After tying this in we move onto the body which simply consists of a length of chenille ribbed with tinsel. The body should be tied so that it falls short of the eye by ¼in (6mm) as it is in this space that the most important part of the fly lies. The head is actually quite heavily leaded, although this is usually done with lead wire, we still prefer to use foil as it is easier to put the greatest bulk of the lead on the underside of the hook shank forcing the fly to swim the right way up. After the leading has been completed cover up the unsightly lead foil with either peacock or ostrich herl wound over a layer of wet Vycoat to make the herl a little bit more durable.

Although the Dog Nobbler is a very effective style of fly it does tend to be rather large which can be a distinct disadvantage when dealing with some wary trout. For this reason Bob Church has come up with the more delicate Frog Nobblers which are being dressed on much smaller hooks. These patterns still have the long flowing tail and the leaded head of the Dog Nobbler, but being that bit smaller and more quietly dressed they can make all the difference to trout that have been bombarded with conventional patterns as they still have the superb ducking, diving action of the original Dog Nobblers. The main difference apart from the smaller hook, is the body which consists of a sleeve of gold or silver mylar tinsel. From this description of leaded patterns, particularly the Dog and Frog Nobblers, you can see that there has been a great deal of development in the field of leaded flies over the last few years. But we are sure you will appreciate there is still plenty of scope for the adventurous fly dresser, and we can only hope that we have helped stir the inventive into concocting the next generation of killing patterns.

9 Specialist dubbing mixes

The real beauty of a perfectly dubbed body is the way the various fibres transmit the light giving an overall life-like sparkle to the fly. For this reason, dubbed bodies have always proved very effective when dressing imitative patterns such as nymphs and dry flies. A common mistake is to form dubbed bodies with a single colour. Even when two or more colours are used on a body, this has been in separate sections rather than being mixed. This is no solution when tying exact imitations for when an insect's body is observed closely it will be seen that its colour is not a single shade but is made up of various colours. This can be best illustrated by the case of the olive nymph, which in reality is not olive at all but a mixture of greens and browns, giving an overall olive effect. So to produce good imitative patterns we must use a mixture of dubbing materials to copy the various hues of the natural. Although the commercial production of dubbing mixes is a fairly recent event, their actual use by both amateur and professional fly dressers is most certainly not. Dick Walker has used mixed dubbing to create a number of new and effective patterns such as his Shrimp and Damsel Nymph, both patterns using dyed lamb's wool as their main material. This is by no means the only material you can use for mixed dubbing. Any kind of fur or man-made fibres can be mixed together in various combinations to create a wide range of new and exciting patterns.

The first and most obvious material that springs to mind when it comes to dubbing mixes is of course seal's fur which comes in a wide range of colours and has the unique advantage of being superbly translucent which makes it perfect for imitating the gossamer-like bodies of the natural insects. Other natural furs include rabbit, hare and mole which between them provide a wealth of shades in the grey to brown ranges. These natural colours are ideal for tying nymphal and suggestive patterns which are very often brown to grey in their make up. The hair on a rabbit or a hare is made up of two layers, the underfur which is usually grey in colour, over which lie the coarser guard hairs, which in the rabbit are greyish brown and gingery brown on a hare. Because each type of hair has a different texture, each offers a different property. The fine underfur makes very neat and tight bodies, whilst the coarser hair forms life-like nymph patterns, especially when the spiky hairs are picked out with a needle.

Mole fur on the other hand is of one single texture and, whilst being a very nice material to work with, was until recently rather limited in application. This is no longer the case as it is now possible to bleach and dye the skins into a whole range of colours. This is particularly useful when it comes to dressing flies which require tightly dubbed bodies such as dry flies. American fly dressers explore every avenue in their search for more natural and man-made dubbing mixes and their list is too long to mention.

Natural furs and hairs though are by no means the only option open to the fly tyer as many excellent synthetic dubbing materials are now available. A great many man-made fibres such as nylon and polypropylene have their uses. Originally these materials were only available in the form of yarns which could be bought in any wool shop, though as could only be expected the more progressive tyers and material sellers have been quick to see the potential of these new materials and now they are available to the fly tyer in a dazzling array of colours and forms.

Polypropylene in particular is a material which has been exploited extensively in the field of fly dressing. It is non-absorbent making it ideal for tying bodies on dry flies and emerger patterns which need to float either on or in the surface film. It is available as a dubbing material under various brand names both as a rather coarse yarn and also in a finer blended form. It is a good substitute for seal's fur which we suspect will soon be difficult to buy because of pressure from the conservationists.

The mixing of various colours and textures of dubbing materials opens up a whole new set of avenues for the adventurous fly dresser and it is to these that we are now going to pay most attention. The first point to consider is the actual mixing of the fibres. Try to achieve a smooth mix and even colour rather than a lumpy, poorly mixed effect. By far the best method is to use a food blender, or from the point of view of marital harmony, a specialist dubbing blender. The only problem with this method though is that it really works best when the materials are mixed in bulk which is inconvenient if you only want to experiment with a new mix. When it comes to actually producing your first mix you will find it best to use a much smaller less complicated piece of machinery than the blender. The equipment which fills this task admirably is a small teasel or wire equivalent which enables the tyer to mix very small quantities of materials. The teasel brush, because it has sharp prongs which catch the various fibres allow even relatively coarse fibres to be teased out and mixed. Unfortunately it does have the drawback of being rather time consuming and does not mix the fibres as evenly as the blender.

When using the food blender, you will find that you need to use a certain amount of water, usually around half a pint, if the fibres are going to mix. When mixing different coloured wools you will find it best to cut the wool into short lengths so that the fibres fall apart and mix properly, around half an inch being the best length. With other fibres, especially the natural furs, you will find that they need little preparation other than to be cut from the skin. Other materials, such as polypropylene or nylon, unless they are already in the form of a dubbing, also need to be chopped up into manageable lengths so that they will break down and mix together satisfactorily.

To mix the different materials together in the blender, pour in half a pint of water to the blending jug, add your ingredients, put on the top and then blend away to your heart's content. It is difficult to give an exact time for blending, as different materials such as nylon tend to take longer to break up than natural furs. As a rough guide you will find that if you switch on the machine in thirty-second bursts and then check the progress of the mixing after each burst, then you will not go far wrong. If you do find you still have some large lumps left, turn on the machine for another thirty seconds and repeat the process until all the lumps have disappeared.

The actual mixing of the dubbing is the easiest task to master. What is the more difficult is the judging of the various proportions of colours and shades to use, and it is here where experience and a good deal of experimentation really yields dividends. You can of course take the easy way out and simply purchase whichever blends of dubbing you require, but it is far more satisfying to mix your own and is more fun to boot, so for this reason we will attempt to give a few hints without going into a whole range of recipes for dubbing mixes. Basically, you need to think first of the exact effect you are looking for; is it a green, a brown, a rust or whatever? Take an olive green for example. Your main colour is going to be green so the

A well picked out seal's fur body. This gives a wonderfully translucent and sparkling effect.

Mixing various colours of dubbing gives nymph imitations the beautiful mottled hues of the natural.

Mixing a small amount of fluorescent wool into a normal dubbed wool body gives already killing patterns even more fish catching attractiveness.

first thing to do is to obtain some dubbing quite close to the colour you are looking for. Then look at the colour and see how it can be altered to suit your purposes better. It may be too bright, in which case add a little bleached seal's fur to tone the colour down. Going back to the olive nymph, you will notice on close inspection that the olive colour is made up of brown, green and sometimes a hint of yellow, and so you can add a few pinches of a brown material and just a hint of a yellow one.

What is very important, especially in the initial stages, is to keep a careful record of the proportions of materials used, as otherwise you will find it very difficult, if not impossible, to repeat a mix you find to be very effective. Once you have put together your intended mix, the next thing to do is to blend the different materials together and see what happens. If the mix turns out to be just what you wanted you have been either very skilful or very fortunate. Usually, after completing this initial mix, the next step is to see what needs to be done to improve it. You may find that you have used either too much or too little brown, in which case you can remedy the matter, remembering of course to make careful note of any extra material used. One point which may help you to save time is to remember that very bright colours can totally swamp a paler one so a much greater amount of the latter may be needed to tone down a brighter colour. The main points to consider when attempting to mix dubbings are the basic colour, the shade, underlying colours and texture. If you take all these points into consideration then you will be on the right course.

Remember what sort of fly you are dressing when it comes to choice of material and texture. If it's a dry fly, then you will find buoyant, non-absorbent materials best, whilst with nymphs and wet flies the reverse is true and you will find it best to use materials that soak up water quickly and help the fly to sink. Another very important point to remember is that when judging a colour, judge it wet rather than dry as this is how the fish are going to see it. This is only a small point, but it is a very important one which is very often overlooked. One subject we must touch upon is that of the use of fluorescent materials in dubbing mixes. Such materials, whether in the form of wool, floss or hair, can be very effective indeed. It is possible to become a fluorescent fan and to over-use the material to the detriment of the fly into which they are incorporated. When using fluorescents in imitative and suggestive patterns, the watch word should be little at all times. What fluorescents are very good for is adding that extra little sparkle to a fly. A small amount of finely chopped fluorescent green or yellow wool added to a mix can work wonders at times. If used sensibly most colours available can prove very killing, though patterns incorporating fluorescent blue materials seem to be the odd ones out.

We hope from this description of how to use and produce dubbing mixes we have given you the idea of trying it for yourself as it must be one of the most versatile yet under-used of all fly dressing techniques. It is without doubt a method which lends itself particularly well to producing really life-like patterns, and for this reason is of inestimable help to those anglers who prefer the imitative approach be it on river or stillwater.

10 Using deer hair

Deer body hair forms the base of what must be the most famous of all streamer lures the Muddler Minnow, a pattern which has killed countless numbers of trout throughout the world. The pattern was devised by Don Gapen of the USA to imitate a small fish known as the Cockatush Minnow. Since its inception, the technique of spinning deer hair has spawned a whole host of flies, lures and bugs.

The real beauty of deer body hair is that it is hollow, and can be used to give buoyancy to any pattern. This property opened up whole new avenues of fly dressing, particularly in the imitative fields where the hair's natural

First form the body and wing, which in this case is for the standard Muddler Minnow. Then cut a small bunch of deer hair from the skin and hold it along the hook shank taking two or three loose turns of silk over it.

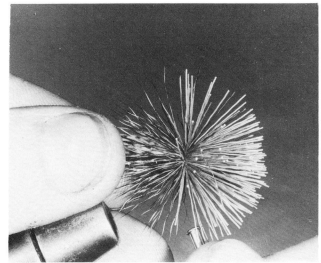

Pull the silk tight and continue to make more turns. This will cause the deer hair to flare, as in the illustration.

Pack the hair back and repeat the process with more bunches until the eye is reached.

The finished hair before trimming.

With a pair of sharp scissors, trim the hair to shape. Leave the tips of hair around the wing to form the hackle.

The completed Muddler.

colour lends itself perfectly to natural looking patterns. While the original Muddler Minnow was designed to imitate a specific small prey fish it also provides a pretty good representation of our own Bullhead. If dressed small though, say on a Size 12 longshank or even an ordinary Size 10 wet fly hook, it makes a very nice little fly suggesting all sorts of creepy crawlies that trout find irresistible.

The best known application of deer hair is in the form of the bubble shaped head which is the mark of a muddler pattern. There are many muddler patterns in a wide range of colours limited only by the materials and dyes available. Among the best known are the Texas Rose, the orange, yellow, white and black Muddlers which all take their fair share of fish. Most lure dressings are suitable for conversion to muddlers. All that needs to be done is to finish off the dressing a short distance from the eye to accommodate the deer hair head. Because of the shape of the muddler head, it lends itself well to fry imitating patterns and it is in this field where the Muddler really scores its greatest success. Lures that are basically white and silver work best at fry time fished around weed beds and any other general cover where the small fish can hide. When the trout are taking three-inch plus roach or bream, it is surprising just how effective a large tandem white Muddler can be.

Whilst still on the subject of fry imitations, there is yet another method of using deer hair that has become increasingly popular over the last couple of seasons. This is an extension of the normal muddler head to cover the whole of the hook shank with deer hair after which the resulting mass is trimmed into a life-like fish shape. White deer hair is more useful as it can be coloured to imitate the various species of prey fish such as perch, roach and bream. Why this style of lure is so killing is quite obvious if you watch what happens when trout are taking fry. When trout are fry feeding, they make headlong dashes into the shoals of small fish crippling as many as they can before returning to mop up the dead and dying. These small crippled fish tend to float to the surface where the trout pick them off with hardly a ripple, and a floating fry imitation fished on the drift with a floating line proves very effective indeed particularly where the larger browns are concerned.

A further application of deer hair comes in the tying of various dry flies, particularly the sedges where it can be used for both the body and the wing. One particularly well known sedge pattern which incorporates deer hair in its dressing is a fly devised by John Goddard and Cliff Henry and appropriately named the G & H Sedge. It is a very simple but well thought out pattern with a combined body and wing of natural deer body hair spun on and clipped to imitate the profile of the natural insect. The body is further enhanced by dubbing green seal's fur onto a strand of tying silk which is then stretched along under the hook shank. The beauty of this particular pattern is that it floats without the addition of a flotant. This pattern is often pulled quite fast across the surface, imitating the struggles of the natural in its attempts to become airborne.

Deer hair can be used as a winging medium in the same way as you would with any normal type of hair, except that you must be careful not to pull the silk too tightly otherwise the hair will flare into a mess. In this way you can make some very effective sedge and emerger patterns as the deer hair wing will help to make the fly float in the surface film which is particularly appropriate in the case of emerger tyings. Yet another application is the use in making detached bodies for mayfly imitations. As far as we know there are few if any British patterns using this technique which only goes to show we don't always pick up some of the best American ideas.

To construct a detached body out of deer hair, the basic technique is to lay a number of hairs together lengthways, the actual number depending on the size of the intended fly, and then to bind them all together with turns of silk every few millimetres. The whole thing can then be given a couple of coats of Vycoat, both to improve durability and to help the hairs to resist waterlogging.

Over the past few seasons we have seen the use of popping bugs on many of our stillwaters. Unfortunately these have tended to be fashioned from very hard materials such as plastic or cork. As a result, anglers using these poppers have found they produced a high proportion of abortive takes with the fish grabbing hold for a split second only to let go again. It is possible to tie bugs out of tightly spun deer hair, giving the desired buoyancy, but now the soft texture of the hair allows the bug to be compressed when the fish takes it increasing the hooking efficiency. Because the bug is so soft and life-like it also tends to be sucked in better and you may find that you have to retrieve it from the throat.

Having dealt with the uses for deer hair we think perhaps that now is a good time to explain to those who are not yet conversant with tying muddlers actually how to spin deer hair properly. Look for hair which is bright and glossy with brown points to its tips, and which looks quite bulky in the individual fibres as this will be the most easily compressible and the easiest to spin. To do this first tie your main materials in, which in the case of the Muddler Minnow are a tail of oak turkey, a body of goldflat tinsel ribbed with oval gold tinsel. The wing is grey squirrel tail overlaid with slips of oak turkey. This dressing should only cover the rear three-quarters of the shank, the portion of the hook nearest the eye left bare to facilitate the spinning of the deer hair. Cover this bare section with an even bed of strong well waxed tying silk to give strength to the finished head and prevent it from twisting. Cut a small bunch about ¾–1in (19–25mm) long depending on hook size. Lay this along the hook so that half projects back over the wing to form a sort of hackle. Now put two loose turns of silk around your bunch of hair. When this has been done slowly pull the turns of silk tight causing the deer hair to flair and spin around the hook shank. When this particular bunch of hair has spun itself evenly all the way around, make a few more tight turns of silk through it to make it secure and then repeat the process with yet another bunch of hair.

Continue until the whole gap between the dressing and the eye has been filled. When first starting to tie Muddlers it is best to use small bunches of hair until you become more experienced.

When you have completed spinning the deer hair what you will have sitting in the vice is something not too far removed from a hedgehog, so we have to trim this mess into shape. Take a sharp pair of scissors and be brutal, cutting away quite large chunks at first rotating the fly so that the hair is removed evenly. When you have achieved something a little more manageable, be a little more careful with your trimming, using the scissors to form the hair into a nice neat bubble shape. You will find it best to remove a little more hair from beneath the hook shank than from above. This is to improve the stability of the lure, helping it to swim straight and upright.

When the head has finally been trimmed to shape, take some Vycoat and run it into the whip finish at the eye. Apply plenty as it will run into the bed of silk at the base of the deer hair to strengthen the head. This is a worthwhile precaution as the mark of a really well tied Muddler is its durability.

11 Common mistakes in fly tying

Like most crafts, the tying of an artificial fly requires some degree of practice and experience before a high level of expertise is reached so the novice must accept that he is going to make mistakes on his road to mastering the problems involved. That said it should not be thought that learning to tie a fly is in any way above anyone's abilities. We assure anyone who has never tried fly tying, that after only a few hours' practice they will be tying flies quite good enough to catch fish. Some budding fly dressers are put off by the combination of the small size of the hooks used and the apparent fiddliness of the whole business of fly tying but these fears are soon overcome. Of course mistakes will be made but we hope that by listing most of the more common errors, along with remedies we will give the prospective fly dresser the encouragement to

take the plunge.

It is a good idea to start right at the beginning, as it is in the actual choice of materials that the beginner can often come unstuck. We know from our own experience that the novice feels that to buy expensive materials is a waste because he will only spoil them with his inexperienced hands. This though is nothing less than false economy and will only lead to frustration as cheap materials are often very difficult to work with even for the expert. For this reason it is by far the best idea to buy the best, particularly hackles, wings and tinsels, as it is in these areas where the novice is most likely to encounter difficulties.

A basic mistake is the failure to form a nice neat bed of silk onto which the rest of the fly is fashioned. The

Wrong! Tinsel body is uneven and is not butted up well to cover exposed tying silk at the tail. Also the ribbing itself is loose and wound unevenly.

Right! Tinsel body is smooth and even and the ribbing is wound in a neat even spiral.

importance of this foundation cannot be stressed too highly as it is the key to a well tied and robust fly. To form the bed all that needs to be done is for tight touching turns to be wound onto the hook shank from eye to bend. Why so many fail to do this is a mystery.

After completing the silk bed we then catch in the tail and, as with any other part of the fly, attention should be paid to proportion. A general rule of thumb concerning tails is that they should be about half the length of the body. What is more important though is that they are straight and even, with no twists and kinks. If a tail is too bulky or twisted it can affect the balance of the fly. Making tails too bulky is particularly easy when using wool, whilst hackle fibre tails are usually dressed far too sparsely by the beginner.

It is when we move on to bodies that we first encounter the main problems faced by the novice. It is here where a well formed bed of silk pays dividends. Materials used to tie bodies include floss, wool, chenille, tinsel and seal's fur. Each offers its own individual problems. There are a number of different types of floss silk, the most popular being Pearsall's marabou floss and rayon floss. Marabou floss comes as two strands twisted together which must be separated before use if an even effect is to be achieved. Rayon floss on the other hand is single stranded but, unlike marabou floss, is rather prone to fraying. Whilst winding, great care must be taken to ensure it does not snag on any rough skin on your fingers. The best way to wind floss is actually to catch it in at the eye, winding it down to the bend and then back up again to the eye allowing any bumps to be evened out.

From floss we move on to chenille which, as long as a

couple of simple rules are followed, is a very easy material to work with. The main thing to remember is to remove the fibres from the core for about ¼ in (6mm), catching in just the bare core. If you simply catch in the chenille unprepared you will create a nasty lump at the tail of your fly or lure. After catching in your length of chenille in the correct manner, all you need to do is to wind the strand up the body towards the eye, butting each turn up neatly against the previous one and taking care not to overlap any turns as this will only produce a lumpy body.

We will treat both wool and seal's fur in the same section, as although you can wind wool on you can also dub it on in the same way as seal's fur. The most common fault with dubbed bodies is to overdo things creating a messy bulky effect which not only looks bad, but which also prevents hackles and wings being tied in neatly. By far the best way is to use well waxed silk and small amounts of fur at a time rather than too much. When dubbing the seal's fur to the silk, you must always twist the fibres in the same direction. If you don't, they will simply refuse to form the tight rope which is so important when forming a neat body. Although wool can be teased out into its original fibres and dubbed on, it can also be wound onto a hook shank in its yarn form. Because wool is fairly coarse it is best suited to lures, where it forms the bodies on many famous patterns, probably the most famous of them all being the Baby Doll, fashioned from white Bri-nylon baby wool. As it usually takes two or more layers of wool to form a body you will find it best to catch your strand of wool in at the eye, winding it down to the bend and then back up the hook shank again in neat touching turns. The most common fault of wool bodies is

Wrong! Tail is uneven, whilst the hackle is wispy and too long. Also the wing slips are poorly matched and have been twisted when tied in.

Right! Tail is even and the hackle is the correct length and well spread. The wing slips are also perfectly matched and lie straight along the top of the hook shank.

allowing the turns to overlap causing a ridged, uneven effect. The simple procedure of ensuring that each turn lies next to the previous one eliminates this trouble.

It is when attempting tinsel bodies that the beginner is most likely to come to grief as this material, especially the metal kind, is one of the most difficult of all to apply well. It is here where care to form an even bed of silk is really important. Without it, it is all but impossible to keep the tinsel body smooth. Two types of tinsel commonly used on fly and lure bodies are the traditional metal strip and the more modern sort which has a plastic base. The beauty of this material is that unlike its metal predecessor, it does not tarnish. Its only drawback is that it is not all that strong, so it is virtually useless as a ribbing material on its own, and when used for bodies must be ribbed well with either wire or oval tinsel.

The plastic based tinsels such as Lurex and Mylar are so much better than the metal types that we always use them except when dressing large traditional salmon flies where we like to try and keep to the original tying which means using metal strip. The usual faults in tinsel bodies include allowing the turns of tinsel to overlap causing lumps and gaps and not winding the tinsel tight enough so that it slips down the hook shank. To prevent both these problems remember to butt each turn of tinsel up perfectly against the previous one making sure that each turn is good and tight. Always remember that if you fail to form a smooth base to start with you will find it very difficult indeed to get the effect you are looking for.

The most used ribbing materials are oval, round, flat and embossed tinsels, and wire. The main problems encountered with ribbing is unevenness in winding and where the rib is not wound tightly enough allowing it to slip, so failing in its function to protect the body materials. There are no real short cuts to forming a good rib, the requirements being simply practice and the ability to analyse what is going wrong. The main things to remember are to wind the tinsel in the opposite spiral to that in which you wound the body material and to keep those turns even and tight.

What most often lets the average fly dresser down is not the tying of them which is quite easy, but the choice of hackle they use. Because hackles tend to be quite expensive the inexperienced fly dresser tends to buy cheap hackles which, except in a few cases, usually proves to be a false economy. The cheaper hackles, both in packets and on capes, include so much waste that much has to be thrown away. It is a far better idea to buy good quality hackles, which are all usable and much easier to use being rather longer and less prone to breaking.

When looking for a good hackle, it is most important to remember that the feather is the correct size for the fly you are dressing. This is best judged by bending the hackle stem so that it is easy to judge if the fibres are the right length. For a wet fly this is the distance between the eye and the point of the hook. Make sure that the hackle is supple and bright and that there are no damaged and frayed fibres. If you don't the hackle will never look right when it has been wound. Not only that, if it is old and brittle it may well snap whilst being tied in so that it needs to be replaced. The most common faults with hackles are that they are either too long or too short or are too sparse or bulky.

Of all the parts of a fly, it must be the wing which

causes the most frustration for the budding fly dresser, and even some quite well experienced tyers still find winging the most difficult technique to master. The real art in forming a good wing stems from providing a good base on which the wing will be mounted and in not making the body of the fly too bulky or too close to the eye. The easiest of all wings to tie in is the hair wing so we will deal with that first. The main trouble with hair is that because it is relatively incompressible, it tends to fall out after being tied in. For this reason you must take care to make the turns of silk as tight as possible. You will also find it helps to give the butts of hair a dab of Vycoat which will help to glue the fibres together.

Hair wings are used on a variety of flies and lures. Other materials used for lure wings include hackles and turkey marabou, both of which pose their own problems. Hackles in particular are often tied in poorly by the novice simply because the nature of the feather is not properly understood. Hackles have a distinct curve depending on which side of the bird's neck they come from. Because they are curved and the wing you want is straight, you need to take two or three hackles from each side of the cape laying each group back to back in order to cancel out the opposing curves. It is surprising how many tyers forget to do this ending up with a wing that is lopsided and which has a poor action in the water. Marabou is simply tied in as a bunch of fibres and has none of those problems. The only possible problem with tying marabou wings is that some tyers forget that marabou slims down a great deal when it is wet and tend not to use nearly enough, which means the fly does not possess that wonderful action when underwater.

From winging lures we now move on to wet and dry flies, which seem to pose greater problems to the novice. The main reason for this is that wet and dry flies' wings are that much smaller and as a consequence are more fragile than those used on lures. The easiest of all small fly wings to tie in are almost certainly those incorporating duck wing quills as these have the strongest webbing and as a result are less prone to splitting than many other materials. From duck quills we next move on to duck flank feathers such as teal and bronze Mallard which can be a little tricky at times. The real beauty of them all is hen pheasant tail which can be very awkward to use unless you choose your feathers well. To achieve good winging the first thing to make sure of is that you have prepared your wing slip correctly before tying in. Use just the right amount of feather and make sure that the slip is not twisted. If it is it will be impossible to tie in straight so you may just as well throw it away and start again. With paired slips make sure that both slips are taken from left- and right-handed feathers and are the same width. If one is slightly wider than the other this will cause the finished wing to twist. With rolled wings this problem does not really occur, but it is still easy to twist and split the wing if a little care is not exercised. When picking the feather for a rolled wing look for one that is well webbed where the individual fibres stick together well and even when split apart, will re-marry with ease. The best way to prepare such a wing is to cut a slip three times the width of the intended wing, folding one edge to the centre and folding the remainder over that. This way you will have a wing which holds together well. Once you have prepared the wing to your satisfaction, the next step is to tie it in and this is where all your preparation can come to nothing unless you are careful. The best way to tie in a wing is with what is known as a winging loop. This is where the wing slip is held in position above the hooks with the fingertips and a couple of loose turns are thrown over it at the head. When these turns are tightened with a downward pull the slip will be pressed onto the top of the hook shank. Any sideways pull with the silk will only cause the wing to twist.

As far as proportion goes much rests on personal preference but we like our lure wings to be about one to one and a half times the length of the hook shank, whilst wet fly wings should be just that little bit shorter. Dry fly wings should be about the same length or slightly longer than the gape of the hook.

12 Tying a whip finish

There is little point in going to all the time and trouble of tying a well-dressed fly simply for it to fall to pieces after a few casts. What is needed is a method of finishing off a fly so that the loose end of tying thread will not come undone. It is possible to use a number of half hitches daubed with varnish to glue them all together, but the five turn whip finish is far more satisfactory.

With the whip finish, the loose end of the tying silk is trapped under a number of turns of silk before the whole thing is pulled tight and the waste end is cut off. This makes for a very secure finish which is unlikely to come undone even if the tyer hasn't gone to the standard precaution of coating the turns of silk with varnish.

The whip finish is carried out after the dressing of the

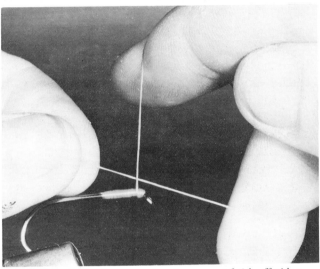

Once the dressing has been completed, you must finish off with a robust whip finish. The first step is to take the silk in the left hand and with the first and second fingers of the right, form a figure 4 shape with the silk.

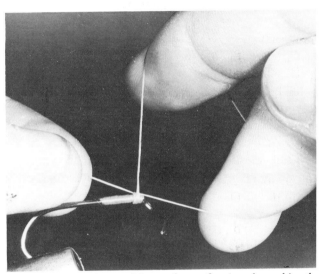

Wind the loop made round the eye four or five times by pushing the first finger over and round.

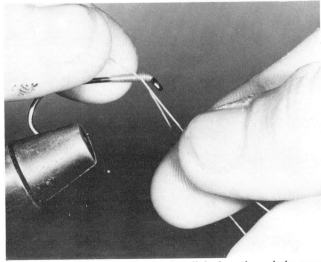

When the turns have been completed, pull the loop through the turns with the left hand.

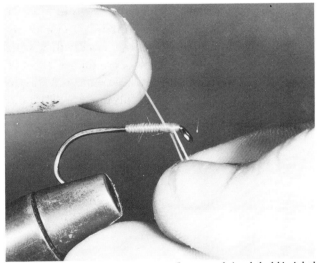

As the loop disappears, remove your fingers and simply hold it tight by pinching it. If you simply let go, the turns will often spring off over the eye.

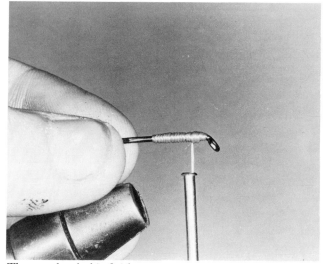
The completed whip finish.

fly has been completed, and in the illustration we have used a thicker silk than normal in order to demonstrate the processes.

The first step is to form a loop into which the first two fingers of the right hand should be inserted. Then, holding the loose end of the silk in the left hand, form a figure of four with the silk, using the first two fingers of the right hand. Once this has been achieved the silk should be wound over the hook shank five or six times using the two fingers of the right hand. To complete the whip finish the loose end of the silk should be drawn tight by pulling with the left hand. Whilst pulling tight care should be taken to keep tension on the loop to prevent the turns from falling off over the hook's eye. Once the loop has been pulled tight the loose waste silk may be trimmed off and a coat of varnish given to the whippings.

ENTOMOLOGY AND THE ARTIFICIAL

1 Corixa

Glancing into the water at the margin of virtually any stillwater one cannot help but notice small beetle-like creatures forever rising up to the surface only to shoot back to the bottom in the wink of an eye. Not beetles these but the ubiquitous *Corixa*. Abundant in all forms of stillwater from the smallest pond right up to the very largest of our lakes and reservoirs they are an important source of food for the trout and must be given due regard by the trout fisher.

Corixa are common in both stillwater and slow moving rivers due to its ability to survive in water with a low oxygen content allied to the fact that it is an accomplished flyer able to cover long distances. If it feels that a particular water is unsuitable, although considering its distribution this is extremely unlikely, all it has to do is take to the wing and fly to another more acceptable lake. If you doubt that a *Corixa* can fly, catch a few in a small net and then hold them out of water in the palm of your hand. As they begin to dry out they will start hopping about and after a moment will open their wing cases and expand their folded wings. A split second later they will be on the wing.

It is not perhaps the powers of flight which make the *Corixa* such a wonderful creature but their ability to colonise water containing little oxygen. The *Corixa* does not actually obtain its oxygen from the water but uses a form of aqualung to carry its own individual supply of oxygen in the form of a bubble on the underside of its abdomen. This supply is gradually used up and the *Corixa* must make repeated journeys to replenish its supplies. Unfortunately this bubble of air has two important side effects. The first is that it makes things rather difficult for the *Corixa* to dive and stay down when its aqualung is full and it is only able to stay submerged by holding on to a stone or a piece of weed. It finds this task of holding on a

bit difficult which is why they can be forever seen scuttling along the bottom trying to find something to grab hold of.

That the *Corixa* needs to be forever rising to the surface brings yet another drawback in that it is unable to venture into very deep water where it might not be able to get to the surface. During its forays to the surface it must break cover and so be at the mercy of any cruising trout. Although it takes only a split second for the *Corixa* to recharge its air supply this is quite long enough for a fish to snatch it up.

The *Corixa* when viewed closely is a striking creature, its back beautifully marked with dark brown or black dashed with bands of gold. Its air supply when at full capacity looks just like a bead of mercury held between the legs. These are also very interesting, with each pair specialising in a particular task. The front pair are short and stubby and are used for feeding, being fringed with hairs to help manœuvre food towards the mouth parts. The second pair are much longer, and are used specifically to cling on to vegetation to prevent it from floating to the surface. It is to the third pair that we should pay most attention. This last pair of legs are specially modified to aid its movement through the water, each one being fringed on both edges with stiff hairs which turn the legs into efficient paddles. These paddles allied to its boat shape has led to its name Lesser Water Boatman. The funny thing is that as anglers we prefer to use the scientific Latin title of *Corixa* rather than the more common name.

There are quite a few different species of *Corixa*, but their colour and markings are very similar and so we do not have to go to great lengths to cover all the species. They do vary a little in size ranging from 5mm to over 10mm, though the larger species tend to be less

Spooning a trout is essential to see what they have been feeding on.

abundant. The most common and the one usually imitated is around 7mm.

When it comes to imitating the *Corixa* there is often some confusion. Some anglers state that patterns should be tied in a range of colours including green. At first I (Peter) could not understand why because there simply are no green *Corixa*. Later I realised that what these anglers had seen was not a *Corixa* at all, but a closely related species known as *Notonecta* or the Greater Water Boatman. In its immature nymphal form the *Notonecta* is about the same size as a *Corixa*, but has a pale green abdomen, hence the confusion. Although *Notonecta* is related to the *Corixa* family being of the same Order, Hemiptera, it does differ in a number of important ways. Firstly, when adult it is much larger than the *Corixa*. *Notonecta* on the other hand is a voracious predator able to catch quite large creatures as big as a tadpole or water beetle larva.

Once captured *Notonecta* pierces the skin of its victim and sucks out the juices with a beak sharp enough to give a human a painful jab. Because *Notonecta* is a predator it is much less common than *Corixa* and so even though trout do take them at times there is little point going to the trouble of imitating them. Whenever I have taken trout with *Notonecta* in them they have also contained large quantities of *Corixa*.

When it comes to tying *Corixa* imitations there are a number of points to consider. These include size and form. There are three other main points to consider. The first is the creature's beetle-like shell back which may be tied with the correct coloured feather fibre or some other similar material. The second is the body colour which, to suggest the air bubble that the *Corixa* carries, should be either white or silver. The third point is of course the paddles. These may be imitated in a number of ways including the use of hackle fibres, goose biots or even short lengths of nylon monofilament. To confuse things Bob has done well with a pale yellow bodied pattern. Why this dressing often works better than a more life-like imitation is not fully understood, and is probably similar to using an over large midge pupa in a buzzer rise. The fish is used to seeing thousands upon thousands of the naturals and when it sees something quite similar, but a little different from the rest it goes for it. The yellow body makes the fly stand out in the crowd.

Because *Corixa* inhabit the shallow margins, they are only taken in specific circumstances. Trout do not like entering shallow water during daylight and for this reason most *Corixa* feeding takes place either around dawn and dusk or when the day is especially dull. Indeed it was during one very dull stormy day that I (Peter) had a rather good catch on *Corixa* imitations. It was at Eyebrook reservoir which is only a couple of miles from my home in Corby, and I was fishing the bay above The Island on a cold blustery day in April. There were few anglers about so I had plenty of room, but conditions were bleak with a fine drizzle. I tackled up with a slow sinking line and a small lure looking out all the time for surface activity.

After a couple of hours I had not even had a pull and things began to look a little desperate. Then suddenly I had a fish swirl at my lure close in. Quickly I flicked out again in the vicinity of the swirl and was rewarded for my speed with a take. As the fish was hooked in only a couple of feet of water it shot off out into the reservoir at a rate of knots. The hook held and soon a nice brown trout was safely in the net.

The reason I had done so poorly was that my casting meant that I was fishing past the trout feeding on *Corixa*

right in the margins. I quickly switched up to a floater and a team of three Size 12 *Corixas* with a lightly weighted goose biot version on the point. Instead of casting out I angled the line obliquely to the bank allowing the wind to blow the line towards the shore. This kept the flies in the feeding area for as long as possible and a twitched retrieve brought the required response. After a patchy start I packed up at mid-afternoon with twelve nice browns up to 2 lb and an overwintered rainbow of 2 lb.

2 Chironomids

Although an insignificant looking creature, the Chironomid or non-biting midge is certainly the most important of insects to the stillwater fly fisher. It is difficult to overstate the importance of an insect which in its various stages provides by far the greatest proportion of the diet of stillwater trout. The Chironomidae family is a large one and up to the present some 450 separate species have been identified in this country alone and I am sure there are quite a few others yet to be properly categorised. Luckily for the angler this wide number of species can be virtually ignored and a far more reliable categorisation can be used by dividing the various species up into groups by size and colour. Even if it is your intention to take things to extremes and try and identify all the species, our advice is to forget it. Not only is it a very difficult task with even the expert entomologists running into problems, it will probably not help you catch one single trout more than if you kept things simple.

From this point on we will not mention any specific species, but simply class all midges as Chironomids, the name incidentally coming from that given to the most popular Genus *Chironomus plumosus.* The size range of these insects is hardly outstripped even by the diversity of species and midges may be anything from a mere speck right up to meaty specimens of nearly an inch long. Luckily the average seems to be around a ¼–½in (6–13mm) which is a happy circumstance as it allows the

insect to be imitated on hooks large enough to give us a good chance of landing a fish.

Before going deeper into the realms of imitation perhaps now would be a good time to delve a little further into the fascinating life cycle of the midge to show how imitations should be constructed and fished. The life cycle may be broken down into four stages; the egg, larva, pupa and finally the adult, after which mating takes place and the whole process begins again. The eggs are laid in a gelatinous mass which floats on the surface of the water. After a few days the eggs hatch and the tiny larvae drift with the currents until they find a suitable area in which to settle. As far as we know no one has yet bothered to imitate the egg mass and so we can disregard it from our list of favourite imitative patterns.

It is only when we move on to the larvae that we have the first stage of real interest. The larva vary greatly in size from the very smallest of thread-like organisms right up to the inch-long worm-like creatures found in the foul-smelling silt on the lake bed. To say that the Chironomid larva is like a worm is rather misleading as it takes only a close look to see that it has a very distinct head and tail end. Not only do the larva vary in size but also in colour. Apart from one notable exception they tend to stray towards the autumnal colours with yellowish green to brown being the most abundant hues. The one notable exception is of course the bloodworm, so named because of its startling blood-red colour.

This bright showy appearance goes part of the way to explaining why it should also be the most well-known of all the Chironomid larvae. Incidentally, the bloodworm, which many of you will know as a superb bait for coarse fish, is aptly named as it gains its colour from the very substance which goes to make our blood red, namely haemoglobin. Haemoglobin enables the bloodworm to make the very best of what little oxygen there is, allowing it to survive in an environment of decaying organic material.

As a group, the different species tend to fill their own separate niches. The bright red bloodworms seem to prefer building their homes in the thick black silt, while the more drably coloured and therefore more camouflaged types live higher in the water, often on the leaves of aquatic plants or tangled mass of silk weed. The larva are also able, by emitting mucous as a cement, to build protective homes out of particles of detritus. They do this by slowly joining the particles of rubbish together to form a fine tube in which they spend the greater part of their lives prior to pupation.

At this point I (Peter) must admit, that of the larvae I have studied, the largest proportion of these has been the bloodworm though for the most part the same conditions relate to many of the other species. I have over the years kept many hundreds of larva bringing them on through to the pupal stage, then on to the adult, so I feel confident that I have at least a reasonable knowledge of the various stages, even if the most detailed study has taken place under artificial conditions. The larvae themselves undergo four moults or instars before they are ready to pupate; after each moult the larva increases in size until it is fully grown.

The trout feed avidly on all the various types of larva and I have often spooned many a trout jam-packed with these little creatures. Although at times trout do feed heavily on the large red bloodworms, it is the more sombrely coloured types which fill the bulk of the autopsies. The small green larva is often found in great quantities, particularly during the warmer months. The reason for this stems from where the larva are found. As I mentioned previously, many small green larva live in the silk weed which forms in the shallower water. As the water temperature increases, these mats of weed become filled with gas bubbles and, becoming buoyant, eventually rise to the surface, a phenomenon which most anglers will be aware of.

The small Chironomid larva trapped in the algae begin to move about, lose their hold and fall back down towards the lake's bed. It can be seen from this that a small creature in such a predicament is easy meat for the hungry trout. Indeed trout make the habit of cruising around these weed mats feeding on the descending larva along with any other unfortunate creatures which might be given an unexpected trip to the surface.

Along with what might be called involuntary migration, the larva itself is capable of movement. This is accomplished by sinuous lashings of its body which gives it mobility, though it is difficult to see that this is a controlled movement. It has been recently discovered that Chironomid larvae are able to move around their habitat by swimming up into the currents and being carried to different parts rather than staying in one place as was previously supposed. You can observe the larva moving about if you peer into the margins of a lake, although by far the greatest part of this migration takes place under the cover of darkness. Once it has moulted for the last time, it is possible to observe the outline of the pupa lying underneath the skin of the larva.

Visible are the slim abdomen, bulbous thorax and the white filaments on the head which later will become so prominent. To be honest it is a little contrived to be able to observe the larvae at such a stage because at this time it stays well hidden in its mucous and silt tube where it develops in peace well away from the prying eyes of any predator.

Once the pupa has developed fully, the rigorous stage of pupation takes place, again well within the confines of its protective tube. Luckily the larva will still go through the motions of pupation even if it is not within its tube, which allows us to observe this wonderful transformation. Once ready, it begins a waving action and the skin just behind the head splits as the pupa begins to emerge. The old skin is reminiscent of a sausage skin and is gradually worked back down the body of the pupa until it comes free. This is a hazardous time for the pupa and there is a particularly high mortality rate at this point, with quite a proportion failing to free themselves properly.

For those pupa which do manage to free themselves, the next step is to develop into the creature that we all know as the buzzer. Whilst on the subject, I think it would be a good idea to try and clear up any confusion which might arise as a result of the various names which pupal stage has come to be known. The names Midge Pupa, Buzzer Pupa, Buzzer Nymph and even the Duck Fly

A nice brown trout which fell to the allure of an artificial midge pupa.

Nymph are all used to describe the same creature.

When it first emerges from its larval skin, the wing buds and legs of the pupa are still unpronounced and the creature looks somewhat like a cross between a larva and a pupa, a form of hybrid if you like. After a few hours the pupa darkens and the thorax, with its wing buds and legs, becomes more obvious. The creature now has the slim abdomen, pronounced thorax and the white filaments on the tips of both the head and abdomen we all recognise. It keeps up the lashing movement for anything between 30 and 70 hours, until it is ready to play its final part as an aquatic creature.

Remembering of course that although we are able to observe the development of the pupa in laboratory conditions, all this usually takes place within the confines of the pupa's tube. In the natural state once it has become fully developed the pupa starts to emerge slightly from its home so that merely the head is visible, the most conspicuous parts of which are the white breathing filaments. After a few hours in this state, the pupa finally leaves its tube for the first and last time and for a while simply lies there on the bottom twitching away. There it stays whilst changes occur within its body which will help in its one great journey to the surface where it will hopefully emerge as the winged insect.

Once an hour or two has passed the pupa darkens quite considerably and in some cases even changes colour. The wing buds also become much more pronounced and the body as a whole starts to take on a rather sparkling silvery appearance. This effect is caused by the pupa absorbing gas which will eventually make it buoyant, so aiding in its long haul towards the surface. It is often said that the Chironomid pupa swims to the surface and from watching many hundreds of pupa emerge, I can state that this is simply not true. What they do is float up rather than swim. The pupae take on so much gas that they become very buoyant simply rising to the surface quite impassively though they often twitch on the way up so giving the illusion that they are swimming.

It is whilst they are at this stage of positive buoyancy that the Chironomid pupa is at the mercy of its predators. It is totally unable to avoid capture and must simply run the gauntlet of the hungry fish. To say that midge pupae are picked off in their thousands must surely be the understatement of the century. If you used the term billions you would not be too far off the mark. Just to illustrate the point, during the 1983 season we managed to catch quite a few large brown trout at Rutland Water, with fish up to six pounds all taken deep down. When we came to clean them out we found that these fish had been gorging themselves on large dark brown pupae to such an extent that each fish contained not just tens but hundreds of them. One fish was found to contain, after counting only about a third of its stomach contents, over 200 and it was by no means an exception.

As can be seen from the availability of the pupa, it is at this stage that the Chironomid is of the most interest to the fly fisher, so I shall attempt to describe as fully as I can the final stages just prior to and also during the act of emergence. If the pupa has been particularly fortunate and has actually managed to reach the surface, its troubles are still far from over, indeed it would probably be true to say that the hardest part has yet to come. Once the pupa does reach the surface it has quite a few problems other than the constant chance of being snapped up by a trout. A flat calm or an out and out gale are neither helpful nor required by the pupa. Conditions which are extremely cold and unsettled are not good days on which to expect a favourable hatch which is quite understandable. Neither are very still conditions for reasons that will soon become apparent. When the surface is particularly still a surface film builds up with dust particles and other rubbish, and the relatively feeble pupa finds it very difficult to break through. This means that the trout now has a sitting target with the pupa neither able to break through the surface nor sink back down to the bottom.

The best conditions for a good hatch are when the weather is warm and there is a slight chop on the water to keep the surface film down to a minimum. At such times the pupae are able to break through and emerge quite easily. Once the pupa has reached the surface and the conditions for emergence are favourable, it will hang motionless for as long as two or three minutes. More often than not it will go for an immediate emergence which has the added advantage of keeping the time when they are vulnerable to predators down to a minimum. As the pupa arrives at the very point of emerging, instead of hanging down vertically from the surface as is so often illustrated, the pupa actually clings to the surface film with its thorax and then lies with its abdomen parallel to it. Once this manœuvre has been accomplished, the pupa then starts to pump its body in order to build up the pressure needed to split the pupal skin. This takes place along a pre-determined line of weakness which runs along the back of the creature's thorax. During this period it is quite easy to observe the adult fly's body pumping within the now defunct cuticle of the pupa, working away trying to break out.

Once the required pressure has been built up, the skin of the pupa parts and the adult insect extricates itself from what must be very much like a strait-jacket. Though yet again the Chironomid does not pull itself out with its legs but uses a form of motion known as peristaltic movement. This particular motion is of the type used for moving food around our own intestines and may best be described as working by rippling the body in the opposite direction to that which the body of the insect needs to move so forcing it forward.

As the adult Chironomid emerges from the pupal shuck, its wing buds are expanded by pumping them up with blood and for this reason as the fly pulls itself free its wings are orange in colour rather than the more normally expected translucent form. This unexpected flash of colour passes quickly and after five or six seconds the wings alter to their fully developed form and the adult insect stands by the now empty pupal shuck for a second or two before taking flight.

Once airborne, the adult insect heads towards the cover of bankside vegetation where it rests before beginning the performance of mating and egg laying. In shape and colour, the males and females are very similar though there are slight differences which allow the layman to tell them apart. The females are slightly larger and fatter than their mates though the real distinguishing feature emerges when you observe the insects' antennae. In the male the antennae are much more feathery than those of the female, which in many cases are quite hard to see. As with the pupa, the adult is known by one or two other names such as Midge, Duck Fly and also Buzzer. Incidentally the term Buzzer comes from the humming sound that the male insects make as they form dense swarms which I am sure we have all seen at times hovering around the tops of trees and bushes lining the lakeside. These large swarms of males make a high-pitched buzzing sound used as a means of attracting the attention of the females, and there they hang in large swarms, until the females arrive and mating can take place.

Mating completed, the now fertilised females return to the water's surface to carry out their final act, that of laying their eggs. At this time the female takes on a hooked shape and many anglers are familiar with the silhouette of the egg-bearing fly which may be carrying as many as 3,000 individual eggs in the package held at the tip of her abdomen. The egg laying usually takes place during either the early morning or late evening period. It is at such a time that the trout take advantage of the females, which having delivered their cargo, fall dying on the surface. It must be said that this is one of the few times that trout take the adult Chironomid in any quantity.

This fine brownie was stuffed full of small brown midge pupae.

Because the Chironomid is such an important insect there are a great many imitations, though these are mostly for the pupal stage, the larva with the adult being a little neglected. Taking matters in chronological order, we will deal with the larva first as on occasion we have found their imitations to be very effective. As the natural creatures vary in both size and colour, so should our imitations if we are to cover most eventualities. It is never a good idea to make things too complicated and so we prefer to keep our patterns to a minimum, sticking simply to two trusted ones.

The first is a bright red imitation of the bloodworm incorporating Copydex which gives a wonderfully translucent effect very similar to the natural. Copydex is flexible and the addition of a dyed red hackle gives the pattern the required life. Obviously it works best when trout are taking the naturals, which often occurs in windy weather.

What seems to happen is that the bloodworms, disturbed by heavy waves are forced to leave their protective tubes, at which point their conspicuous colour makes them an easy target. Fishing this imitation correctly is not always an easy matter especially from the bank. To be most effective it should be fished from the bottom to mid-water along the bank of coloured water formed by wave action. This can be difficult as it may mean casting slap-bang into a strong breeze, but it is well worth the effort. It is best to use either a floating or a sink-tip line and if a floater is used, a long leader with a weighted point fly will be needed to get down to the right depth.

Fishing from a boat is an easier proposition as it is possible to anchor off shore and cast in towards the bank. Whichever it is the retrieve should always be slow, keeping the flies as close to the bottom as you can. When fishing in this manner a typical three fly cast would be a weighted Pheasant Tail on the point, the bloodworm imitation of the middle dropper and perhaps a midge pupa on the top dropper. This allows the bloodworm imitation to be fished just off the bottom where the naturals are to be found lashing away.

A similar technique is used for fishing the second of our larvae imitations. This is the small green pattern used to imitate the similarly coloured natural which abounds in stillwater. As mentioned earlier, there is a phenomenon, where these small larvae rise up to the surface in buoyant mats of algae. As they fall out, the trout mop them up and

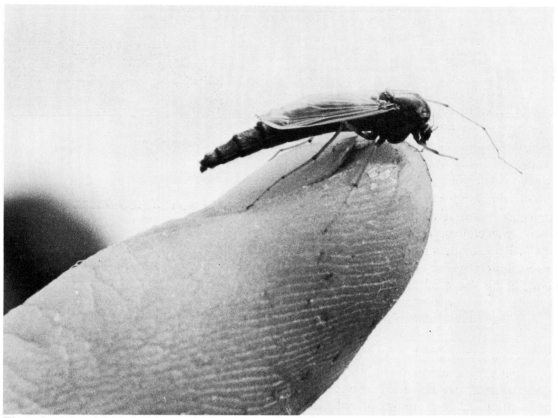
The early season adult black Chironomid. These hatch in their billions in late April.

it is here that an imitation can prove a real killer. The best time to use such a pattern is during the height of summer when fly life is at its peak.

Again using a floating line this imitation is best fished around weed beds but, unlike the bloodworm pattern, this smaller one should be retrieved near to the surface. As this imitation itself is small and is best used when conditions are calm and difficult, this in turn means fine and long leaders are necessary in order to be successful.

When we consider the pupa though we move on to the stage most important to the stillwater fly fisherman. Being so important you can understand just why there are so many imitations around. This was not always the case as it has only been in recent times that anglers have realised their true significance. Patterns range from the simple to the complex, all of which have their place. Simple dressings are none the less extremely effective and a plain wool bodied pattern with a peacock herl thorax catches a lot of fish.

Over the years we have developed a range of patterns including both marabou bodied and a true to life version which fills the gap left when fish are proving difficult. The usual advice when fishing midge pupa is to use a floating line and a team of three imitations in a range of colours. Looking back at the life cycle of the midge we can see that fishing our pupa near to the surface does not

always guarantee results. We tend to obey the adage that says that the evening rise often begins at 10 a.m. This may sound a shade daft but does have sound practical backing. Let us explain.

A few seasons back I (Bob) had been taking some very good fish from Draycote on a variety of techniques so consistently that it was becoming almost routine. I was brought down to earth one day when I arrived to find a water becalmed and the trout very difficult. Virtually nothing was rising and few fish were being caught even on delicate tackle. The reason for this was the calm conditions and the crystal clear water, a combination which always proves difficult for the fly fisher.

It was during the last week of April, a period when fly life should have been blossoming which made the apparent lack of insect life difficult to understand. Nevertheless I persevered with the usual deep water methods used when nothing is showing and though they accounted for a few fish, results were still well below par. Peering down into the clear dark water, I noticed thousands upon thousands of tiny white specks hanging a couple of feet below the surface. At first glance I assumed them to be some sort of Daphnia, and only closer inspection brought home their true significance. It was a sight I will never forget. These flecks of white were not Daphnia at all, but the white breathing filaments of large dark Midge pupae,

40

thousands of them.

It seemed likely that these were what the fish were taking, but how to make my imitation stand out from the multitude? In the end I plumped for a Size 8 Black Buzzer which although much larger than the naturals, had the advantage of standing out in the crowd. I also used a home-made slow sinking sink-tip in order to get my imitation down those two vital feet. Just to give it that bit more attraction, I also retrieved quite fast, a trick which often works as it certainly did in this case. And now in no time at all I had built up a really nice bag finishing off the day with a limit including browns to 3lb and some superb rainbows in the 2¼–2½lb class.

Other anglers using the normal tactics of floating line and a Black and Peacock Spider or a Black Pennell still struggled. The trout were as I suspected jam-packed with midge pupae all of which they had taken well down, picking them off during their ascent to the surface. Incidentally the actual emergence only took place as evening fell, even though the trout had been feeding heartily on the pupae all day.

Since then I have experienced similar occurrences on a number of waters including Grafham, Pitsford and Rutland. Thoughts of Pitsford bring back memories of another day which backs up the Draycote experience. During early season a year or two back, the initial onslaught had finished and the fish were proving very difficult. I had been fishing Pitsford mainly in the evenings and was finding things tricky coming away most times with only the odd fish. The curious thing was that one chap was doing very well indeed. He had taken an early season holiday and was fishing from a boat over a period of three days or so. Each day he caught good limits with trout up to 3lb even though everyone else was struggling. Eventually I managed to have a word with him and he let me into his secret. He was fishing in deep water along the Gorse and was using a team of Midge pupae but, and this was the point, fished hard on the bottom. The trout he was taking were full of big black Midge pupae, eaten as they were leaving the bottom. From this you can see how the evening rise can begin during late morning.

The midge pupae have a long way to go and must begin their rise to the surface early on in the day, well before we see them emerge on the surface. The trout, ever watchful, pick them off whilst they are still near the bottom, following them up to take them eventually on the surface at which point what we see is a typical rise.

The original Arthur Cove Pheasant Tail Nymph.

Once the pupa has reached the surface it is a different proposition and a stage on which the trout may become pre-occupied. I (Peter) remember one instance also at Pitsford where the trout, although rising freely, were proving very difficult to catch. In this case a floating line and a long leader were the obvious combination. There was a good emergence of Chironomids, but hardly a breath of wind and the water was as still as could be. No one was catching a thing until I managed to take a nice rainbow more by luck than judgement. Spooning the fish I saw to my surprise just what they were taking.

The trout had been taking pupae at the very point of emergence so that the body of the adult was half in and half out of the shuck. Indeed all the pupae I spooned from that particular trout were exactly the same. As luck would have it, I had been working on a pattern which imitated just this stage. I had taken a few fish on it at Eyebrook and it had found a dark corner in my fly box in which to hide. With trembling hands I tied it on, dipping it in flotant before casting out. It had hardly hit the water and settled before a fish took it and soon a second nice rainbow was placed in the bag.

This spectacular success continued until I had seven lovely rainbows including a 4lb specimen which is still my best ever from Pitsford. I cast out again and like a trained dog, up came yet another fish and took. This was no puppy though as in the clear water I could see a beautiful rainbow the best part of 6lb twisting and turning a few feet down. How it happened I don't know but after a few minutes of tough scrapping, the line suddenly went slack. I retrieved my line to find that not only had the fish gone but so had my fly – the only one I had. I managed to catch my last fish but it hardly made up for the disappointment of losing such a tremendous rainbow.

The pattern in question was dressed on a Size 14 dry fly hook, but with an extended body of nylon monofil which was wrapped in pheasant tail fibres. The idea was that the extended body would penetrate the water's surface imitating the shuck of the natural whilst the fly was kept floating by a normal collar hackle. Other patterns which work well are an ordinary green bodied pattern and also John Goddard's Suspender Buzzer. The Suspender in particular works very well when the trout are taking pupae right in the surface film. The beauty of this pupa is that it is supported by a ball of buoyant foam at its eye which keeps it floating right on the surface even without the use of a flotant in a heavy chop.

The main thing to remember is that when trout are taking pupa watch the water closely. Although it is by no means easy, especially when the pupa are being taken at depth, there are signs which give clues as to how the fish are feeding. For instance, if you do see a good hatch of Chironomids but little activity, it is likely that trout are feeding on the pupa deep down. The tactics to use on such occasions range from a floating line and leaded nymph, to a sink-tip or even a full fast sinker should the pupa be deep down.

Even though the intentioned imitation of Chironomid pupae and adults is quite a modern thing, there are many traditional wet flies which work very well. Whether their originators had the midge in mind when they put feather to hook I don't know, but many spider patterns work very well when trout are knocking off midges.

Two patterns which have worked well for us are the Black Pennell which is a hackled fly closely related to the spider patterns and a traditional winged wet fly, the Blae and Black. The Black Pennell, being a simple wingless pattern, works well when trout are taking the pupa. It seems that the bright yellow golden pheasant tippet tail gives the fly just the right amount of sparkle to be attractive. The Blae and Black also has the same material in its tail but unlike the Pennell, is winged with slips of grey starling primary. It works best when the trout are taking emerging pupae and adults.

Both patterns may be fished either from bank or boat. In the latter case they work best when fishing traditional loch style with a long soft-actioned rod and a light floating line. From the bank they should be likewise fished on a floating line and I have done particularly well at Eyebrook reservoir using both patterns on the same cast. To be honest, both patterns are a transitional phase between the pupae and the adult winged midge. The only trouble is

Always tie a good strong knot to your fly. It pays to take time over this as Arthur Cove shows.

that the adult midge turns up infrequently in autopsies and as a result it is of limited importance.

There is only one time when the adult Chironomid is taken in any number and this is when the female returns to deposit her egg mass. This usually happens towards evening time at which point we have had some success with one of Bob Carnill's patterns. It works best fished on the middle or top dropper of a three fly cast and suggests the spent female submerged in the surface film. Bob dresses the pattern in a range of colours but we find black and brown to be the most effective. It also has the advantage of working well when the trout are taking the emerging adults, which makes it quite a useful fly. Although it is always worthwhile having a few few adult midge patterns they are certainly the least useful. Sticking just to larvae and pupae imitations you will find that there are few times when you are caught lacking.

3 Daphnia

Trout have catholic tastes at the best of times and will readily take a wide range of food items. They have been known to eat feathers, stones and even cigarette ends. In the main though trout eat those insects we try to imitate to fool them into taking our impostors. Indeed the imitation of the various food forms is the whole basis of fly fishing and without it trout fishing would be all the poorer. On stillwaters there is one creature which though a major food source is impossible to imitate. This is the animal plankton Daphnia, and the reason it is impossible to copy is its size, or to be more correct, the lack of it.

Daphnia are very small indeed and, of all the species found in Britain, the largest is little more than 3mm in diameter. It is not the size which makes it such a popular food, but its incalculable numbers. Many lakes and reservoirs have a good population of these tiny creatures and in many cases the growth rate of the trout, particularly the rainbows, is linked directly to its numbers. Waters such as Rutland and Queen Mother Reservoir both contain immense concentrations of Daphnia at the height of the season providing an easily exploited source of protein. The fish from both waters are noted for their superb quality and large size. Trout simply take Daphnia in like soup when feeding on it.

It is often said how difficult it is to catch Daphnia feeding trout, but nothing could be further from the truth. Daphnia feeding trout form the basis of those taken by the boat fishing lure angler hitting brightly coloured flies and lures with abandon. Because they are so small Daphnia are seriously affected by water currents and light levels and we must be observant if we are to take full advantage.

Daphnia feeding trout are a superb example of the type of thoughtful approach needed by lure fishers. Daphnia blooms are not only pushed around a water by wind and currents but they also move up and down from the surface to the bottom. They don't seem to like bright sunshine one little bit and sink deeper to avoid the light. This means that they will alter their depth throughout the day. In the morning they will be near the surface, sinking deeper as the sun rises, only to return to the surface as light levels drop towards the evening.

When trout are taking Daphnia they follow the blooms and we must alter the depth at which we fish our flies in order to prevent them at the correct level. If we don't we may either fish too deep, or what is even worse, too near the surface. You can see that there are many factors which govern our tactics for catching the Daphnia feeders.

Perhaps the most perfect conditions are the grey, cloudy warm days when the Daphnia will be high in the water. If there is also a good wind they will get funnelled into the various bays into which the wind is blowing. Fish on the drift if you are in a boat, starting some 200 yards or so from the shore. Presentation of your lure at the correct depth is crucial and you must experiment with a range of depths until you hit fish. There is no point whatsoever in trying to imitate the Daphnia, simply use a single Size 6 or 8 longshank lure, tied in either white, black, green or orange. Colour is an important consideration which varies throughout the year.

In the early part of the season when the water is cold, a Black Chenille is as effective as anything. As the water warms though it is the more gawdy patterns which work best. Lures such as the Whisky Fly, Orange Marabou Muddler, Mickey Finn and the Leprechaun all catch well during the summer, particularly the first three.

In the 1981 season I (Bob) had been fishing regularly with England International Dave Allen and we had decided to fish loch style on each of our outings. It is a method I love, but the weather had been cold and on our last trip we had managed only four fish between us. This would not have been quite so bad if our friends hadn't consistently taken good bags of big trout throughout this period.

I didn't want to lose complete touch with lure fishing so on our next trip to Rutland we decided to cash in properly and fish deep. Instead of motoring straight down one of the arms with the armada, we drifted along from the Normanton Church towards the valve tower in the southern corner of the Dam. Keeping the boat some 150 yards from the shore, we drifted along carried by a stiff westerly breeze. As we passed the Three Trees, a well known landmark, we started to catch using a method that proved so deadly at Grafham. This meant drifting the boat point down the wind using the rudder for control

Spooning out a Daphnia feeding trout.

and casting with medium fast sinking shooting heads out from each side of the boat. What actually happens is that the line is cast out at right angles to the boat, allowed to sink for a few seconds and then pulled in quickly. This causes the line and therefore the lure to follow a curved path of swing which the trout find irresistible.

The day was windy and overcast and we started to pick up fish four to five feet down. As the boat was moving fast and we were also retrieving swiftly the trout took with a real bang. They were all beautiful rainbows around the 2½lb mark which put up a good fight. Virtually every one fell to a Nailer Fly, a lure with a gold body and red hackle and a wing overlaid with a few fibres of brown bucktail. We did so well in fact that by mid-afternoon we had returned to the lodge to buy second tickets. It was then that I decided to spoon the fish to see just what they were feeding on, and to my surprise they were stuffed to the gills with Daphnia.

Now after explaining all about Daphnia feeders, you may find this a little strange but there is a good reason. When Rutland first opened there were virtually no Daphnia which in turn meant that the rainbows did poorly; so badly in fact that it was generally accepted that Rutland was unsuitable for them. This was the first instance that I realised that Daphnia needs time to become established. Since then the Rutland rainbow has thrived and it reminded me that it took five years for Daphnia to get established at Grafham.

There is a strange phenomenon during mid-summer when Daphnia feeding trout go really daft for bright gaudy coloured lures. It has become known as Orange Madness for obvious reasons, and you will find the most effective flies during this period have at least a little orange in their make up. Why this is so it is difficult to be sure but even wet flies and nymphs incorporating orange prove real killers. The Grenadier is one such fly as is the traditional Teal and Orange, but there are other modern patterns which work well too. Palmered flies are effective fish catchers at all times. Use one with hot orange hackles during Orange Madness and you are on to a sure fire killer.

A few seasons back well known Northampton angler Nick Nicholson and I (Peter) were developing a range of palmered flies for use in International competitions. We came up with a variety of colour combinations, many of which took fish but there was one outstanding pattern which proved particularly good during the difficult mid-summer period. Like most Palmers, the fly was simplicity itself having just a gold tinsel body and a hot orange wing and collar hackle. It caught really well for both of us, taking some very nice browns up to 4lb even when others were struggling. I suppose Grafham was the place where the importance of Daphnia feeding was first recognised by anglers. Although it has suffered from a drop in Daphnia levels in recent years in the past both Bob and I have experienced some wonderful fishing there. During the 1980 season I had been concentrating heavily on loch style fishing virtually to the exclusion of all other methods though I couldn't complain as I had taken some lovely rainbows up to 4lb as well as some good browns.

Rutland was fishing well but I have a soft spot for Grafham and decided on a trip there during July. Fishing had been good, particularly off the surface, and catches of sixteen fish a trip were being reported even by anglers taking an evening boat. It was a late start but undaunted we set off towards Savage's Creek where some good fish had been turning up. The breeze was light and warm, the sky overcast and breaking, making for perfect conditions. Or so I thought because after three hours of pleasurable messing about we hadn't caught a thing. On such a supposedly good day it was difficult to understand our lack of success. It would have been easy to put on a fast sinking line and go deep, but we decided to stick to floating lines and teams of wet flies whatever the results.

We kept moving around gradually working our way towards the Dam and in one small bay I took a nice brown on a Soldier Palmer which at least raised our spirits a little. It proved a false omen though as five hours later it was still our only fish. The breeze now was getting up a little and blowing into the far corner of the Dam and white slicks were forming. The light was also beginning to fail and a definite touch of panic was setting in; after all, we only had one solitary brown trout in the boat. Drifting in towards the corner of the Dam I made a long cast and immediately I felt a take. As I lifted the rod, a trout leapt clear of the water in front of me and gingerly I played it to the net. While doing so I glanced at my father who had two fish on at once.

From then on we took short drifts into the Dam and on each drift caught fish, good ones too, silver rainbows up to 2¾lb. The wind had concentrated the Daphnia right into the corner. The fish knew this and were gorging themselves as a glimpse in the trouts' mouths easily showed. On this occasion the bulk of the fish fell to a palmered Dunkeld fished on the point. After taking a further fifteen beautiful trout in this evening frenzy we packed up delighted and relieved.

In closing we think it would be a good idea to look back at Grafham's Daphnia problem. Grafham was once the top trout water in the country. This was basically because of the huge concentrations of Daphnia which made the fish grow at a tremendous rate. At one time there were plenty of rainbows in the 3 to 5lb class but sadly this is not the case now. The rainbows just do not seem to grow so fast and whilst each season there are plenty of fish in fine fettle, they just do not reach those heady weights. It is interesting to note that this decline has also befallen the Daphnia and it looks highly likely that the two factors are linked. Of course there is little we can do about it, but it is a good explanation why we do not see those superb rainbows of the 1970s. Let's just hope it is merely cyclical and that the Daphnia will return with a vengeance.

4 The Olives

Although perhaps of not quite the same degree of importance to the fly fisher as the Chironomids, the various members of the Order Ephemeroptera or as they are sometimes known the upwinged flies play a significant role during a typical season on stillwater. That the upwinged flies are of less importance to the stillwater fly fisher than to his river counterpart is quite true, but it would be foolhardy to believe that such an important insect could be ignored. Indeed at certain times the various stages in the life cycle of the upwinged flies play an important part in the diet of the stillwater trout.

Stillwater anglers will need far fewer imitations of the upwinged flies and will use them on fewer occasions.

The Order name Ephemeroptera is derived from the same Latin word which gives us ephemeral, or short-lived. Many species do live longer than a single day but not much longer, their only task being to mate and breed. The adult insect's mouth parts are so poorly developed that they are unable to feed. Taking things in order we will deal initially with the nymph which is the creature's longest stage by far and the one of most interest to the trout. The nymphs of the various species are all basically the same design, each having a segmented abdomen with three tails, a thorax, three pairs of legs, and a head holding the eyes, mouth parts and antennae. To categor-ise the variations on the basic shape the late Oliver Kite divided the nymphs into six main groups using the criterion of habitat rather than species to identify them. Those groups are the bottom burrowers, silt crawlers, moss creepers, stone clingers, laboured swimmers and the agile darters. For the task of quick identification this grouping holds good today.

Although there are a fair number of species of up-winged flies found on the various types of stillwaters throughout Britain and Ireland, there are only five, not counting the Broadwing or Caenis which are common enough to make their inclusion in this book worthwhile. These include the Claret and Sepia Duns, Blue Winged Olive and the Pond and Lake Olives with the last being the most important.

The Claret and Sepia Duns are closely related species being *Leptophlebia vespertina* and *Leptophlebia marginata* respectively. They both belong to the laboured swimmers group.

The nymphs of the Claret and Sepia Duns are similar enough for the same imitation to be used for both flies. The nymph is a little flattened with a row of feathery gills running along each side of its abdomen. It has three very long tails spread wide apart. When fully mature the

nymph of the Sepia Dun is that little bit larger than the Claret and its gills are rounded, while being pointed in the Claret.

When fully mature they climb up vegetation or even crawl up into the bank to emerge into the adult insect. Those I (Peter) have kept have climbed up the sides of their plastic dish before emerging leaving their empty shucks for me to see in the morning. Both adults are quite similar, especially in the Dun stage, though on closer examination there are quite distinct differences. The wings in the Claret Dun are very dark grey and pale fawn or buff on the Sepia. Although designed to give the reader a trout good eating guide rather than a species identity parade we will describe the differences between the spinner stage of the two species though it will probably never influence your catch rate a great deal. In the female spinner, the Claret and Sepia both have very similar coloured wings, though the abdomens do vary, the Claret being dark brown tinged with claret while the Sepia's is more a dark brick red.

The main reason we have included these two species in this chapter is that although they are relatively un-common they do at times offer interesting fishing when the fish are taking the naturals though this is far more likely to occur on the smaller Southern waters than it is on

A bright summer's morning at Eyebrook Reservoir, a water where pond and lake olives abound.

our big Midland stillwaters.

Another species that also falls into the category of being more common on the rivers is the Blue Winged Olive, *Ephemerella ignita*. Like the other two as well as occurring in rivers it also inhabits a number of stillwaters, though again these tend to be either large natural lakes or smaller waters close to rivers. The Blue Winged Olive is quite a simple insect to identify as it is virtually the only actually olive-coloured Olive stillwater anglers are likely to encounter which has three tails. It is quite large and its wings have a definite backward slant.

The Blue Winged Olive nymph is a curious little creature and belongs to the Moss Creepers group because of its habit of crawling about under stones and pieces of sunken wood and mossy vegetation. It grows quite large and is a decent bite for any trout, and as a result is taken quite frequently. As far as imitation goes, any brown nymph such as a Pheasant Tail is effective when trout are taking the natural which is basically a brownish hue.

It is only when we move on to the Pond and Lake Olives that we hit upon the species that are of the greatest importance to the stillwater fly fisher. Both belong to the genus *Cloeon*, whilst the actual species title is *dipterum* for the Pond Olive and *simile* for its lake counterpart. As this is not a book to help the angler identify the exact species but simply to give him an idea as to the type of insect and how best to go about imitating that creature we have decided to pair the two together and treat them as the same insect. For this reason we will refer to both species as the Pond Olive and hope that you will bear with us in understanding that we are talking about two very similar species.

As the season progresses, so the average size of individual specimens tends to decrease. Again, like the Blue Winged Olive it is quite an easy insect to identify, as apart from the Caenis it is our only upwinged fly without any hind wings.

Dealing with the nymph first, the Pond Olive Nymph belongs to the group of Agile Darters. When the nymph decides to move it really can motor, so fast that it is often difficult to follow. Of all the nymphs to be encountered frequently on stillwater they are probably the most rapid movers and it is often a wonder the trout manage to catch them, but catch them they do in quite large quantities. When fully grown the nymphs are about 9–11mm long and up until the very point at which they are about to emerge as the winged insect they are basically an olive green in colour. As their time to emerge beckons the colour darkens, especially round the wing cases which

Ex-England World Cup winning centre half Jack Charlton has turned his sporting attentions to trout fishing. Here he lands a good rainbow at one of the small fisheries.

turn almost black, whilst the body becomes more of a brown shade particularly in the male. This is probably one of the reasons why a Pheasant Tail Nymph can be so effective during a hatch of Pond Olives.

Just prior to their emergence, the body of the nymph suddenly changes to a silvery hue caused by gas being trapped between the old cuticle of the nymph and the body of the winged insect. At this point the nymph becomes so buoyant that it has problems staying beneath the surface and has to grip on to any available vegetation. After a short while though the nymph does eventually rise and after a few seconds, the skin along the thorax splits and the winged adult emerges. It is now in the stage known as the Sub-Imago or as we anglers call it, the Dun. A dull creature with opaque wings edged with a row of hairs it has yet another moult to undergo before it is sexually mature. Once the dun's wings have dried, they sail along on the surface before eventually taking flight for the nearest bank-side vegetation which brings with it some degree of protection.

Once a few hours have passed, the dun then completes yet another moult which is all that more incredible if you consider that it even sheds a layer of skin from its already fragile looking wings. The creature that emerges from the dull skin of the dun might just as well be another separate species being so different. The dull wings have been replaced by clear, sparkling new ones and the body colours are much more vivid and alive. It is now that the Pond Olive is ready to mate.

Harking back to the Sub-Imago or Dun it is at this point that the Pond Olive is actually olive in colour, particularly in the case of the females, which may range in shade from a bright green olive to a darkish brown olive depending on the time of year and individual variation. It is now that the Pond Olive may best be imitated by such patterns as the Olive Quill and Greenwell's Glory which suggest the Pond Olive in its winged form so very well. Although fish taken during a hatch of Pond Olives are not often the largest in the lake there is some terrific sport to be offered to those willing to fish the Olive.

One of the best waters in Britain, I (Bob Church) know of for regular Pond Olive hatches is Pitsford Reservoir, a water only a few minutes' drive from my home in Northampton. It probably fishes best during June and July and as a result I rarely bother to fish it until then when fly life is at its peak. Although I had not been fishing the water in the 1983 season, a good friend of ours, Nick Nicholson, had. He was a season ticket holder and spent most of his free time on Pitsford and informed me that fishing had begun to improve with the first of the season's Pond Olive hatches.

My first boat was booked for 22 May and I wondered whether it might have been just a little too early with the rain having already spoiled the hatches of flies we had come to expect at this particular time of the season. But, because of the unexpected wave we set up loch style outfits. Nick had tipped me off that the Scaldwell Arm was fishing particularly well so I decided to stay in the shallower area of the reservoir. Making my way out towards the direction of Scaldwell I noticed the occasional rise on the far side of the Walgrave Arm. I watched closely as the odd fish rose among a whole armada of Pond Olives sailing down the wind.

To keep things simple I used only two flies on the cast, the June Fly with its pale green body on the point with my favourite all rounder, the Queen of the Water, on the bob. In no time at all two good-sized brownies took a liking to the bob fly and were boated within my first few casts, a very pleasant way to start what looked like being a very uncomfortable day. Unfortunately my initial enthusiasm was soon dampened as for the next half an hour it thundered, hailed and then finally poured with rain. As soon as the rain abated, the obliging Olives were soon hatching again and the fish continued rising until 3.30 p.m. when we packed up with a very nice double limit of sixteen fish. Incidentally, the catch was half rainbows and half browns. It was interesting that it was the browns which fed in the morning with the rainbows taking over later in the day. As far as the most effective flies were concerned, the bulk of the fish did fall to the Queen of the Water followed by the June Fly with just two fish falling to a standard dry Pond Olive pattern.

It is not just our large Midland reservoirs which can provide good Pond Olive fishing. Eire's Lough Carra is a unique water in that it is so alkaline that the bottom and the aquatic vegetation is covered in a thick milky white deposit. The gin-clear water makes the fishing particularly difficult, especially during the middle part of the day.

On one occasion a couple of years ago I was fishing the water during a lean spell and it had been quite a few tiring hours since my last take. Suddenly from nowhere the odd fish began to rise in small patches. The fish were quite happily knocking off the emerging duns and, using a traditional Irish pattern the Sooty Olive, we were soon into some of the very silver brown trout for which Lough

Carra is famous. So, after what had initially looked like being a rather poor day, we were pleasantly surprised to end the session with several fish in the 1¼–2lb class, most of which fell to the Sooty Olive, the Olive Quill and the Greenwell's Glory. Incidentally in Ireland they have the habit of calling the green coloured flat winged chironomid midges olives.

If the Pond Olive Dun manages to avoid the fish until it is able to take to the wing, it still has to run the gauntlet of birds and the literally millions of spiders which lie in wait for any hapless insect which might stumble into their web. The Pond Olive is now at the Imago stage, the sexually mature adult best known to the angler as the Apricot Spinner because of its pale orange or apricot colour strongly marked with reddish blotches. The wings are also particularly striking being perfectly clear and translucent and edged along the front with a yellow olive band. To avoid confusion we have only described the female insect. In the Dun both sexes are very similar although in the spinner there is quite a large degree of difference but as it is only the female which returns to the water there is little point in going into a great detail about the male which few fish see anyway.

When mating has taken place the now fertilised female returns to the water not to deposit her eggs as you might expect, but minute larvae, which have already hatched in her oviducts. This task completed the now exhausted female falls spent and dying on the water's surface. This return to the water often takes place either during late evening or even during the hours of darkness. As a result it is often only until the next morning that both fish and angler can take full advantage of the fall.

As far as imitating or at least suggesting to the trout the various stages in the life cycle of the Pond Olive, there are quite a few patterns which cope well indeed with the problem. When it comes to the nymph, any green or brown nymph, such as the Pheasant Tail, the Spring Favourite or the Olive Nymph will prove effective if fished around weed beds and the like where the naturals are to be found. Fished slowly on a floating line, imitations of the nymph can prove very effective indeed as can the Olive Quill, Greenwell's Glory and the June Fly when the fish are knocking off the emerging Duns. Dry olive patterns in similar colours to the wet flies also prove very effective at times, as can the dry imitations of the spent Apricot Spinner. For such times both Dick Walker and John Goddard have devised very killing patterns with the necessary spent wing profile and apricot coloured body.

Midway through the summer of 1983 Peter stumbled upon an excellent dry fly pattern to imitate the Pond Olive. He passed a few on to me and I had quite spectacular results with them at Ringstead Grange. It is amazing how experiment at the tying bench with new materials can pay off and I must name this fly for him, Peter's Olive. In closing, fishing the various imitative stages of the Pond Olive can prove very profitable throughout summer though its main period as the winged insect peaks in June and July.

5 Crane Fly

There are a number of insects eaten by trout that are not aquatic in origin. These terrestrial insects get blown onto the water or sometimes land there under their own steam. One such fly is the Crane Fly, a large insect known more popularly as the Daddy Longlegs. There is hardly a person, let alone a fly fisherman, who has never seen a Crane Fly. With their long gangling legs, and large size, they are an unmistakable sight. They belong to the family Tipulidae, which is very large, containing nearly 300 species in Britain alone. In this family species vary considerably in both size and colour and, whilst some are very small, one, *Tipula maxima*, is so large that it is only exceeded in size by the larger dragonflies. *Tipula maxima* although large is not the most abundant of species, and is

Fishing during a blustery autumn day. A perfect day for trying out the Crane Fly

not the one usually seen on stillwaters.

Although Crane Flies are not aquatic in the strictest sense of the word, neither are they wholly terrestrial. The larvae of the various species of Crane Fly vary somewhat in their habitats. Some are totally aquatic, feeding on plant material and rotting organic matter and breathe by means of an extendable tube which reaches up to the surface from the tip of their abdomens to take air from the atmosphere. Others live in the damp ground at the margins of rivers and stillwaters. Another type is wholly terrestrial and lives amongst the root systems of many plants nibbling away around the ground level. Gardeners will immediately recognise the creature described as the Leather Jacket. This dirty greyish coloured grub is the bane of many a horticulturist as it satisfies its appetite on his prize plants.

When it comes to the time for pupation, the larva migrates to a dry piece of ground. When the pupae are fully developed, they wriggle up through the soil to the surface, until they protrude for a short distance into the air. At this point the dry brown skin of the pupa splits and the adult insect emerges, leaving the shuck empty and forlorn. The sight of these shucks incidentally is a very good sign of the start of a mass hatch. Crane Flies will emerge throughout the whole of the spring, summer and autumn, depending on the species. The angler though, is only really interested when they are at their peak. This

tends to be around the last week in August and all of September, when the weather is usually still mild but damp, with strong winds.

I am sure that we are all familiar with the sight of Crane Flies around our windows, attracted during the night by our lights. When this occurs it's time to watch closely for Crane feeding trout. The terrestrial species offer the best chance of sport, particularly those which inhabit the large grass pastures which are so common around most of our reservoirs. In these fields the numbers of individual Crane Flies may be counted in thousands, the grass seethes with them, both singly and in mating pairs.

Crane Flies are rather weak flyers, and when a good strong breeze gets up, they are often uncontrollably blown onto the water's surface. At first the trout take a while to get used to them, as is quite common with large creatures. For a while at the beginning of the Daddy season dozens of Crane Flies are blown helter-skelter over the waves without a single one being taken. It does not take long though before the trout realise that here is a new source of protein, at which point the fireworks really start.

When the trout are hard on Daddies, you'll see them being blown past you onto the water, and into the mouth of a trout. Strangely when the fish are taking the natural you must watch the water carefully to see them being sipped in. Trout do not often take Daddies in a violent

50

manner, but with a gentle rise, which in a large wave is hardly noticeable. Now a suitable artificial can produce some wonderful results. Although it is not always the big fish that come to Daddy Longlegs, there are enough large fish up after these meaty insects to warrant the use of a leader of at least 6lb breaking strain.

Although it was mentioned at the beginning of this chapter that the family Tipulidae contains a great many species, this affects the angler very little. Like so many creatures we have come across in fly fishing the various species are so similar as to warrant only a handful of artificials.

When tying imitations, the main points of recognition are the large meaty-looking body and the long gangling legs. All our patterns are tied on either a Size 8 or 10 longshank hook.

The first pattern has a body of grey brown feather fibre, wings of Plymouth Rock hackle tips and eight legs of knotted cock pheasant tail fibres. It may sound strange having eight legs on the imitation of an insect, but there is method in our madness. When the trout take, their sharp teeth often break the fragile legs. As it is these straggly legs which give the pattern its effectiveness, once they have gone it's useless. If you tie on a few more in the first place, it lasts that little bit longer, and the trout don't mind at all as they are unable to count.

This pattern can either be fished wet or dry and has caught some nice fish for both of us. It works particularly well fished dry as I (Bob) found out one breezy day in early October. I was out in a boat at Rutland Water on this occasion working my way down to the bottom of the South Arm. The breeze was blowing off Lax Hill carrying with it numbers of big Daddy Longlegs which were dropping onto the water. The trout were out in force to take advantage. It is funny how these large insects can bring up those good brownies which have been skulking around the bottom all summer. Trout usually take Daddies quite gently, but on this day they were crashing about all over the place. It is not often that we are lucky enough to see rises which include a porpoise roll and a great splash as yet another Daddy is engulfed by a big brown. Exciting stuff.

I used a 6lb breaking strain leader and two dry Daddies, one fished on a dropper 2 yd from the point fly. It would have been folly to go any lighter with such big fish about. The trout's antics were amazing and on one rise the fish jumped a good 2½ft (76cm) out of the water only to splash back down onto my dropper fly. Clearly he

was trying to drown the Daddy by slapping it, but in doing so he fell on the hook and foul hooked himself.

With the trout feeding so well it was the signal to fish loch style, drifting and covering as many fish as possible. We drifted quite fast not using a drogue, and we began to catch well. It was very pleasant fishing taking these fish right off the top. They were a good size too and we ended up with several in the 2½–3½lb class.

Apart from the ordinary wet and dry patterns, we have also developed a buoyant bodied dressing. It is very similar in make-up to the previous dressing, but the body is of bird quill covered with dyed latex rubber strip. The quill, which is usually fine peacock, provides the buoyancy needed to keep the fly up even in a good chop. Remember you are using a heavy Size 8 longshank hook and you need all the flotation you can get.

The third pattern is used exclusively for dapping, a style which is only really applicable to boat fishing, but catches a great many fish on all our big lakes, lochs and loughs. The fly is tied in a very similar manner to the previous two, but lacks wings, these being replaced by two long fibred hackles. They are tied in long to catch the breeze, and let the fly be worked over the water's surface.

Dapping is not only very effective it is also very exciting. Use a long rod in excess of 12ft (3.75m) and, instead of a normal fly line, about 6ft (1.8m) of dapping floss. The dapping floss is now usually made of polypropylene, a material which billows out well to take advantage of even a light breeze, and doesn't absorb water as easily as silk floss. Instead of casting you simply allow the wind to catch the floss and blow it out in front of the boat with the fly in tow. You need only a 3 or 4ft (91 or 122cm) leader as the floss doesn't touch the water until you hook a fish.

I (Peter) have used the method on a number of occasions when the fish have been on the Daddy and done well. At Grafham in particular, I have had some very nice browns and rainbows. On one occasion fishing in a boat with Duncan Currie from Corby, we had some tremendous sport on the dapped Daddy. Grafham allows the use of the natural Crane Fly and as we wanted to see if it worked, this is how we started off. It's the only time I have ever fished after spending half the morning catching flies. We finally got out onto the water and our efforts were rewarded with some nice rainbows up to 2½lb. The takes to the natural insect were very delicate, and if you didn't watch carefully all you would notice was your line suddenly shooting under.

Unfortunately we soon ran out of Crane Flies so we

continued dapping, but with artificials. The trout seemed to like them just as much. The fishing remained steady and whilst we did not catch anything huge we ended up with a nice bag of rainbows up to 2½lb.

It was very nearly a different story though as Duncan had the misfortune to miss a beautiful brown trout in the 6–7lb class. The fish took just as we finished a drift, in about 3ft (91cm) of water, and Duncan in his excitement pulled the fly right out of its mouth not letting it turn down before striking. It was understandable in the circumstances, but nevertheless robbed him of a superb fish. Rainbows to 6½lb have been landed at Grafham on natural Daddies.

6 Fry Feeding Trout

Most lakes and reservoirs contain high levels of coarse fish which are forever having to be removed by netting. Whilst regarded as a nuisance competing for food with the trout, they themselves make up quite a high proportion of the trout's diet particularly on large reservoirs.

Whilst the administrators often think little of these coarse fish they do provide us with some very interesting fishing. When trout are on fry they often become preoccupied and if you do not have the right pattern to imitate the particular small fish that the trout are eating you may well go home fishless. Over the years many so-called experts have denounced lure fishing as a merely chuck and chance it game, proving their own lack of experience. When the trout are on a particular stage of fry they can become very selective and to be successful you too must be selective in your lure choice. This is much the same way as a chalk stream fly fisher who chooses his tiny pattern carefully. You too will need to use a lure of the right size, colour and just as important, action.

Each year on our lakes and reservoirs millions upon millions of coarse fish eggs are laid to hatch out into tiny fry forever on the hunt for food. Unfortunately Nature is a cruel mistress and of the incalculable number which hatch, only a very small proportion are destined to reach adulthood. When the fry are at a very small stage they lack any colour, their bodies being virtually transparent, and shows their intestines quite clearly. Their eyes are large and pronounced. Because of this we do not need a whole range of patterns to cover all the various species, simply the odd one or two. The main points of a good imitation should mirror the natural's small size, translucency and pronounced eyes, the latter point incidentally is important but often overlooked.

As the fry grows it gradually assumes some colour varying of course depending on the species. Because the fish is still small though it is still very pale and even though the body may be coloured the fins are still colourless. Because of the lack of colour general fry patterns are just as effective as the more imitative ones. An interesting point at this stage is that as the fry grow, they appear in their thousands around the margins in the shallow water. This is typical of all small fish which use this safety in numbers as a protection against predators.

Fry feeding takes place in a number of ways which should all be observed by the fly fisherman if his imitations are to be fished properly. The most frequently described method is when the trout attacks the shoal smashing through the small fish to cripple a few before returning to mop up the dead and dying. It is difficult to actually see the trout when they do this, but by watching the water there are pointers towards its occurrence. The main thing to watch for is the movement of the small fry.

When a trout charges in on an attack, the fry, desperate to get away, jump clear out of the water in small groups. Such a sight is of course an indication that trout are on the prowl. You may even be lucky enough if the trout are feeding hard to see them actually break surface right in the margins spraying fry everywhere. I suppose you could call these typical fry feeding instances. They do not offer the angler too many problems other than to get the size of

A sunken hedge. A perfect spot to find small fry sheltering amongst the flies.

lure right. Size does matter a lot. For instance, in the case of the tiny pinhead fry you will need a small, finely dressed imitation, two very good ones being the Jersey Herd and Sinfoils Fry.

The last pattern is a very close copy with its silvered hook wrapped with clear polythene, a speckled grey mallard wing, bold head and conspicuous painted eye. One point that is worth mentioning is that when trout are on tiny fry it may not always show up in autopsies unless you know what you are looking for. Because their bodies are so fragile they are quickly digested. This means they do not last long in a trout's stomach before being broken down. If you spoon a trout and all you find is a grey nasty looking soup, suspect fry. Search for the tiny backbones which are the last parts to be dissolved and these will confirm your suspicions.

When the fry are tiny their imitations need to be dressed on similarly sized hooks, Sizes 14 and 12 long-shanks being about right. As they grow, we need to scale up our patterns to Size 8 or 6 longshanks. Dressings which are effective when these larger fry are being taken include the Appetizer, Badger Matuka, Missionary, Chenille Bodied Baby Doll, Mylar Bodied Fry, Squirrel and Silver, White Muddler and the ordinary Muddler. As you can see it is quite a range, but they all have their place. They all have the same pale bodies being either white or silver and most are backed with a darker material which imitates the countershading of the natural fry. This countershading is very important, as it makes the fry look simply like a greyish floating object underwater. The dark

back and light belly merge when the light is coming from above and break up the fry's outline making it appear less solid. So it is with lures such as the Appetizer which while looking totally improbable lying dry in our hand takes on a natural ghost-like quality when fished a few feet down.

When fishing these patterns the most obvious point is to track down the big shoals of fry in the first place. Now neither of us have a great liking for seagulls but they do come in useful for fish spotting. Watch the flocks carefully and if you see them constantly diving in one area, suspect fry as the cause. Remember, where there are fry there are usually trout. It sounds very easy, but it is not always like that.

A few years ago I (Bob) had the pleasure of taking two *Angling Times* prize-winners Fred Russell and Ralph Williams out on a boat at Grafham. Murphy's Law was at work and the August day we chose was very hot and the water flat. I was desperate to catch fish for them but after trying virtually all over the reservoir, by mid-afternoon we had only two fish in the boat between the three of us. As a last resort, I thought it would be a good idea to have a look around the valve tower as a few fish often hung about there. We approached carefully on the oars and as we got closer I began wondering if the fry might be early this year. When we were only 35–40yd (32–37m) from the tower the small fry could be seen dimpling all over the place. It made me think that flat calms were not so bad after all.

I was just thinking that the trout might be feeding around this area when there was an almighty crash as a big trout smashed through the fry on the surface. With trembling fingers I tied on a big White Muddler and cast out, dropping my lure just short of the concrete. After only a couple of pulls I had a tremendous take, and after a great tussle I landed a perfect rainbow weighing almost 5lb. Interestingly it was hooked not in the mouth but just under the chin. This occurs quite often with fry feeders and does not mean it is foul hooked. What happens is that the trout rushes at the lure and tries to kill it rather than actually eat it. We continued to catch trout on sinking lines and Muddlers, casting these so they hit the stone-work and dropped into the water. To cut a long story short we finished up with fourteen immaculate rainbows, the smallest fish being a two-pounder.

For my next trip I arrived totally prepared and a few minutes after leaving the Grafham Lodge, was anchored 35yd (32m) upwind of the tower. The day could not have been more difficult and a stiff wind had concentrated the fry at all depths tight up against the tower. Using a fast sinking line, a 5yd (4.5m) leader and a White Tandem Muddler, I cast as before so that the lure hit the tower each time. The line would then sink to the bottom but the long leader and buoyancy of the lure meant that it remained on the surface. Only when I began to retrieve did the lure sink, swimming right down the side of the tower. Being more visible than the other fry the lure was taken time and time again and we finished with sixteen fish for 41½lb, the best two being 4lb 12oz and 4lb 4oz.

We were not the only anglers to have a good catch, as another Grafham regular from Wisbech took some good fish topped by a magnificent 7¼lb rainbow, which took a tandem Appetizer. It is interesting to note that Grafham's big brown trout population is receiving very little attention in the 1980s, most anglers now happy to fish on the top with small flies which have little chance of being taken by a really big fish. The big browns which made Grafham so famous are still there though. At the end of the 1983 season I (Bob) took part in a two day pike fishing experiment. Whilst we took few pike, a number of big browns were caught.

Fishing around the Dam Wall with a 7in (18cm) spoon I connected with a powerful fish which turned out to be a 5lb brown. Luckily it was hooked in the front of the mouth and I was able to return it. Further along the Dam two other anglers caught magnificent fish of 7lb and 9lb, the larger falling to well known pike man Bill Chillingsworth. This means the big fish still exist at Grafham. Whilst the water has had its problems of late with daphnia levels falling, brown trout live a long time and it is quite possible that a 15 or 16lb fish could fall to anyone prepared to stick to deep fishing methods with large tandem lures.

Thinking of fry feeders let me (Bob) turn the clock back to pre-Grafham days when a 3lb fish was a specimen. I used to fish with Fred Wagstaffe and John McLelland quite a lot and it was Mac who taught me to tie flies. I remember building the first glass fibre rods in his workshop when the material was virtually unknown in Britain.

Mac was a great fly tyer but very secretive about his new inventions. He was so secretive that Fred used to tease him saying that the contents of his fly box was so secret that even Mac himself dare not look inside.

He did invent one good pattern, the Squirrel and Silver which has caught consistently throughout the years. One day in August I did very well with it using the

A late season fry feeder. In this case the brown trout had been taking both small roach and perch.

continuous overhand retrieve achieved by clamping the rod between the arm and the body using both hands to pull the line in. It imparts a smooth retrieve which catches the better fish which are used to the normal jerky style, either ignoring it completely or following then sheering away at the last minute.

As the season continues so the fry grow until at the back end there are vast shoals of fish 2–3in (5–7.5cm) long. If you are going to catch trout taking this size of fry you need to use similarly sized artificials. When trout are gorging themselves on great big mouthfuls of fish they are hardly likely to look at a Size 12 longshank Sinfoil's Fry. The small fish hang around weed beds for protection and it is here that we should concentrate our attention. From the bank the best times are during the early morning and evening when trout are less timid and will move into shallow water where the bank angler can reach them. For the boat angler, things are a little easier as in deeper water the trout's feeding binge will continue throughout the day.

What happens is that there are short periods of frantic activity followed by long periods when the trout are digesting their meal. Why most people fail to take full advantage of fry feeders is that they find a good spot, catch a couple of fish and when things go dead, they move. This is a mistake. If you are to be in with the chance of a big catch you must sit it out. If you find an area where big trout are fry feeding, anchor up and wait for the fish to come back on the feed. Like as not they will, though it might take a few hours.

During the 1982 season I (Peter) had been fishing Rutland Water with my regular partner Duncan Currie. We had been fishing well all season and had taken a great many big browns topped by two fish of 8lb 15oz and 9lb 12oz. The interesting point was that there had been a huge surge in the perch population. There were thousands upon thousands of them, and as usually happens when there are population explosions, a compensating disease broke out.

Towards the end of the year, the perch fry began to die off in large numbers and the trout, always ready to take advantage of an easy source of food, were packing them down their throats. They become so preoccupied with the perch that some good trout were found dead with perch as large as half a pound stuck in their gullets.

At first the trout were easy to catch but as they became even more selective they began to prove tricky. Duncan and I had witnessed this tailing off and so one day set off down the South Arm to try and settle the score. We had come to the conclusion that the most productive areas had been given too much of a hammering and so new spots needed to be found. It was a rough windy day so we tried a few drifts but to no avail; there appeared to be no fish at all more than 50yd (46m) from the shore. At this time the bank anglers were doing really well and it was the boatman's time to struggle. Most times he just could not get close enough to the bank to catch fish.

Using fast sinking lines and tandem white lures we anchored up in the shallow water of Manton Bay and whilst we took a few nice rainbows of around the 2½lb mark, the large browns were conspicuous only by their absence. We continued picking up nice rainbows for the rest of the day, until Duncan pointed out that lower down towards the Gorse Bushes he had noticed a great deal of seagull activity. It was now getting quite late and as we only had three fish each we decided to move. At first we just drifted along carefully trying to get a better picture of what was happening. We could see that the gulls were picking up the dead and dying perch being blown into the corner.

Dropping anchor close to the area we watched the huge swirls as the trout took the dead perch. We were still not close enough but decided to remain stationary as we had already caused enough disturbance. Casting out,

Duncan immediately had a take and soon a fine 4lb brown lay glistening in the landing net. Apart from a few follows from big fish we didn't get another take so we decided to let out more rope and to drift in closer towards the activity. The results were nothing if not spectacular. In no time we were catching good brown trout packed to the limit with small anaemic looking perch about three or four inches long. This was the reason our tandem Appetizers had proved so effective. We were still catching good fish when I had a big brown follow me right up to the boat. Luckily it was in a killer mood and crashed into my lure on the surface splashing me with a great thrash of its tail. It then shot off in a great powerful rush and took quite a while before being beaten and ready to be netted. It was a tremendous fish and whilst not as big as some of the monsters that had been caught from Rutland, it weighed in at 6lb 1oz. As darkness fell we packed up with sixteen superb trout including rainbows to 4lb and browns to 6lb.

The main point to remember is to try to keep your patterns of the same size as the fry the trout are taking. This may mean using lures as large as 4in (10cm) and, although the fry may be a little larger, it seems this size is ample. They are also the largest lures which may be cast properly even with heavy tackle. Many of the normal fry patterns tied on Size 6 longshanks in tandem work well and there is a tandem White Muddler with a blue and black over wing which is also effective at times.

The only other factor to be considered is colour which may be important in certain instances. It all depends on the species of fry the trout are taking. For example, if they are on either roach or bream fry, basically white patterns with perhaps a touch of red at the throat are usually best. Patterns such as the Missionary, Orange Throated Baby Doll and Jack Frost are ideal.

Perch are another species high on the trout's menu and lures like the Appetizer and Badger Matuka all work well, particularly as the small dying perch look rather pale with little colour in their bodies but with distinctive fins. The Mylar Bodied Fry is also good for stickleback feeders which is more prevalent on our smaller stillwaters. In closing it is interesting that a lure first designed to imitate a small bottom grubbing fish also works on trout taking Bullheads as they do at Draycote Water. The lure is of course the Muddler Minnow.

7 Shrimps & Hoglice

When we consider the diet of the stillwater trout we invariably think of stages in the life cycles of aquatic insects. We also tend to think of all those terrestrial insects which either fly or are blown to a watery grave. What we often neglect are the whole host of small aquatic creatures which at times figure very high on the trout's menu. Two such small bugs are the freshwater shrimp and the hoglouse, both of which are taken in huge numbers at particular times of the year.

Both are extremely abundant in virtually all stillwaters and you do not have to take our word for it. Just pull up a few handfuls of weed from the shallows of any water and that weed will virtually move on its own due to the huge numbers spilling out from within the fronds. Both creatures are crustaceans rather than insects and this is quite easily recognised by the fact that they have far more legs than the insects which have six. In general form and habitat both are very similar, though there are of course some differences which we will now consider.

The more common of the two to turn up in autopsies is the shrimp. This is not because it is the more abundant but more to do with the habitat and the way the shrimp forever scuttles about amongst the weeds. The hoglouse on the other hand moves rather slowly and tends to keep itself well concealed beneath the rubbish on the lake's bed.

There are a few species of shrimp in Britain, the most common of which is probably *Gammarus pulex*. Like so many creatures which we anglers know we have to imitate, all are so similar that they may be treated simply the same. Although the species do vary in size, this is not a problem as all are of the same shape, but there is a slight variation in colour.

The adult *Gammarus* ranges from 10 to 20mm long. Its body is translucent with the actual colour showing through. One colour which is often mentioned is the orange mating shrimp, although I (Peter) have yet to see a naturally orange shrimp. The point that makes me suspicious as to their existence is that they are quoted as appearing during mid-summer in their mating season. In reality the shrimp has no particular season and breeds throughout the whole of the year. I may be wrong, but I have a feeling that the orange shrimp simply does not exist even though some anglers have assured me it does. Anyway until I actually see a live specimen I remain unconvinced.

The main point of confusion seems to arise from the fact that when a shrimp dies decay tends to turn it a pinkish orange. So, when a fish is spooned and its stomach contents examined if it contains dead shrimps they will often be this pinkish orange. This gives the impression that the fish have actually been eating shrimps of this colour. An understandable mistake it's true, but nevertheless a mistake.

Trout take them in large numbers especially in spring. Like one or two of the other species of aquatic fauna, the fish take shrimps usually when they are eating nothing else. When either at rest or just moving slowly whilst feeding the shrimp is basically arched in appearance with its many hair-fringed legs held in the curve of its body. When it wants to put on a quick burst of speed, it straightens its body using all its legs for maximum propulsion. This is an interesting point from the view of imitation as it means that not all shrimp patterns need to be dressed in the usual curved manner to be life-like.

There is also some variation in colour amongst individuals ranging from a pale washed out olive to almost transparent. Shrimp feeding seems to follow a specialised pattern. You very rarely find trout with a stomach full of midge pupae plus the odd shrimp. In large waters you often catch good brown trout in deep water which contain large numbers of *Gammarus*. Although it is of course difficult to be certain we have the feeling that this feeding does not take place in deep water.

As the bulk of the food is in the shallower water where weed and aquatic fauna is at its most prolific it is here that the trout must hunt. Shallow water means danger to fish and so they will only venture into this zone when light levels are down. It seems by the state of the shrimps to be found in many autopsies that the trout feed on them in the shallows at dusk, moving out into deep water during the day where they are then caught.

When fishing from the bank shrimps tend to turn up in fish mainly during spring and early summer, usually when other food items are scarce. For this reason imitations may prove very effective but the same cannot always

Shallow weedy bays like this one are a perfect habitat for both shrimp and hoglice.

be said for the hoglouse. In stillwater both creatures fill virtually the same habitat though as previously mentioned the hoglouse tends to be much more secretive. That trout eat them is undoubted. On quite a few occasions we have found them in autopsies carried out on fish from a number of waters but we feel that imitations are of limited use. This does not mean that imitations are going to be totally ineffective, just perhaps not as killing as might be thought, particularly considering the huge numbers of naturals to be found.

The hoglouse is known by various names throughout the country including the water slater and the freshwater louse.

The only problem when it comes to fishing hoglouse (Asellus) imitations is actually finding trout feeding on the naturals. Because they are so secretive trout do not appear to feed on hoglouse all that often. Most of the times we have encountered them in a trout's stomach is actually when we have caught large fish from deep water. At Rutland Water a few seasons back we were catching some very nice brown trout deep fishing with fast sinking lines fished out of the back of a drifting boat. These fish were actually lying about thirty feet down in over sixty feet of water. Virtually every one we caught was chock full with really huge hoglice, some only a little under 2cm long, though when we caught the fish they were not actually feeding on them at the time.

On smaller waters hoglice crop up in autopsies on

quite a few occasions and of course in such circumstances an artificial may prove effective. Indeed, when we come to fishing both hoglice and shrimp imitations, they both may be fished in a similar manner. One pattern which has accounted for a few fish is actually one of Peter's own tyings and is not available commercially. It has a body of brown rabbit or hare's fur, a hackle of brown partridge and a shell back of dark speckled grey turkey. The interesting thing is the way the hackle is tied. Instead of being wound on, it is laid along the body and bound down with either gold or silver wire. In this way it imitates the legs of the natural hoglouse.

Unlike the hoglouse, the shrimp has no lack of imitations, though most of them are relatively modern. It seems that up to twenty years ago fly fishers virtually disregarded the shrimp. Perhaps the most well known pattern is the one devised by Dick Walker. Like many of Dick's patterns, its body is composed of various coloured dyed wools giving an overall pinkish olive colour when mixed together thoroughly. It is usually dressed over a lead underbody, but this is optional. The beauty of the lead underbody is that because most of the weight is on the top side of the hook shank, the completed fly fishes upside down. This means that it can be bumped along the lake bed like the natural without forever catching up on bottom weed.

Other patterns include one of Peter's more life-like dressings using olive marabou and another similar pattern using brownish tan seal's fur, which imitates the light coloured naturals. When it comes to fishing them effectively, we must look back to how the natural moves. Like most imitative patterns it should be retrieved slowly. The real shrimp scuttles about along the bottom and that's just how our copies should be fished. This means either using a sinking line on a floater with a long leader and weighted fly. If you are in a boat and you find fish in deep water then a sinking line will be your best bet. From the bank or if you are anchored up in shallow water, the floating line and leaded shrimp is more controllable and more effective.

When we catch trout feeding on shrimp it tends to be by chance when fishing deep. During the cold weeks of April and early May it is quite possible to fish a shrimp imitation, catch fish on it and convince yourself you are really imitating a shrimp. At Rutland Water I (Peter) have taken some quite respectable trout on deeply fishing imitations twitched slowly along the bottom.

8 Dragon & Damsel Flies

Surely the most striking and spectacular insects to be encountered by the angler are dragon and damsel flies. With their beautifully iridescent bodies and translucent glistening wings they have the ability to brighten up even the most dour fishing days. Both belong to the Order Odonata. As can be expected both are similar in form although there are some quite distinct differences. Though both belong to the same Order, they may be divided into two further Sub-Orders. In the case of the dragonfly, this is Anisoptera and may be easily distinguished from the damsels by the fact that they have two pairs of wings which are unequal in length and held open when the insect is at rest.

The dragonfly is an accomplished hunter taking a wide range of flying insects on the wing. They are also extremely territorial in behaviour defending an area from other individuals. Their voraciousness is matched with their ability for flight. Their flight is strong and swift, darting in and out of marginal reeds and bushes. I (Peter) have observed a dragonfly take a large butterfly which is no mean feat. Once the prey has been captured there is virtually no escape and the dragonfly will return to a favourite perch in order to devour its meal.

Although the dragonfly is a very conspicuous creature it is also quite scarce and so is low on the trout's menu. For this reason it is of only passing interest to the fly fisher at least from the point of view of imitations. We must move on to their smaller cousins to find the more effective species to imitate.

The damsel fly belongs to the Sub-Order Zygoptera and may be distinguished by their much finer bodies and the fact that their wings are of equal length and held pressed together when at rest. Although they are much more numerous than the dragonfly, they too seem unattractive to the trout in their adult winged form, and apart from the very occasional instance are rarely taken. The nymphs on the other hand are quite a different proposition and these are high on the trout's menu in summer.

Like the adult winged insects, the nymphs of the two Sub-Orders of Odonata also differ quite considerably in appearance, although their general structure is very similar. Dragonfly nymphs, like the adults, are large robust creatures with stout bodies, and in the larger species may attain as much as 50mm or more in length when fully mature. Again like the adults, the nymph is an accomplished predator.

Because the damsel nymph is not quite so large and strong it is unable to prey on such spectacularly sized creatures as its larger cousin and prefers to feed on smaller, softer bodied creatures such as the larvae and nymphs of the Chironomids and 'mayflies' which do not put up quite the same struggle as a small fish. Both nymphs use the same apparatus to catch their prey. Their large eyes hardly miss a trick, being acutely aware of movement. Once the prey has been located, the nymph slowly stalks up to the creature and in a flash shoots forward a specially designed pair of jaws which have become fused together. These contain a wickedly sharp pair of pincers which grasp and hold the prey in a grip from which few escape. The prey is then pulled towards the true jaws to be devoured.

Both nymphs are equally adept at camouflage and come in a whole range of browns and greens which blend in perfectly with their weedy habitat. They are capable of a rather untypical burst of speed should the need arise.

Trout do undoubtedly take both nymphs at certain times of the year. Because the damsel fly nymphs are very much more abundant it is to these that we must pay most attention.

The damsel nymph is unlike the dragonfly nymph quite happy to emerge during the day when both the trout and the angler are about. This is an obvious but important statement. To emerge, the damsel nymphs must break cover from their protective weed bed and swim to the margins. This exodus takes place over a long period as the various species have differing times of emergence ranging from June to the end of August.

I (Peter) can well remember the first time I encountered a good emergence of damsels. It was on a small fishery near my home on a hot August day. Trout were rising well, often making slashing takes on the surface. At the time I had no idea what they were taking but I kept trying with little success until at my feet I noticed some damsel nymphs wriggling about in the margins. I was already fishing a floating line, so on went an imitation of the natural. I cast out and immediately began to retrieve, keeping the imitation moving quite fast just below the surface. It was not long before I got my first take and duly landed a small rainbow weighing about one pound. I didn't even need to spoon it as it still had nymphs at the back of its throat. Some were even alive though a little the worse for wear.

By now the hatch had really hotted up, so much so that two nymphs actually crawled up my boots as I waded. There they sat and to my surprise suddenly split open, the adult emerging from the skin. I didn't know whether to continue watching the nymphs or carry on fishing, it was fascinating.

Although there are not all that many nymph patterns available commercially there are a few which catch well. Among these are patterns incorporating wool, seal's fur and floss in their make up all in the appropriate olive hues. We also use a very life-like imitation fashioned from olive dyed marabou dubbed on. All work well fished close to the surface when the naturals are about. The only part of the insect which is tricky to imitate is its wriggling action. When swimming slowly it appears as if it is hinged in the middle and whilst some fly tyers have tried to imitate this action by using jointed nymphs they are basically unsuccessful. We prefer to stick to normal long-shank patterns finding them just as effective.

Leaded nymphs are also effective and are particularly useful for tempting big fish in small clear stillwaters. Dick Walker's pattern, dressed with mixed colours of wool dubbed on and wound over an underbody of lead foil, is one of the best for this sort of fishing. Trout feeding on nymphs are not always so fussy about what they take. A few years ago I (Bob) was fishing at Blagdon with three friends, Peter Dobbs, Peter Wood and Jim Collins, chairman of the Mid-Northants Trout Fishers Association.

I was in a boat with Peter Dobbs though and we were struggling a little. After several fly changes Peter hooked into a good fish which turned out to be a cracking 3½lb rainbow. Thinking we might get some clues I suggested he spooned the trout to see what it was eating. As it had been taken deep down we were both surprised to find it stuffed to capacity with green damsel fly nymphs. The interesting thing was that it had taken a bright fluorescent green Leprechaun Lure invented incidentally by Peter Wood. Surprisingly the Leprechaun worked better in this instance than more imitative damsel fly nymphs. We eventually ended up with a quite respectable catch, but

Peter Gathercole lands a hefty 3½lb rainbow from a small fishery. Here you can clearly see the tail erosion on the fish, the result of intensive rearing and most certainly recently stocked.

we were more pleased because we had solved the problem on a difficult day, albeit in an unconventional way. It shows though that lures might be more imitative than is generally realised.

The only stage that has not been dealt with is the adult. Now, although adult dragonfly imitations work in America they are all but useless in Britain and neither of us have ever seen a trout eat a natural. The damsel is also very rarely taken as the trout prefer the nymphs. But take them at times they do as I (Peter) proved one bright July morning. I began with a floating line and a Pheasant Tail Nymph which quickly took a fish. I soon had another nice trout in the bag and continued to catch, returning a few others until lunch time. Around mid-afternoon I started to see the odd damsel nymph wriggling about in the margins and I popped on an imitation. Nothing much happened at first but the trout began to make big splashy rises right along a fringe of reeds.

After that all hell broke loose. One fish even poked its head out of the water to take a nymph as it began to climb up out of the water along a reed stem. Apart from one rainbow though nothing had fallen to my imitation even with all this incredible activity. The rise became more and more intense with the trout now leaping clear of the water in an effort to drown the adults which were skimming low over the surface.

More by luck than judgement at the time I had been reading up on the insects and had tied one rather complicated artificial which to be honest I thought would never even get wet. I could not really work out how to fish it so I simply cast it out and twitched it back slowly. The fly had not moved more than a yard before I was fast into a nice rainbow which leapt all over the place. It was full of crumpled blue adults so I was right, they were taking the adults. After my initial quick success it took a while before I hooked another fish but I did take another three nice rainbows and very satisfying it was too. It is a super feeling to work out what the trout are taking and then to catch them on an imitation of your own design.

Though trout will pluck the adults out of the air, it is interesting to note that the adult is more available to the trout than might be realised. You see many species actually enter the water and move around under the surface during egg laying when the female needs to cut a slit in a water plant stem in order to insert a single egg. This has been a well known scientific fact for many years now but no one bothered letting us anglers into the secret!

9 The Sedges

For many a fly fisherman the sight of his first sedge hatch of the season tells him that summer has well and truly arrived. Bobbing and weaving in small groups above the bankside vegetation the sedges or caddis flies are an unmistakable sight. Their form and method of flight is so distinctive that even if the angler is unable to put a name to them, he is almost certain to have observed them at some point.

There is little more reassuring in stillwater trout fishing than to sit on the bank observing the start of a sedge hatch confident in the knowledge of things to come. In Britain there are a great many species of sedges but a large proportion of these are either too small or uncommon to bother about. I suppose this is just as well, for if it were not so we would have to carry a suitcase full of artificials. The sedges belong to the Order Trichoptera and in general appearance resemble moths. This is not total coincidence though as they are closely related to certain moth families, but there are very specific differences. Firstly, even though both moths and sedges have four wings, in the moth's case these are covered in very tiny scales whilst those of the sedge are endowed with fine hairs.

Like some moths certain species of sedges are quite happy to emerge throughout the day or at least during the evening hours. We have all at one time or another observed the day-flying sedges. These species tend to be either small or medium sized and are to be seen hovering in swarms around the margins. The most well known of these must be the Grouse Wing and the various types of Silverhorns, of which the latter are probably the more common.

Although there is the odd exception for the angler's purposes all sedge flies begin their lives as aquatic larvae. Some make protective homes for themselves and some prefer to live free-swimming, using a camouflaged body to protect them. Others have a sort of halfway house in the form of leaves curled over and bonded with a silken material which the larvae exudes. Although the non-casemaking types of larvae are encountered in stillwater, on the whole they do not turn up in autopsies and so are of lesser importance. Because of this there is little point in going to great lengths over their description. They are much the same as the casemaking type except they tend to be darker and slimmer, more resembling a caterpillar, though they have only six true legs. Also the type which makes the leafy home is bright green and very quick moving which makes it a rather distinctive creature.

Of the casemaking species, once the larvae have hatched they begin on their career of master house builder. It is by no means uncommon to see very tiny examples of sedge or caddis larvae trundling along with their homes in tow. Although these homes may seem spartan, they are both beautifully constructed and very functional, fashioned as they are from all manner of rubbish, they work very neatly from the point of view of camouflage.

The larvae case as well as being well camouflaged is exceedingly tough, particularly when either small stones or sand have been used. Whatever the materials used they are held in place by exactly the same method though the case shape does differ. The larva exudes a sort of glue which when set is very tough. It uses this glue not only to stick all the pieces together but to line the case and seal all the gaps. And, because of the method of construction it is able to add on new sections to accommodate the growing grub.

The caddis larva uses many different materials in the construction of their cases ranging from leaf debris, sand and small stones, and even snail shells. Unfortunately for the snail, the caddis larva does not always check to see that the shell is unoccupied. More than once I (Peter) have seen a poor snail stretching and struggling to remove its home from that of the larva. The design of the case also depends on its habitat. Because of this, shape and materials vary considerably amongst the species. Some are quite large whilst others are very small indeed. The larva of the largest species of all, the Great Red Sedge (*Phrygania grandis*), makes a case up to 2in (5cm) long. On the other hand the cases of some of the Silverhorns, which are the smallest species of interest to the stillwater fly fisher, may be only ½in (13mm) long or less. The cases are also tapered, becoming wider towards the creature's head.

Unfortunately because individuals of many species will use identical materials this cannot be used as a positive identification of the species. Caddis larvae will use any material going and if there is no sand available they are quite happy to use another material readily to hand. The larva live within their mobile homes for up to a year though this may differ amongst varying species. They will eat any organic material they can find, some preferring leaves after they have begun to decompose. Some are carnivorous though it must be difficult to catch prey with such an encumbrance on your back.

One final point which may be worth adding is that perhaps the caddis case is not as ungainly as might be imagined. There is one type of larvae which, far from being tied down by a weighty home, is actually able to swim free, case and all. This larvae doesn't grow all that large and the case it builds is very slim and light. It is able to swim with two legs flattened into paddles like those of a Corixa. This type seems far too uncommon for it to be worthwhile imitating.

Once the larva has reached full size, the time has arrived for pupation. Like moths sedges have a complete metamorphosis. This means that they go through four distinct stages during their lives. These include the egg, larva, pupa and finally the adult winged fly. Unlike moths, sedges pupate under water, so when it is time to make the change, the larva finds a suitable stone or a piece of sunken wood, and it sticks itself firmly to its chosen site.

This 5lb superb rainbow is the type of fish the late Cyril Inwood was used to catching.

This gives the pupae at least some protection. Certain large stones and sunken fence posts may be particular favourites. Amongst the smaller species, it is quite common to see a sunken branch or similar outcrop festooned with thousands upon thousands of caddis larvae cases. These cases are not just from one year group though and comprise many generations, a great number of them having been abandoned in previous years.

Once anchored securely, the larva goes to the precaution of covering up the open end from which its head and legs once protruded. It completes this with either its normal house building material or with a fine gauze formed from the adhesive substance. Shut away it lies there in its protective home whilst its body undergoes a miraculous change. The case is never sealed completely and there are always minute holes left in the plug at the case end to allow water to pass over the gills while the larva begins a swaying action which presumably assists the flow of water through the case as an aid to respiration.

Over the next few weeks the pupa goes through a series of changes. At first the changes are only slight, but as time progresses they become increasingly pronounced. Once the final stages of pupation have been reached the creature hidden away within its case is far different from that which sealed itself in. The legs and wing cases are now fully formed and the pupa resembles a sedge fly but with short stubby wings. Unlike the moth, the sedge's pupal legs are quite functional and carry out a specific task in the insect's emergence.

Once the pupa has reached the end of its development, its final task is to break free of its larval case to emerge as the adult. With its sharp pair of jaws it breaks through its tough casing and, pulling itself free, swims to the surface using specially flattened legs. When I (Peter) observed my first emerging sedge pupa, I thought it was a weird looking Corixa. On closer examination, the differences are quite obvious, particularly as the one I was watching emerged into a Grousewing! With its paddle-like legs, the pupa is able to swim quite comfortably either simply to the surface, or, in the case of some species, to a likely looking stone or reed stem on which to crawl out. The other four legs of the sedge pupa are also well developed especially in the larger species, some of which are quite capable of crawling around on dry land.

As the pupa reaches the water's surface it must emerge quickly if it is not to end up in the stomach of a trout. Because the pupae move at speed the trout have to move fast as well giving us the spectacular rises which are so evident during a rise to sedge pupae. Once the pupa is on the surface, its skin splits along the line of the thorax,

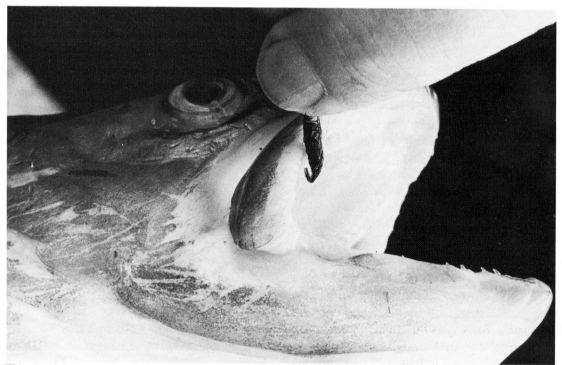

This nice fish took an artificial caddis larva trundled slowly along the bottom.

head and mandibles, and the adult emerges. The fine hairs which cover the rapidly expanding wings and body are water repellent and help to prevent them from becoming waterlogged.

The adult sedges come in a wide range of sizes and colours, from the diminutive Silverhorns which may be less than ½in (13mm) right up to the giant of the family, the aptly named Great Red Sedge. Again like the adult moth, the sedge is unable to take solid foods, though it may take liquids in order to prolong its rather short life. There is virtually no difference between the two sexes in sedges so from the angler's point of view both may be treated the same.

Of all the three stages, the adult insect is perhaps the least useful, but probably the most exciting to fish. Sedges may be divided into two distinct groups, these being day hatching and secondly night hatching species. On the whole, the day hatching species are much smaller and darker than those which emerge at night and include such types as the Silverhorns and Grousewings. A funny thing though is that of all the autopsies I have carried out, I have yet to find more than the odd Grousewing in a trout's stomach. From this I can only surmise that they are not very tasty.

I have often encountered fish feeding on large numbers of adult sedges of the paler night-emerging types. Whilst many sedges do emerge under the cover of darkness, a proportion venture out around dusk.

Due to its great importance anglers have developed a wide range of patterns to imitate the various stages in the sedge's life. Up until recent times, most of the imitations have been just of the adult flies, probably because of the great influence of the river fly fisher. Since the advent of the first big stillwaters at the beginning of this century, imitations of both larval and pupal stages have blossomed.

Dealing with the larval stage first, we now have quite a few very effective patterns most of which have been designed over the last twenty years. The main consideration of the effective imitation is that it should be quite large. Three patterns which we find work well are the Stick Fly, Brer Rabbit and a Brown and Yellow seal's fur pattern. Funnily enough we have had little success with what might be termed true to life imitations formed from real sand and such. Anyway if the imitation you use is about 1in (25mm) long, dark and scraggy looking it should work well. What really makes for an effective larval pattern is the way it is fished. Apart from the one notable exception, caddis larvae are bottom dwellers and that's just where the imitations should be fished.

Where the trout are grubbing about for them it is often a good idea to lead your patterns to get them to fish really hard on the bottom. If you do use heavily weighted patterns, fish them on the point of a long leader in conjunction with a floating line. That way you can twitch them slowly along the bottom in a life-like manner. If the water is quite deep, you will have to use either a sink-tip or a full sinker in which case the retrieve should be as slow as possible. You can see from the way caddis larvae patterns are fished that they make ideal early season patterns when the trout are bottom feeding.

Although caddis larvae work well in the spring we tend to think of sedge fishing as a high summer pursuit. There is little more pleasurable than fishing in a good sedge rise when the trout are splashing on the surface taking the pupae. This usually happens towards the evening and can often turn up the odd surprise in the form of a big fish or two. When the trout are knocking off the pupae we have a range of flies which take many fish for us each season under varying conditions. These include the Emergent Pupa, Latex Grub, Invicta and of course the Amber Nymph. This last one, devised by Dr Bell of Blagdon was probably the first attempt made at imitating the sedge pupa and is one that has stood the test of time. We have also included a true to life pattern which works when the trout are proving just a little difficult.

Going back to Dr Bell's pattern I (Peter) have a great affection for this very simple nymph, as it has taken a great many good fish for me from a wide range of waters. The first time I used it was at Eyebrook when I had only been trout fishing for a few seasons. When you have little experience you are forever trying to make the pieces fit. Often you catch a fish and are desperate to know just why that fish took that fly. So it was on one difficult August evening. With the sun sinking slowly a few fish began to rise. Just the odd one at first but steadily they increased until there was a respectable rise in progress. I was using a team of wet flies on a floating line at the time and making one of my few accurate casts put them in front of a fish which obliged. At the time I was just getting into the imitative approach and I reached for my newly acquired marrow spoon which showed that the trout had been eating orangy yellow blobs with legs. I had no idea at the time that these were sedge pupa.

Anyway, I looked in my box and came across an Amber Nymph which looked just like the things in the trout's stomach. I tied it on the point and cast out. I did not even have to retrieve because a trout took the Amber Nymph on the drop. From then on it was just like magic and I finished up with ten lovely fish, all browns, which up to that point was my best catch ever.

Since that time I have had other good bags on Dr Bell's nymph including some quite big fish. Fishing Rutland Water one evening with my regular partner Duncan Currie, we were drifting about at the bottom of the North Arm. Again it was getting dark when we encountered a shoal of big browns rising madly. Sedges were coming off in quantity, but as the rises were to a subsurface creature we tied on large Amber Nymphs. The results were instant and we both hooked into big browns around 3½–4lb.

Unfortunately up to that time Duncan had been an affirmed lure stripper and was more used to hooking trout at depth on heavy tackle. He was not used to the instant hooking of surface fishing with lighter leaders and tended to strike a little hard.

Whilst pupal patterns are the most effective of all the stages, when trout are up and taking the adult sedges the fishing is spectacular. After emerging, the adults skitter across the surface and the fish hit them in an explosive swirl. Because fishing the adult sedge is limited we have included only a few patterns but have chosen those which have taken fish for us from the smallest of stillwaters right up to the largest of Irish loughs. One traditional pattern is the Wickham's Fancy which we would never be without. Others are the Inwood's Ginger Palmer, Superla Sedge and perhaps unexpectedly, a tiny natural Muddler.

Only three of the above patterns are fished dry, but nevertheless, they all catch sedge feeders. Fishing the dry sedge can be really superb and I (Bob) have memories of Draycote when it proved so successful it beat every other technique hands down. It was late one July and we had been having tremendous sedge hatches. The method of the moment was the typical wet fly approach with floating line and patterns like the Invicta. This was helped by the prevailing warm summer breezes ruffling the water's surface.

We then had the misfortune to book a boat on a day when it was flat calm all through the day. To say conditions were difficult would be an understatement. They were diabolical and no one was catching a thing. As evening approached a few sedges began to emerge, their efforts dimpling the still mirror-like surface. Fish began to rise but even now as fish after fish broke surface we still could not induce a single take. We figured that the continuous casting was making the trout wary as even 4lb breaking strain nylon stands out like a sore thumb in these conditions.

I decided to try as a last resort a dry palmered sedge soaking it in silicone flotant, remembering to degrease my leader. Casting out towards the area of greatest activity I retrieved a little slack and sat back. After a few moments a fish simply popped up and took the fly in a perfect rise. My dry sedge simply disappeared in the splash. In the next two hours I had taken a very unexpected limit and packed up well content. It just goes to show that the dry fly does have its place on our big reservoirs.

On Irish loughs perhaps the most well known sedge pattern is the Murrough. It is an imitation of the Great Red Sedge and like the natural, it is big. It can be dressed on a Size 8 longshank which is quite a mouthful for any trout. In Eire we have both caught plenty of beautiful wild browns on these big flies pulled through the wave tops. Like Mayfly fishing, it is truly a wonderful sight to watch the trout porpoise over the fly before taking. The beauty of the Murrough is that it works just as well on our reservoir trout and often sorts out the better fish.

Finally we would like to tell of one pattern which is a real killer when trout are taking sedges. Dressed on a Size 10 or 12 ordinary wet fly hook the Muddler makes a superb wake fly, imitating just the type of disturbance which the adult sedge makes and the trout find so irresistible.

10 Phantom Midge

There are a number of creatures which, though they are relatively minor food forms, crop up in autopsies from time to time. For this reason they can never be totally ignored. One very good example of such an organism is the Phantom Midge, which can be an important food item on many smaller stillwaters. The Phantom Midge is closely related to the Chironomid Midge which it resembles closely in the adult form. The Phantom Midge's season is a good deal shorter than the Chironomid's, and it will mainly be found between May and August.

There are very few species belonging to the genus *Chaoborus* to which the Phantom Midge belongs. The most common species is *Chaoborus flavicans*. The adult insects are around 4–5mm in length and vary from a pale green in the females, to a greyish hue in the males. The adult stage is very limited in interest to the angler, as they tend to emerge at night although the female returns to the water to lay her eggs, usually in the late evening. We have never been lucky enough to encounter a time when the trout have been feeding on the adults. As we have yet to meet anyone else who has, we will move swiftly on to the two stages which are of real interest.

Like the Chironomids, the Phantom Midge has four stages to its life, the adult we have already dealt with and as the eggs are not taken, this leaves the larva and the pupa to be considered. In overall shape the *Chaoborus* larva closely resembles that of the Chironomid, though it is here that the similarity ends. I (Peter) well remember the first time I came across this curious creature. It was when I was about twelve years old and I had been collecting various bugs from a local pond. Like most small boys, I had this love of messing about in any mucky puddle I could find, usually laying any interesting items out on the dining-room table. After tipping out the results of my latest expedition into a water-filled tray, I noticed a number of creatures, which I thought at first were some kind of fish fry.

These creatures were over ½in (13mm) long, transparent, and seemed to hover in a horizontal position in the water. On closer examination I could see that the body contained two pairs of bubble-like objects which I assumed were swim bladders. As there were two pairs, one at the end of the abdomen and another nearer what

Bob Church has a method of changing his rod hand which he occasionally uses when landing fish from an awkward bank spot.

was obviously the head, I concluded that the creature I was observing was definitely not a fish fry. By using a number of identification books I soon realised that what I had was the larvae of *Chaoborus* or as they are known to aquarists the Glass Worm. This title is a very apt one as the creature is so transparent that you can see every one of its internal organs.

The *Chaoborus* larvae does not lay in the mud feeding on detritus, but is an active predator. It feeds on a number of small creatures such as the Water Flea (Daphnia), which it grasps with a hooked device at its head. The fact that it feeds on Daphnia sometimes means that it turns up in autopsies even though the trout probably were not actively feeding on them at the time. This is because *Chaoborus* larvae are often to be found in the vast Daphnia swarms and when the trout scoop up the Daphnia, some *Chaoborus* are often unwittingly taken too.

Another very interesting point about the Phantom larva is the way it moves. When at rest its swim bladders enable it to hang motionless in the water. There it hovers virtually invisible ready to snap up any unfortunate tiny creature. All of a sudden the larva will twitch and vanish, only to reappear a few inches away, a movement which is difficult to follow. Because they are so transparent they also offer quite a few problems when it comes to their imitation, though we will go into greater detail in due course.

Once the larva has reached maturity, it must then pupate. Luckily for the angler, the pupa does at least contain a little colour on which to base imitations. It is very similar in shape to the Chironomid pupa, but it differs in that it is an active creature, and whilst it does not feed, it is able to alter its depth and position at will. It hangs there motionless in a vertical position for long periods, but when disturbed is capable of moving quite quickly.

The pupae are a good deal shorter than the larvae, usually around ¼in (6mm) in length. They gradually darken in colour as they mature and towards emergence the abdomen turns a translucent creamy white, whilst the thorax becomes a pale orange or amber colour. The pupa also sports ear-like appendages on its thorax and plates on the tip of its abdomen which are an aid to respiration. Over the years Peter has kept many of these interesting creatures observing their movements, trying to learn what he can about them.

The pupal stage usually lasts around four days though light levels and temperature can alter this period. When emergence takes place the pupa rises up to the surface film, and like the Chironomid pupa, it splits and the adult emerges to start the life cycle all over again.

When tying larval imitations the most important thing is to keep your dressings fine and use a material that makes a transparent body. Polythene strip is ideal for this, and along with a Size 14 silvered longshank hook and a white hackle, it makes up the imitation devised by Dave Collyer. This pattern is probably the only one which really looks like a *Chaoborus* larva and does catch fish.

The pupa is also a difficult creature to imitate properly, though it does have a little more to it than the larva. We have included a life-like imitation devised by Peter, but there is yet another very simple pattern that proves just as killing.

The late Bob Glennon was both a superb angler and a talented but practical fly dresser. His local water was Pitsford Reservoir and it was here that he set to solving many of the niggling problems which dogged the water's regulars. Bob was particularly skilful at fishing the nymph, his forte being catching difficult and preoccupied trout. On one occasion though, it took even an angler of his calibre two days to solve the problem. In fact it took him two whole days before he caught a single fish, during one very difficult period. The fish were rising quite freely, but no matter what Bob and other anglers threw at them, they just didn't want to know. Luckily he managed to catch one by a fluke, and in doing so found out the reason for their dismal failure.

The trout had been gorging themselves on the Phantom Midge pupa. They were all of ¼in (6mm) long. Bob's answer was to tie up a very simple fly which used a strand of pale green floss for the body. The pattern was completed with just a shell back of grey feather fibre, simplicity itself. It didn't take long for Bob to realise that this pattern was the answer, and it still is.

As trout often take both larvae and pupae in calm conditions, and as the dressings have to be quite small, you need to fine your tackle right down. Use a light floating line and as fine a leader as you dare, cast out into the area of general activity, and fish the little nymphs back slowly giving the odd tweak to induce a trout into taking. Fishing Phantom Midge imitations is not easy, but when they are preoccupied on the naturals, it is the only way you are going to catch anything.

11 Leeches

It could never be said that the leech is as important as the Chironomid, but we have on numerous occasions found trout with stomachs full of big dark brown and black specimens. The curious thing is that these fish always seem to be large browns. The only possible reason for this is that as these browns feed more on the bottom than the rainbows, they pick up the leeches in deep water. These big black leeches live in the rubbish on the lake's bed, feeding on soft bodied creatures and decaying organic material.

At Rutland Water we have caught plenty of leech-feeding browns, though they have not all come on bottom fishing tactics. During the 1982 season I (Peter) took quite a few nice browns over a three-week period. All came to short lining with a floating line using patterns such as the Soldier Palmer and Wickham's Fancy. To be realistic though, if we are to catch trout actively feeding on leeches, we are going to have to go down for them.

To say we have taken large bags of browns on leech patterns would be a lie, though we have taken enough to make further investigations worthwhile. Black Lures are often mentioned as leech imitations, but we find this is often merely a way of justifying their use. Whilst a tandem black lure will catch fish it does not always mean the fish has been eating leeches. We've included two leech imitations, one of which was devised by Terry Williams of Bristol. It's dressed on a Size 6 longshank with a carrot shaped body of brown suede chenille and a tail of brown marabou. This marabou tail is very important. When the leech wants to move fast instead of its usual inch worm gait, it's able to swim quickly by undulating its body with a sinuous motion. The flowing marabou gives the pattern its necessary life and imitates the natural's motion well. We've also included a second pattern which is similar to the previous one, but has a body of dubbed seal's and hare's fur mixed. Incidentally both patterns may be leaded at the head similarly to the Dog Nobblers which gives a better action.

Even if the patterns are weighted, they still need to be fished on a fast sinking line. As you will probably be fishing at anchor over 20 to 30ft (6 to 9m) of water, if you used a floating line you would need a very long leader to get your imitation near to the bottom. A fast-sinking shooting head, such as the lead impregnated type, is the ideal line for the job.

We've not mentioned any particular species during this

Fishing deep water from a boat is an ideal way of picking up early season bottom grubbers. The fish might be taking a whole range of creatures, including caddis larvae or leeches.

chapter, as that is totally irrelevant, all that matters is the creature's size and colour. Though the specimens we have found in fish have all been quite large and dark, other leeches vary considerably in both size and colour. Some are quite unsavoury in their habits including the Medicinal Leech, which sucks the blood of both animals and, given the chance, humans alike. There's also another large species called the Duck Leech, which actually lives in the nasal passages of ducks. As it may be as long as 6–8in (15–20cm) when stretched, it's got to be uncomfortable for the duck.

Most leech species are quite inoffensive, feeding mainly off snails and dead organisms. Some are also very pale, or even white, and this has led to confusion. I (Peter) remember reading once about a chap who said he had discovered the reason why trout take Baby Dolls. He had caught a trout with a stomach full of what he thought were white leeches. Unfortunately he let the cat out of the bag by saying that they were still alive and would expand and contract in a dish. It's likely that they were not leeches at all, but parasitic worms in the trout's stomach.

12 Caenis

Whoever it was who first coined the phrase 'good things come in small packages', was obviously not thinking of the *Caenis*. These diminutive upwinged flies offer the stillwater fly fisher no end of problems. There are a number of *Caenis* species to be found on stillwater but *Caenis horaria* and *Caenis robusta* are probably the most common. The different species though are so similar that they may be all treated as one.

Caenis are the smallest members of the Order Ephemeroptera. In fact they have an average abdomen length of only 4mm. They are also very easy to identify, being our only Ephemeropteran to combine a lack of hindwings with three tails. They range from an ivory to a greyish cream, and the wings are rather broad in comparison to their length.

Like most upwinged flies, the *Caenis* has four main stages in its life cycle. These are the egg, nymph, dun and spinner. The nymph, like the adult, is very small, even when fully developed, and lives in the bottom silt and soft detritus on the bed of most stillwaters. The tiny nymph is easily hidden and for most of the year they are rarely found in autopsies. Imitating the nymph is consequently a very minor fish catching technique.

The duns are small pale flies which are also very short lived. *Caenis*, like other Ephemeropterans, must transpose from duns to spinners, before they are sexually mature. In most species the dun stage lasts a number of

hours. In the *Caenis* though, it may last only a few minutes, and the transposition may sometimes be so fast during big hatches that the angler can be covered with myriads of tiny empty white skins.

When hatches of *Caenis* occur fishing can be difficult. It's not that there are no fish about, far from it. When there is a good hatch of *Caenis* just about every fish in the lake seems to be up on the surface taking part in a feeding orgy. The only problem is that, like as not, the fish simply will not look at your offering.

Two factors make the fishing so difficult. The size of the insect and the staggering numbers of them. Hatches may be so profuse that they get into your eyes, ears and mouth. *Caenis* may be a tasty morsel for a trout but not for an angler. Calm warm evenings produce the largest hatches. Because *Caenis* are so small you hardly notice them at first, then all of a sudden there are millions of them, everywhere.

After the Dun has emerged it quickly transposes into the sexually mature Imago or Spinner. *Caenis* Spinners are unique in that when they transpose their wings are still fringed on the trailing edge with a row of hairs. They also have very long tails or setae which gives them a very delicate appearance. In colour they are virtually the same as the Dun although the body is a little paler and more translucent and so similar imitations may be used for both.

Preparing to fish the evening rise. During calm conditions like this the diminutive *Caenis* may prove a real headache.

It is the Spinner that causes the angler the most trouble. Once it has mated it returns to the water's surface to lay its eggs, and then like all other Ephemeropterans once spent, it dies. When this happens the fish go berserk. With thousands of flies littering the surface like a fall of blossom, the trout have to expend very little energy to eat them. It can be very frustrating to fish for trout that are feeding on these Spinners as they do so in a unique way. Instead of head and tailing or sipping them in, when the flies are at their peak, the trout simply cruise along the surface swallowing the trapped insects like a whale feeding on krill. Instead of taking flies individually they seem to scoop the *Caenis* Spinners up in clumps which makes their imitation that much more difficult.

Over the last few years patterns have been developed which go a little way towards helping the fly fisherman. The main point to remember is that *Caenis* feeding fish are never easy. They can be extremely frustrating, but trying to catch them can still be an enjoyable challenge.

It is not that the fish are shy, far from it. They seem to lose all caution and will rise within a rod's length from the angler, and because of these advances in patterns and techniques when we hit a heavy *Caenis* hatch now we don't have to take the usual age-old advice, 'pack up and go home'.

Because *Caenis* are so small we have to use a similarly sized artificial, which means dropping as low as a Size 16 or 18. This also means a fine leader of as little as 2lb

breaking strain. Although using imitations of the nymph is a minor technique, we have included two patterns to fill the gap. Both should be fished slowly on a floating line and a fine, long, degreased leader. Degreasing is particularly important when it comes to fishing tiny patterns in calm conditions. A leader with any grease at all will float and cause the fly to drag through the surface. Grease also thickens the monofilament and that scares fish.

The two patterns are very simple. The first is just a body of dubbed white wool and a soft badger hackle at the head. The second is a little more complex having a silver tinsel abdomen and a pale yellow wool thorax with a shellback of grey mallard, the points of which are left projecting over the eye. Both are tied on Size 16 hooks.

Because the Dun and Spinner stages are taken more often, it is these imitations which catch most fish. Trout often take *Caenis* in clusters and one rather crafty pattern takes advantage of this. Unlike other *Caenis* patterns this one is dressed on a longshank silvered Size 14. It doesn't just imitate a single insect, but a whole mass. It has another advantage as the larger hook gives a better hold and fewer fish are lost. The idea is not a new one, and several similar patterns have been published before. The dressing we find most effective has small bodies of dubbed white wool or fur divided by white cock hackles short in fibre. This fly can be fished as a normal dry fly, or if that fails it may be fished damp using a short twitch retrieve.

In the five years before his death the master angler Cyril Inwood spent many trout fishing days with the then much younger Bob Church.

There are also traditional dry flies which work well in *Caenis* hatches, including the Grey Duster and the Tups Indispensable. Both have taken fish for us in such conditions tied in small sizes. These are not the only dry flies which work though.

I (Bob) have a particular affection for Chew Valley Lake and it was on one of my visits there that I first tried a new approach to *Caenis* fishing. On this occasion I decided to use a boat, my partner being Peter Dobbs, a friend from Northampton. The day had started well enough, and although they were proving none too easy with a lot of shy takes and on and offs, we had taken some trout, good ones too, with rainbows up to 3lb.

As evening commenced the breeze eased off completely and a hatch of fly began, a hatch which at its peak was one of the heaviest I have ever witnessed. Sedge, Chironomids and *Caenis* were all coming off together in their millions, and the trout responded in the now flat calm.

At first they were willing to take a stripped Muddler, but as they became more preoccupied, it was a small Wickham's Fancy and a Golden Olive which did the trick. Towards the latter half of the rise though, the fish concentrated their attentions on the *Caenis* Spinner, taking the spent fly from the surface. In these cases, I usually use a Grey Duster, but instead tried a fly which really works for the Americans during hatches of similarly sized flies. It is a near perfect match for the *Caenis*

and naturally it caught fish.

The pattern is just one of a range of no-hackle dry flies made famous by Doug Swisher and Carl Richards in their book *Selective Trout*. I have a feeling that more of their patterns would work in difficult conditions. The particular one we used had a white body, wings and tail. As there is no hackle it is the wings and tail which support the fly. Consequently it must be fished in very calm conditions as it is easily swamped.

Anyway it proved very successful on this occasion and the rise brought us eight good rainbows between 1¾lb and about 3lb, which more than made up for the long wait.

I (Peter) have also experienced some interesting *Caenis* fishing particularly at Pitsford Reservoir, a water very close to both our homes in Northamptonshire. I remember one occasion fishing with my father, when we had taken an evening boat. As the weather had been so hot that day, fishing was a virtual waste of time. This day was unusual in that there was a breeze, something that had been lacking for quite a while. As we rowed out, the air was thick with small grousewing sedges and Chironomids, but there was little rising. We decided to use sinking lines to start with, as most fish had been coming from the deeper cooler water, though catches had been modest to say the least.

I was startled therefore to hook a nice rainbow on only the second cast, and even more surprised when I landed it. It was in peak condition and an autopsy revealed it had been taking sedge pupae. Unfortunately after tying on imitations, we failed to get so much as another pluck. Persevering with a variety of methods, we hardly noticed the sun sink behind the horizon, but as it did what little breeze there was died. As the air cooled a rise began, sparse at first, but building up continuously in its concentration, until it seemed every trout in the reservoir was up on the surface. How on earth we didn't realise what they were taking I don't know, but after a while I happened to notice a small piece of fluff dancing in front of my face. Bringing my eyes to focus on the tiny object I saw not one, but a whole swarm. I looked around and saw the air was full of *Caenis.* My heart sank.

In a matter of minutes the air was so thick that they got into our eyes and mouths and our shirts were covered with the tiny white skins of the transposed duns. While we were panicking, the fish were having a feast taking the spent insects in great slurping mouthfuls. We tried everything from tiny nymphs, to huge lures and bushy dry flies, with little more than a few tentative tweaks for our efforts.

It was then that I remembered a small fly I had been experimenting with. Like Bob's previous fly it was devised from an idea I had seen in an American fly fishing magazine. Instead of the usual feather or hair wings, it used polypropylene yarn tied spent. There was no hackle, and the fly was suspended in the surface film merely by its tails and wings.

I only had one, so my father had to try something else. Fishing it carefully on a very light floating line and leader, I managed to tempt four nice rainbows up to 2lb before the air cooled off completely, and the *Caenis* disappeared as if a switch had been thrown.

My father did not end up fishless. Indeed he took the best fish of the day, a 3½lb rainbow, on a Black Lure stripped through the surface just as it was getting really dark. It is interesting to note that this method can often produce the better fish. The trout are still up near the surface looking for food even though the fly life has vanished.

Another interesting point actually occurs during the heat of the rise. We have a theory that there are perhaps not quite so many fish rising as would be assumed. Trout taking *Caenis* do not just rise once or twice, but constantly, following a line giving the impression of many fish. To be effective the best method is to watch carefully for this rise pattern casting your imitation into the trout's path.

13 Snail

It's always worth finding out what trout are feeding on. The usual practice is to look in the fish's mouth and if this reveals nothing, a more involved autopsy using a marrow spoon is called for. There is one food form that requires no such niceties, no careful observation, no marrow spoon. All you have to do is feel the fish's belly, which bulges and virtually rattles with what's inside. You can never miss the snail.

There are many species of snail in our lakes and reservoirs, some of which are eaten in large numbers by the trout. They vary in size from tiny creatures the size of a pin head, right up to the Greater Pond Snail, which is a good mouthful for any trout. All an angler needs to know is the size and colour.

Like many of the creatures eaten by the trout, it is neither the very large nor the very small specimens which are most readily consumed, but those of a more average size. During autopsies carried out on snail feeding trout, you will find that all the snails taken from any one trout's stomach will be roughly the same size. This overall size may differ, depending on the time of year, and where the fish have been feeding. The size of the most commonly eaten snails ranges from around 5 to 10 mm. Colours of individuals vary too, from a dark brown or almost black to a pale translucent olive. There is yet another factor which heavily influences the way we tie our snail imitations, and that's where the naturals occur in the water.

There are two ways in which trout feed on snails and

both offer the angler a few problems. The first is the method which we would most expect. The snail is hardly a fast moving animal and calmly grazes on algae and plant life, scraping away with its tooth-covered tongue. Trout browse the snails from the weed in a calm confident manner. Then all they do is pluck them up shell and all. This form of feeding is most common in the early season and again the back end, when other forms of food are on the wane. Under these circumstances a number of sunken line techniques will prove effective, and a small black or drably coloured lure fished slowly along the bottom will be as killing as any purpose-tied imitation either from boat or bank.

Fishing in this way, takes when they come are mostly good confident ones with the trout securely hooked.

But there are two main ways trout feed on snails and it is the second way that causes all the headaches. At certain times of the season, mainly during the summer, snails embark on a sort of mass migration. This doesn't appear to happen every year, but when it does, look out, because it can make fishing very difficult indeed. This migration is an interesting phenomenon which is so far un-explained. Whatever the reason, when it happens the fish can go quite mad for the snails, virtually to the exclusion of anything else.

Snails suddenly rise to the surface en masse. They are then carried out from the margins by the breeze and currents. Sitting there in the surface film at the mercy of the elements, they are unable to escape, and the trout consume them with abandon. When the trout are feeding in this way it can be a frustrating or an extremely reward-ing time for the angler, depending on how experienced he is. When the snails are on the surface trout rise enthusiastically, but there's no way of knowing what they are taking. The snails are subsurface and there are no emerging adults as with Midge and Sedge pupae. This confusion can be made worse by the presence of other aquatic life forms such as the ubiquitous Chironomid. The main thing to remember is that if you are fishing during the mid to late summer, and fish are rising very well but proving nigh-on impossible to tempt, suspect snails as the cause, particularly if there is little else on the water. But this can be an extremely fruitful period for the angler if he has his wits about him.

Although fish feeding on floating snails will look at virtually nothing else, they can be real suckers for a correctly presented artificial. We have fished a number of waters including Draycote and Grafham when the trout

Always take time to tie a good strong tucked half blood knot.

have been on snails. The only response from the majority of anglers has been simple bewilderment at the number of fish rising and their total lack of success.

Apart from bottom fishing with a small lure, several other patterns are useful, especially when trout are taking the snail just subsurface. Tom Iven's Black and Peacock Spider works extremely well, as does the purposely designed Grafham Snail, which has a body of either black or dark brown chenille. Both should be inched slowly on a floating line, right in the surface film.

I (Bob) had one lovely summer's day with the snail at Blagdon. There were plenty of fish rising as I made my first few casts, but they wouldn't look at a thing. I noticed though, that the rise was concentrated in one small specific area. Try as I might I couldn't find a fly they would fall for and, believe me, one thing I don't lack is a huge collection of flies. Never one to concede defeat, I eventually managed to get a good take. The fish was not in the landing net ten seconds before I spooned it and the cause of my problems was revealed. The trout was full to the gills with tiny black snails. Unfortunately even with my large stocks I had nothing in my box which even came close to imitating them. So I improvised.

72

Peter Gathercole brings in a 3½lb fish to net at Horseshoe Lake.

The nearest thing I could find which looked anything like them was a small Size 14 Black and Peacock Spider. I decided a bit of pruning was needed so I trimmed off all the hackle to make it more lifelike. It still didn't work though, until I worked out how to fish it properly. I used a floating line, but I also had to grease the leader for half its length to keep the fly up within 6in (15cm) of the surface. The method that finally proved deadly was a simple inch retrieve. The trout confidently took the fly with it ending up right at the back of its throat. After starting off so poorly I was delighted to take a lovely bag of browns up to 3¼lb from a small area of Holts Bay.

Since this time we have experienced many occasions when trout were on snails, but it is always the first occasion which sticks in the mind. Grafham was where I (Peter) first encountered snail feeders, though like Bob it took me quite a while to cotton on. I was bank fishing along Savages Creek and it was a beautiful day with a warm gentle breeze. Everything looked perfect and a good rise was in progress. The day was perfect except for one tiny problem. No one was catching. Whatever you threw at the fish, they didn't just refuse, they didn't even give the fly a second glance.

In desperation I stripped through the mêlée with a small black lure, and was rewarded with a diminutive but gratefully received rainbow. The marrow spoon showed that it had been on snails, in this case greyish green ones about the size of a pea. More by luck than judgement, I had been experimenting with deer hair patterns a few days before, and had tied up a few floating snail imitations. I looked through the contents of my box, and eventually came across what I was after. It was tied as a round ball of clipped natural coloured deer hair, but it was all I had so out it went. I fished it soaked in flotant so that it hung just under the surface, and in no time a trout came along and obligingly took it.

The take was more like the run you might get when pike or carp fishing. Instead of just picking up the fly and spitting it out again, the trout took and kept hold, pulling the line along with it. There was plenty of time to hook the fish, and I didn't miss many. From then on things ran like clockwork and by mid-afternoon I had seven more lovely fish in the bag. As I left I handed my well chewed ball of hair over to the chap next to me and, glancing over my shoulder as I walked away, I saw him into a fish.

Since then others have designed a number of patterns which imitate the floating snail. They are all tied out of either cork or deer hair which makes sense, as both are very buoyant materials. We prefer the deer hair patterns though, as cork is a bit hard for our liking. It isn't that they are taken less, but being very hard the fish are able to hold with their teeth, and when you strike they simply let go. With the deer hair being more compressible, when the trout takes, it crushes the body which allows the hook to bite properly. So the ratio of takes to landed fish is much better with deer hair patterns.

A very effective imitation was first devised by ex-Rutland Water Bailiff John Clarkson. 'Big John' as he is affectionately known, tied his pattern with a body of deer hair, but with the addition of a back of brown raffine to imitate the natural's shell. You can of course use other colours if you want to cover the colour range of all snails.

These snail imitations are best fished on a floating line and a long leader. The main thing about the retrieve is that it should be non-existent. Simply fish the fly just in the surface film, allowing it to drift like the natural, carried along on the surface currents.

14 Mayfly

The sight of their first mayfly is one that few anglers will ever forget. Drifting along with their large yellowish green wings held aloft, they resemble miniature sailing boats. There are three species in Britain belonging to the genus *Ephemera* which we as British anglers refer to as mayflies. These are *Ephemera danica*, *E. vulgata* and *E. lineata*. One point of interest is that in Britain we call our largest species mayflies and talk of the smaller family members simply as upwing flies. Biologists and American anglers refer to all species of Ephemeropterans as mayflies. It is only a small point but may help to avoid confusion for those who also read American literature. Of the three, only two, *E. danica* and *E. vulgata* are common enough to be worthwhile to imitate and all three are so similar from the angler's point of view they may be treated as one.

Like all the mayflies they have four stages to their life cycle, egg, nymph, dun and spinner. The first of interest is of course the nymph. Although I (Peter) have seen it described as an ugly creature, I take the opposite view and find it very attractive and interesting. It grows quite large and some I have collected have been as much as an inch or more long excluding their tails.

It is also unique in Britain in that it is the only nymph which forms burrows in the silt on the lake bed. Because it lives for the greater part of its life in a protective burrow, it does not need camouflage to protect it. For this reason, the mayfly nymph is very pale in colour, being an overall yellowish buff, with brown markings. Add to this its large size and a row of gills which run down each edge of its abdomen, you realise that the mayfly nymph is an extremely conspicuous creature.

Over the years there has been some controversy over the length of time the mayfly spends in its nymphal form. Some authorities state one year, others two. For my part I can only state that my experience in the field backs up the latter view. During my sampling I have encountered mayfly nymphs of only 4 or 5 mm, just a few weeks before their emergent period. I must add that at the same time I also found many fully sized and mature nymphs. These very tiny nymphs simply would not have been physically mature enough to emerge during the forthcoming season and point towards a two-year life cycle.

Once the mayfly nymph has reached full size around the period of May to June, it must emerge in order to continue its life cycle. Just prior to emergence it leaves its burrow to make sorties towards the surface and at such times it is under threat from the trout. Its body also changes slightly and the wing cases and tails darken so that they are both virtually black and quite visible giving the nymph a striking appearance.

When the time is right, the nymph rises up to the surface and after pausing for a few seconds, the skin splits along a pre-determined line which runs the length of its thorax and the Dun, or Sub imago emerges. This stage is also known by the fly fisherman as the Greendrake because of its overall yellowish green appearance. It is an unmistakable creature with its very large size cream coloured body, heavily veined wings and three tails. In flight it resembles a butterfly more than its smaller Ephemeropteran cousins.

In British stillwaters it is unfortunately an all too rare creature. Pollution and a general drop in water quality has taken its toll and now it is found in only a few small stillwaters in England. These waters include Lower Moor, Horseshoe, Lechlade, Bishop's Bowl and Church Pool, where it is possible to encounter some really good hatches. If you are prepared to travel, you can still see hatches large enough to make some really interesting fly fishing.

In a few Scottish lochs and nearly all the Irish loughs, mayflies are still abundant. In Ireland, due to the better water quality it is still possible to see hatches of immense proportions. On the biggest loughs such as Mask and Corrib, there are enough mayflies for them to form an integral part of the fishing season.

Once the Dun has emerged from its nymphal skin, it sits on the water's surface for a few seconds before taking flight. From this point it makes its way towards the bank where it gains some protection from the elements and also a perch on which to transpose. As with all Ephemeropterans, the Dun sheds a layer of skin from its body and also, believe it or not, from its already tissue-thin wings. What emerges is the sexually mature adult, the Imago or as we anglers have christened it, the Spinner. This stage is where the mayfly is truly at its most

Corixa

Leggy Corixa

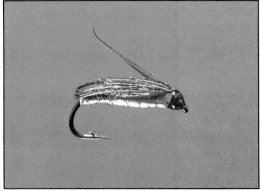
Silver Bodied Corixa

Yellow Bodied Corixa

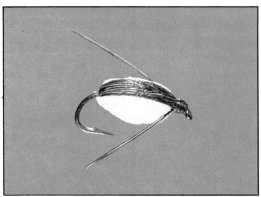
Buoyant Corixa

Corixa

Chironomids

Midge Pupa

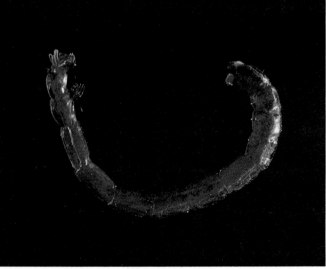
Chironomid Larva (Bloodworm)

Adult Midge

True to Life Midge Pupa

Marabou Midge Pupa

Suspender Buzzer

Adult Midge

Black Midge Pupa

Black Pennel

Bloodworm

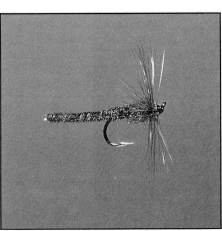

Emerging Midge

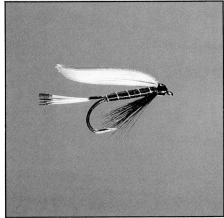

Blae & Black

Daphnia

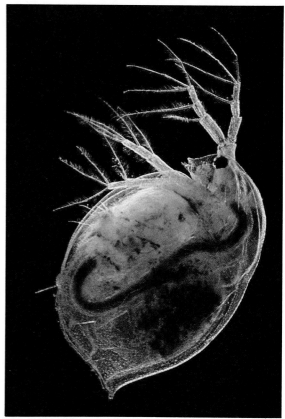

Daphnia Water-flea

The Olives

Pond Olive Nymph

Pond Olive Spinner Female

Pond Olive Dun Female

Whiskey Fly

Black Chenille

Orange Muddler

Old Nick

Jungle Cock Dunkeld

Leprechaun

Greenwells Glory

June Fly

Spring Favourite

Apricot Poly-Spinner

Olive Quill

Peter's Pond Olive Dun

Crane Fly

Fry Feeding Trout

Perch Fry

Roach Fry

Stickle Back

Standard Daddy Long Legs

Daddy Long Legs Dapping Pattern

Latex Bodied Daddy Long Legs

Muddler Minnow

Jersey Herd

White Muddler

Missionary

Jack Frost

Tandem White Muddler

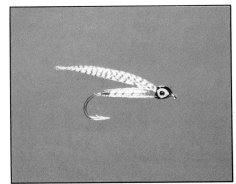
Sinfoils Fry

Mylar Bodied Fry

Appetiser

Shrimps & Hoglice

Hog Louse

Fresh Water Shrimp

Dragon & Damsel Flies

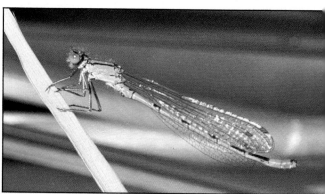

Adult Blue Damsel Fly

Damsel Fly Nymph

Dragon Fly Nymph

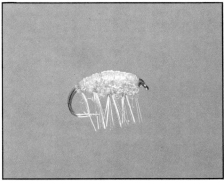

Walker's Shrimp

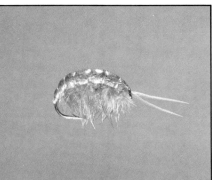

Peter's Shrimp

Hoglouse

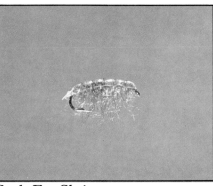

Seals Fur Shrimp

Dragonfly Nymph

Leaded Damsel Nymph

Seals Fur Damsel Nymph

Traditional Damsel Nymph

Blue Damsel Imitation

Marabou Damsel Nymph

The Sedges

Sedge Pupa

Adult Sedge

Caddis Larva

Phantom Midge

Phantom Larva

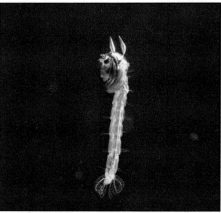

Phantom Pupa

Amber Nymph

Stick Fly

Invicta

Mini-Muddler

Peter's Sedge Pupa

Wickham's Fancy

Latex Grub

Superla Sedge

Murrough

Phantom Larva

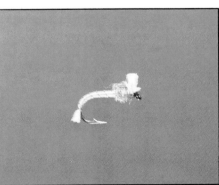

Phantom Pupa

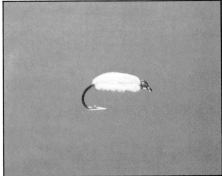

Glennons Phantom Nymph

Leeches

Leech

Caenis

Caenis Nymph

Broadwing or Angler's Curse

Snail

Freshwater Snail

Brown & Olive Leech

Black Leech

No Hackle Caenis

Caenis Cluster

Poly Winged Caenis

Grafham Snail

Black & Peacock Spider

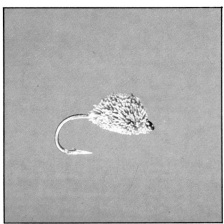

Deer Hair Snail

Mayfly

Female Dun/Sub-imago Mayfly

Mayfly Spinner Female Imago

Mayfly Nymph

Miscellaneous

Drone Fly

Hawthorn Fly

Palmered Mayfly Nobbler

Straddle Bug

Mask Mayfly

Wulff Mayfly

Static Spent Mayfly

Walker's Mayfly Nymph

Bob's Spent Mayfly

Hamills

Drone Fly

Hawthorn Fly

Black Ant

Recent Developments

Original Flectolite Lure

Waggy

Dog Nobbler

Frog Nobbler

American Mylar Fry

Chamois Leech

Deer Hair Perch Fry

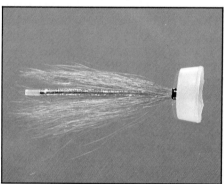

Disc Head Tube

Bullett Minnow

Yellow Fluorescent Palmer Fly

Tandem White Lure with Green Overwing

magnificent. The body of the female spinner especially is a beautiful translucent cream with contrasting dark brown markings. The wings also change from an opaque yellowish green to a wonderful transparent, film impregnated with many very dark veins. When in flight, these veins give the wings a black appearance which looks most striking against the vivid white of the body. The male insect is very similar, but its body is a little darker with patches of grey and its wings are splashed with darker blotches.

The males are often to be seen in swarms at the tops of bushes and trees. They have long tails and their flight is unmistakable as they shoot quickly off into the sky, only to hold their wings still and to float back down towards the ground like so many animated leaves.

The females join these swarms and mating takes place in mid-air. After fertilisation, the female returns to the water to lay her eggs and at this stage she is known to the angler as the Grey Drake. Once her cargo of eggs has been laid, she falls exhausted and dying on the water's surface, at which point she is known as the Spent Gnat. I cannot honestly work out how this name came about because she is not a gnat in any shape or form.

When the mayfly falls spent on the water the trout have a feast. On hitting the surface their wings naturally open and there they lay spreadeagled, trapped in the surface film. Because they are so easy to sip in when in such a predicament, feeding comes easy to the fish. You will need a good imitation tied in this prone position if you are going to have much success.

Of all the insects known to the fly fisher, the mayfly has prompted more imitations than the other creatures put together. Unfortunately for the stillwater angler, particularly those who fish the big Midland reservoirs, they are a little wasted. Dealing with mayfly nymph imitations is an easy matter: there is only one. What we mean by this is that there is only one good one. This was devised by Dick Walker, and, after studying the natural closely we can confidently say that it is the only pattern which actually looks like a mayfly nymph. Although there are many flies available which claim to be imitations, they are most definitely not. Most are simply green or brown nymphs tied on large hooks. Mayfly nymphs are not green at all but a pale buff and only Dick Walker's pattern fulfils this criterion.

Walker's Mayfly Nymph was originally devised for fishing on rivers, but it is just as effective on stillwaters and is a killer even on waters which have no mayfly. Its

Unhooking a fish which snapped up a leaded mayfly nymph.

real beauty is that its colour, large size and gills which run down each side of the abdomen give it a wonderful succulent appearance. If you read the chapter on tying leaded nymphs you will realise that Walker's Mayfly Nymph is heavily weighted. For this reason it is best fished on a floating line and a long leader. Also because it sinks very quickly it is an ideal pattern for stalking fish in clear deep stillwaters.

The technique has accounted for a great many big rainbows in small waters and is easy to master with a little practice. Firstly you must spot your fish, using polaroids to cut down any surface glare and enable you to see deep into the water. Moving carefully along the bank you search for fish cruising close in. Once this has been accomplished you must then check which direction the fish is moving and then cast your fly far enough ahead so that it sinks slowly past the fish's nose. Although this does simplify a relatively skilled task it is exactly what happens.

On the whole, the mayfly nymph has been a pretty neglected creature, probably because many anglers have never seen one. The same cannot be said for the adult. There must be literally thousands of patterns invented over the hundreds of years of fly fishing history. Dealing with the Sub-Imago or Dun, we have found most success on the big Irish loughs by using a yellow hackled pattern which imitates the yellowish green hue of the natural's wings.

I (Peter) have a particular affection for the mayfly Dun as it brings back fond memories of fishing Lough Mask in Co. Mayo. I remember vividly the sight of those elegant duns drifting silently downwind. The trout were feeding heavily on the freshly emerged flies as autopsies proved and every fish we caught was stuffed to the gills with the crumpled corpses. An interesting point was that many of the duns had failed to develop their wings properly which meant the insect could not fly.

I did best with a traditional pattern tied with a yellow body and a hackle of grey mallard flank dyed yellow. Fished in the traditional way, short lining with a floating line and a three fly cast, the normally wily trout took the imitation with gusto. They were beautiful wild browns with wonderful colours and a spectacular forked tail which gave them real power. The take itself was also something to behold. You would be retrieving, skimming your flies through the waves when suddenly a trout would make a leap like a porpoise just in front of the boat. This was actually a take and to hook the fish you had to drop the rod tip and count to five. A simple tightening usually accounted for a hooked fish, though at the time it was something new to me. I was more used to rainbows which chase and nip than these wonderfully confident wild browns. I can tell you, it took a little getting used to.

The Mask Mayfly is not the only pattern to prove effective when fish are taking the duns. There are many other traditionals such as the Straddlebug with its Wood-duck hackle and as I found during a trip to Bishop's Bowl in the 1983 season there are also a few very unlikely modern flies which work too. I (Bob) first visited Bishop's Bowl Lake near Leamington Spa in June. Although it is a small 26-acre water formed by flooding an old limestone quarry it has the great asset of a really superb hatch of mayfly, an unfortunately rare thing for a Midland water.

The water is deep, clear and alkaline supporting a prolific insect population including mayfly. Add to this the many bays and islands and you will realise that the

A hooked fish takes to the air.

fishing can be very interesting indeed. After searching out the most likely looking spots I began to tackle up, trying to ignore the splashes of the trout sucking in the big flies. I suppose if I ever lost that feeling of excitement I get at such times I would hang up my rods for good.

To be honest I was not properly prepared as the last thing I expected was that the lake would be alive with mayfly, so a compromise was called for. I tied on a Mayfly Dog Nobbler. Now before you start muttering about this being a very crude technique for trout taking the regal mayfly, let me remind you that the mayfly nymph may be as much as 1¼ in (3.2cm) long and it is no slouch when it comes to putting on a turn of speed. So why shouldn't my Size 8 Nobbler version work?

My first port of call was in the narrow stretch where a good cast would see my fly falling just short of the far cliff-like bank. As expected after a few pulls, I hooked a hard fighting fish from mid-water. Spooning the fish showed that it had been taking both the nymph and the dun stages in large quantities. I hooked but lost a second fish from this spot and so decided the best course of action would be to walk the bank and try to sort out one of the better fish.

It was at the far end, at a spot called Island Pool that I found the most activity. A great many adult mayflies were drifting on the light breeze and were finishing up in the margins at a spot where no other angler had walked that morning. Because they were not being disturbed the trout were coming in close to take these easy pickings right off the surface, a classic dry fly situation.

Looking in my box I could hardly believe it, there was

not one single dry fly to be found. Yet another compromise was called for. My eyes settled on a small yellow hairwinged Muddler. The question was, would it work on so preoccupied fish? I sprayed the already buoyant Muddler to ensure it would float and cast it out into the mêlée. A few short jerks and my question was answered with an explosive take, the best visual take I had seen for many a day. Now I was into a much better trout which made many long fast runs, before I duly landed a gleaming 3lb rainbow. It was a superb fish just like a bar of silver and had fought more like a trout twice its size.

Another unlikely pattern that has worked well for us is an American fly called the Hamill's Killer which is not a mayfly imitation at all but a lure. It is dressed with a body of yellow chenille and a two-stage wing of grey mallard flank dyed yellow. In the water it looks very like a drowned mayfly dun and has caught some good fish for us, particularly on the large Irish waters.

Trout do not only take the Dun though and have a real liking for the spent females as they lie dying on the water's surface. Again there have been many patterns devised to imitate this stage, a few of which may be classed as real killers. Even though they were initially dressed as river patterns no one bothered telling the stillwater trout which take them with equal gusto.

Our selection of mayfly imitations is completed by two final patterns, both of which are dry flies. The first is like the previous pattern, an imitation of the Spent Female Spinner. It is dressed with a body of ethafoam which gives it buoyancy and wings of Iron Blue cock hackle fibres. It is a wonderfully life-like pattern which lays naturally right in the surface film very much like the natural.

The second is the White Wulff, an American hair wing dry fly which is an exceedingly good general pattern. It is big, bulky and floats very well even in a heavy chop. Because it is big it is also highly visible both to the angler and the fish, which is very useful in a large wave. Like the Walker's Mayfly Nymph, it has the advantage that it takes fish even on waters with no mayfly.

15 Miscellaneous

The Hawthorn Fly

Although the Hawthorn Fly is a terrestrial insect, it's eaten by the trout in large enough quantities to mean it cannot be neglected. It is also known as St Mark's Fly as it starts to appear around 25 April which is St Mark's Day. It is a large black insect about 10–12mm long and it's interesting, because the male and female are different. The female looks just like a large black gnat, and it is only the male which has the characteristic hairy body and dangling legs. It doesn't really matter because when the Hawthorn Fly is about, the sight of these males is enough to identify the species.

The Hawthorn is usually found in mating swarms some distance from the water. As it's a weak flyer any decent offshore breeze sees it blown out over the surface. Because the season is only short, lasting about three or four weeks, the angler has to be lucky to encounter a good rise. If he does he will not be disappointed, as when the fish are taking the naturals they go quite mad.

I (Peter) was fortunate enough to witness a good rise to the Hawthorn Fly during the 1982 season. It was at Wimbleball, a beautiful reservoir set on the edge of Exmoor, one of the South West's top trout waters. Although it is a long way from my home it was not the first time I had fished there, so I had a good idea where to start. I found a quiet bay with a light breeze blowing from slightly behind me and my left, casting out a team of wet flies. Around mid-morning the wind got up and some large black flies began to be blown past my head, and out over the water. Grabbing out at one as it went by, I found I had caught a Hawthorn Fly.

The fish by now had started to rise quite well. Unfortunately I was down in Devon for only a short visit, and hadn't got all my flies with me, and I had no Hawthorn Fly imitations. A compromise was called for, so I searched for and found a thinly dressed Black and Peacock Spider, tied with a long hackle. I hoped it would look enough like a natural Hawthorn Fly to fool the trout, and thankfully it was. Casting out into the area of most activity, I was soon connected to a nice 1½lb rainbow.

With an effective pattern found, it wasn't long before I'd taken a good bag of rainbows up to 2lb. Wimbleball is capable of producing much better fish than this though, and an angler nearer the head of the bay landed a superb full tailed specimen of 4½lb, again on a Hawthorn imitation.

Apart from general patterns such as the Black and Peacock Spider and the Black Pennel, which all work well during a rise to the Hawthorn Fly, there are other more lifelike patterns available. One imitation which we have used to good effect, is dressed with a body of black feather fibre, blue Dun hackle points for wings, and two knotted fibres of black feather to imitate the dangling rear legs. The fly may be fished either wet or dry, and as it is usually dressed with a black cock hackle, more turns will be required in the dry fly.

The Drone Fly

During the summer months you may have noticed a small yellow and black fly hovering around the flower heads in your garden. Although it looks a little like a wasp, it's not a wasp at all but a Drone Fly. The Drone Fly belongs to a family which also includes the Hover Fly, but from the angler's viewpoint they can all be treated as the same. They are basically variations on a theme, with yellow and black or orange and brown abdomens. Because of this they resemble either common wasps or honey bees, depending of course on the species. You can tell the difference though, because unlike the wasps or bees which have four wings, the Drone Fly belongs to the Order Diptera, and therefore has only two. This likeness to the wasp or bee is not pure coincidence. The Drone Fly has few natural defences of its own and uses its mimicry of the stinging insect to gain protection from birds and other predators.

Some species of Drone Fly are aquatic or semi-aquatic in larval and sometimes the pupal stage. One larva which is quite common in the margins of stillwaters is known as the Rat Tailed Maggot. It prefers to live in the black silt, and there it feeds on decaying organic matter. The reason it is called the Rat Tailed Maggot is that it is a grey maggot-like creature about ½in (13mm) long, with an extending tail. This tail, which can stretch up to as much

as 3in (7.6cm) is a breathing tube. It allows the larva to move about freely in shallow water without fear of drowning.

From this you would assume that it's the semi-aquatic Drone Fly which are of most interest but you would be wrong. We've read many times that the trout take the female Drone Fly as she returns to lay her eggs. Whilst this may be true, it does not account for the huge falls of Drone Flies that take place from time to time on waters such as Grafham. The insect which causes all the problems is the smaller terrestrial Hover Fly, which sometimes occurs in huge numbers. Its larvae feed on Greenfly, and when there is an abundance, there is an upsurge in the Hover Fly population.

When this occurs Hover Flies get onto the surface in large quantities, so much so that the trout become pre-occupied. It was the late Cyril Inwood who first discovered how deadly the Hover or Drone Fly imitation could be. It was way back in 1968 when Grafham was in its prime. It was mid-summer in the midst of a heat wave. Hover Flies were falling heavily onto the surface of Grafham, and Cyril was quick to notice the connection between these flies and some difficult to catch but free rising trout.

He invented a pattern which, though now developed slightly from Cyril's original, still catches fish when trout are on the naturals. The fly may be fished either wet or dry, right in the surface film, using a floating line and a fine long leader. Fishing the Hover Fly remains a minor technique, but without the correct imitation you will struggle to catch.

The Flying Ant

Like both the Hawthorn and Hover Fly, the Flying Ant is another terrestrial insect which finds itself on the water from time to time. Like the previous two it also has the ability to preoccupy the trout making a good imitation necessary. It's only the ant in its flying form that gets eaten and the season is also rather short. I am sure we have all seen the mass emergence of winged male and female ants from their underground nests. This usually takes place on those hot sultry days during the middle to latter parts of summer.

It is a funny thing that although ants emerge in great numbers every year, they don't always get onto the water. A combination of a large number of insects, and a good

breeze to blow them out over the surface, is required. It takes the fish a while to cotton on and quite a few naturals need to be available before the trout take an interest.

When trout feed on ants, they can be difficult to catch, and often will look at nothing else. An imitation we have used which works as well as any is tied on a Size 12 hook with a body of floss, and two white cock hackle tips for wings. The body and hackle colour can be varied according to the type of ant that is being taken. There are many species of ant but we only have to worry about the colour, the two main ones being black and red-brown. As fishing the ant is only a minor technique, we only have to keep a few imitations, and three black and three red patterns in the box should easily be enough.

Ant imitations can be used either dry or subsurface. Either way they work best fished in the surface film. The dry fly should be used with a long fine degreased leader. The wet fly is most effective on a similar leader, but greased for half its length, the remainder degreased to keep surface disturbance down to a minimum. Keep the retrieve slow allowing the imitation to drift along on the breeze, just like the natural trapped in the surface.

The Beetles

The Order Coleoptera to which beetles belong is a very large one, and they come in all shapes and sizes from tiniest of weevils right up to Britain's largest, the Stag Beetle. As they are able to fly they do get onto the water, but not often in large enough numbers to make their imitation worthwhile. This is not to say they are not useful at times, particularly on some of the small acid hill lochs where any food item is welcome to the hungry trout.

One very famous species is the Coch-y-Bonddu, which appears in large swarms around June. It is more common in Scotland and Wales than it is in England but when the natural is on the wing the well-known imitation is a real killer. There are other species too, including the prolific orange Soldier Beetle which is seen in huge numbers throughout June to August but we do not feel its imitation is worth worrying about.

More as a guide of what not to imitate, we must also mention the aquatic beetles. Because they are aquatic you would think they would turn up more often in autopsies. But after spooning thousands of trout, we can't remember finding more than the odd Water Beetle. Like their terrestrial cousins they vary in size from tiny individuals right up to creatures as large as *Dytiscus marginalis*, better known as the Great Diving Beetle. Both it and its larvae are fierce predators, even worse than Dragonfly Nymphs. We have not even found many larvae, which are more accessible to the trout, so we suspect Water Beetles as a group are best disregarded.

As terrestrial beetles are totally incapacitated when they fall into water they are much easier for the trout to catch than the aquatic forms. Sometimes small specimens do become trapped on the surface, and trout will take them. In such cases though, patterns like the Coch-y-Bonddu or the Black and Peacock Spider fished slowly in the surface film in a similar way to ants and Hover Flies will prove as effective as any.

RECENT DEVELOPMENTS

1 Rats Tails

I am fortunate in meeting so many outstanding fly fishers on my travels around the country. Some of these may have come up with a very good idea which could benefit our sport in general, but because they do not write in the magazines no one gets to know about them.

One such angler is Roy Parker, a member of the Mid-Northants Trout Fishers Club. Roy and his friend Hector Woolnough are two of the club's most successful trout catchers and often share a boat on their local Pitsford Reservoir. They have one thing in common, they are fanatical dry fly fishers, a method at which they excel.

Roy has a particular soft spot for Pitsford because like me he feels it is one of the best reservoirs in the country for free rising trout making it ideal for dry fly fishing.

Roy's dry flies are rather specialised. They are called Rats Tails and are unsinkable. He developed them when his traditional dry fly patterns refused to float. Rats Tails come in many colour combinations and cover the whole range of natural fly imitations.

Basically he ties a pinch of deer hair along the hook shank, then enough is added so the shank is out of sight which provides the buoyancy. The ends are left protruding to form the tail. Tying silk is used mostly as a ribbing, but fine wire or oval thread can be used if a little flash is required. The body is now combined with anything from one to five cock hackles. When dipped in silicone flotant this fly is impossible to sink in any conditions including the heaviest wave.

Roy first took a limit on a dry fly some six years earlier using one of Hector's patterns, a traditionally tied Green Sedge, and admitted that it was the most exciting limit he had ever taken because he saw the fish come up and take the fly.

Roy likes to fish mainly from a slow drifting boat, in the early part of the season from April to June preferring the shallower water, around 3–4ft (91–122cm). In this depth the trout will rise to these flies confidently from the reservoir bed and if there is a hatch of buzzer on so much the better.

'Sometimes we go as small as Size 18 flies tied to 2lb nylon when the water is very clear and this works well when the larger flies fail', says Roy.

I saw Roy one evening at Pitsford coming off with a heavier than average limit bag from the fishery when many others fishing close by had caught nothing. Those that had failed were either nymphing, luring or traditional wet fly fishing. The fish were taking small smuts in the surface and the little Black Rats Tail had imitated them perfectly.

Asked if he always fished the fly static, or made it wake, Roy revealed that he never moved it except occasionally when a fish rises just a few inches away when he slightly lifted the rod so as to just move the fly. Unfortunately this often brought a smash take which could easily break the fine cast.

While most anglers who fish dry fly use a double taper or certainly a full fly line Roy uses shooting heads as beefy as a number 9 so that he can throw it 40yd (37m) to a fish or could simply drop it in front of the boat as you would traditionally. His winning method is to keep drifting and searching until a shoal of fish is found, then he anchors. Roy stressed that the technique was to cast out and as the boat drifted downwind to just take up the slack line but not to retrieve or skate the fly. Many anglers who have tried the Rats Tails cannot discipline themselves on this point when really it is the key to success.

I have given Roy's flies a fair trial on Rutland and I have proved to myself they really do work well, but what is their record elsewhere? Roy confirmed that they have been tried at Ravensthorpe, Draycote, Grafham and Eyebrook as well as the two other reservoirs mentioned and had worked well.

Roy has dyed deer hair in virtually every imaginable colour to achieve all the different body variations on his patterns which range from tiny Size 18 flies to Size 6 longshank fry imitations. Here is a month by month approach used by Roy at Pitsford.

In April if fish are showing, a little Black Rats Tail is the answer. If this should fail try a natural deer hair with a black hackle, or a brown deer hair with a black hackle. These imitate the early brown or black Chironomids.

Now we move on to the Olives. At the end of April and into May we get the half-hour hatches of this delicate insect. Quickly put on an Olive Rats Tail and take advantage of the short hatch, when it is quite possible to pick up a couple of brace before the naturals disappear.

Into May and it is the time for a Ginger Rats Tail. This is a great time of the year and limit after limit falls to this colour. By June move on to Orange Rats Tails, or even bright red ones. Carry on into July with these bright colours but mid-way through the month the sedges appear in good numbers which means a switch to green, orange or cinnamon versions.

By August, the very small Rats Tails come into their own and the fishing can be tricky but highly satisfying. In September and October Roy uses a natural deer hair bodied Daddy Longlegs. Like the others this is a far more buoyant pattern than the normal dressings and the whole secret of the style's unquestionable success is that the fly must sit right on top of the water.

2 Dog and Frog Nobblers

It was 1981 when Trevor Housby introduced his new lure which he had christened the Dog Nobbler. However, it wasn't until the following season that the general angling public became wise to them.

Head weighted or leaded flies or lures are not new, but all credit must be given to Trevor for capturing the imagination of every stillwater fly fisherman in Britain with his Dog Nobblers.

I (Bob) must admit I made some very impressive catches myself using both large and small Nobblers. I think the most interesting experiences I had while using them was first at Avington in mid-summer. A good big rainbow was spotted in the bottom lake, cruising slowly along and quite easy to cover. It was late morning when I first spotted it but was told by several other anglers not to waste my time on it. Apparently they had covered it with all the obvious leaded nymphs and so on without response. However, I could not resist having a try myself but it viewed half a dozen patterns with disdain.

I opened my fly wallet yet again and tied on a Size 8 yellow Nobbler, wet the tail to ensure quick sinking before casting it out to the middle of the deep hole at the end of the pool. I could clearly see the big rainbow several yards away from where my highly visible Nobbler was sinking.

The big fish's reaction was amazing. It was transformed from a docile sleepy mood to one of fin bristling alertness. I began the figure of eight retrieve coupled with a jigging of the rod top. This meant the Nobbler was hopping along back towards me fairly close to the bottom. I watched the trout race across the pool and the Nobbler disappeared into the gaping jaws. I struck into him before feeling the take and a fine 11lb 11oz rainbow was on the bank.

Now before you start thinking that was a fluke, later in the day Jean Zender, a visiting angler from Luxembourg, copied my tactics to take a 12½lb fish. This was after careful nymphing had failed for him for most of the day. Even pellet fattened large rainbows have this aggressive instinct to kill any smaller nuisances that challenge their territory or feeding area. When standard delicate nymphing failed on a number of occasions throughout the rest of the summer and autumn, on went a Nobbler and out came the trout.

I discerned that colour and hook size could be very important. I did see quite a lot of anglers misusing the

This fine Bayham fish took one of the Frog Nobbler Lures.

Nobblers by fishing them on fast sinking lines. This was a waste of time and defeated the object of presentation.

It was when I led a group to fish in the French National Fly Fishing Championships that I discovered the worth of the mini Nobblers now christened Frog Nobblers. All of the six English anglers competing fished on the permitted practice day. Most patterns caught fish, but it was very noticeable that my Size 12 short shank Nobblers were attracting the most fish. A gold body and a black tailed version was catching browns while a silver body and a white tailed version was taking rainbows to around 5lb. Certainly these Nobblers helped us find the hotspots of the lake. This was used to good advantage the next day when *Trout Fisherman* Editor John Wilshaw drew a good spot. He knew how to fish it and fished the Frog Nobbler to become the French Champion.

I have traced the weighted lure idea back to 1965 when American angler Mike Prorok presented me with some jigs designed for casting with a fixed spool reel. About the same time I used to pinch a soft lead shot in front of my lure when I fished it on a floater from the bank which gave me that hopalong action that seems to trigger off the rainbows' aggression. Then Dick Walker came out with what he called Lead Heads. This was a shot pinched onto a long shanked hook and a normal lure tied over it. Geoffrey Bucknall then came out with his Beastie Lure which had lead wire wound on at the head. It was dressed

with marabou and fished very well as a diving lure again on a floating line. Then came Trevor's Dog Nobbler which put the idea into top gear. Since then I have tried some castable mini American jigs and finally developed the Frog Nobbler. These are weighted with fine strips cut from the lead foil off wine bottle tops. If you tie in more lead beneath the hook shank than on top the Nobbler will fish on an even keel which is important.

The actual dressing of the Frog Nobblers is simplicity itself. The tail is a generous plume of whatever colour marabou you like with a body of silver or gold mylar tubing slid on over the lead underbody and secured with tying silk at hook bend and head. The hook is a Size 10 or 12.

For the tying of Dog Nobbler you need long shank hooks of size 10, 8 or 6. Glue and pinch on a soft shot at the eye of the hook although lead or copper wire can be used as an alternative. Again the tail is generous plume of long marabou fibres. The body is chenille ribbed with fine oval thread. The head is peacock herl to cover the weighting hump. When a shot is used for head weight these are painted and eyes added.

Dog and Frog Nobblers are now working on all waters I have fished this past three seasons and I certainly look to them as an important part of my armoury. Try a red and white tail and silver bodied Frog Nobbler if you want to see how effective they are.

3 The Waggy Lure

It has always been the impossible dream to devise a fly or lure guaranteed to catch fish whatever the conditions. Of course this can never be but it has never stopped us trying all the same. This does not prevent us developing new techniques though. Certainly, if the early reservoir pioneers had lacked the spirit of adventure we would lack the methods we use today.

Fishing deep with fast sinking lines and lures has its fair share of critics. It has been called little more than trawling but this only shows the ignorance of the critics. In many ways, fishing deep on the drift is a very difficult technique to master. Whatever your view, bottom dragging with big lures does sort out the better browns, fish that would simply die of old age if only surface fishing were allowed.

The catching of large browns has always fascinated me (Peter) and although I enjoy loch style fishing as much as anyone, the challenge of catching a big brown from the deep is hard to resist. Sometimes it is difficult to switch up to surface fishing techniques even if the trout are rising well!

About the time Rutland Water first opened, Bob and I were experimenting with methods which might work better on the bigger fish. This meant not only developing the tackle but also the flies and lures we were using. At the time we were concentrating on fishing the drift using the rudder to control the boat on a point down the wind drift either casting or casting and paying out fast sinking lines out behind the boat. The two lines we used mainly were either a lead core shooting head or a 100yd (91m) length of lead cored trolling line, depending both on the speed of the drift and the depth of water we were fishing over.

Although we could cast the shooting head and retrieve the lure to give it a good action, when it came to the trolling line we could only pay it out which meant that it was difficult to achieve an attractive action to the lure other than a straight retrieve back up to the boat. Now big browns are wily creatures and soon get used to the same old method of retrieve. It was all right at the beginning of the year, but as the season progressed catches would taper off simply because they had got used to what we had to offer. Big fish would continue to chase the lures right

up to the boat before turning away in disgust. Obviously something needed to be done.

Big lures work best for fishing deep for two main reasons. Firstly, a big trout needs a good mouthful if it is to take notice and have a go. Secondly, when drifting in a big wind, the boat really moves along apace and the big hooks are essential if you are to maintain a hook hold. Small hooks will hook the fish but will often pull out on the long haul needed to get a good brown up to the net. We had the formula worked out, all we needed was to put the components together in a way sufficiently different to make the trout take properly.

We decided that what was needed was a lure that was both big and meaty, the right colour and had built-in action. At the time we had been catching some nice brownies on the tandem Goldie Lure which is black, yellow and gold so this then was to be our basic colour. We also reckoned that a Muddler type head would be needed to help the lure fish a couple of feet off the bottom and to ride over any obstructions without getting caught up. All we needed then was a way of imparting a natural action to the lure.

After considering many different methods and trying some of the more likely looking ones we soon realised this was going to be more difficult than imagined. It looked like we were going to draw a blank until Bob came up with a brainwave. He had been studying the action of a Red Gill sea fishing lure and asked me if we could use this sort of tail movement. On the face of it, it looked perfect. The tail of the Red Gill beats away from side to side in an extremely lively way. The only problem was how to copy it and to be honest we did not even consider the legalities at the time.

The problem of the flexible tail was easily solved by using wide, white rubber bands which were very thin. After that all we needed was to find a way of forming the 'T' shaped tail to give the lure its action. Again it looked as if we had hit a stumbling block until we came across a material known as Flectolite used for tarting up old cars and which came in a range of colours including gold, silver and green. Its real beauty was that it was both light, sticky-backed and, being metallic, was very stiff. Not only that, but it was finished in a scale pattern which reflected the light in a most attractive way.

So the first prototypes were tied up and I tried them in my garden pond to see if the action was right. They looked fine so I took them along on my next trip to Rutland. Unfortunately the breeze was very light and I couldn't match them against their intended task. I tried them all the same though and soon found a problem. Because they were fashioned by hand some lures worked better than others, and some hardly worked at all. After a bit more experimentation I worked out how the tail should be formed to give it the best action.

Returning to Rutland a week later, I was pleased to see an overcast day with a strong westerly breeze. I could hardly wait. I tackled up right away with a long lead line as I was determined to give the new lure a fair trial. We motored straight up the South Arm to a spot known to produce good browns and I cut the motor and paid the lead line out over the back. This was to be the acid test. I let out enough line to make sure the lure was tripping just over the bottom and waited for a take. We had drifted along for about 100yd (91m) when I had a superb pull but nothing connected. I retrieved my lure only to find to my horror that the fish had pulled the tail clean off. I didn't dare use the other lures in case the same thing happened so I switched back to ordinary tandems. We caught some nice fish but I had yet to succeed with the new lure.

On returning home I decided to make the tail a bit more permanent by stapling it to the rubber band. It looked all right and didn't seem to affect the action. I also added a Size 12 flying treble. So back I went for a third time and thankfully, conditions were as good as the last.

Trying the same drift again we had travelled about 150yd (137m) when I had a lovely take, though this time when I lifted I felt the satisfying double knock of a good fish. To cut a long story short, we ended up with a really nice bag of browns up to 4½lb, virtually all of which fell to the new lure. We had finally proved it really did work.

During the remainder of that season and the subsequent one, both Bob and I took some good bags of both large browns and rainbows on these lures and others which were developed from the original idea. The largest fish I caught was a 5¼lb brown which came when the Rutland record was 6lb 10oz and I would have had another even bigger one on the same day if my boat partner hadn't knocked it off with the net.

Fishing deep for browns with such lures cannot really be called fly fishing in the truest sense of the word. After two seasons of it I became tired of the method and for the

Correct choice of fly or lure can mean the difference between a limit bag or blank.

next two years stuck exclusively to loch style fishing, totally neglecting the lead line and the waggle tailed lure.

One day Bob was fishing with that master of deep fishing Fred Wagstaffe who has taken many large browns from both Rutland and a number of Scottish and Irish loughs even into double figures. Fred noticed one of my original lures in Bob's box which set him thinking. Unfortunately the lure Bob had was one of the early ones which didn't work well. The main thing was that unbeknown to me, it gave Fred the idea to develop patterns based on the rubber sand eel which now prove so effective.

Fred has made the lure his own with his tremendous catches and it has now come to be known as the Waggy. Fred was not only the first angler to gain official approval for the lure, but developed it far beyond our original, handmade lures. Since their development, Fred's dressings have accounted for some really huge limits of specimen browns, some of them nearly into double figures. Whilst all this has been his own work it is nice to think that we had some small part to play in its success.

4 Tube Flies

Tube flies are an idea that trout fishers have adapted from the salmon fishers who fish the big rivers in spring and autumn. Why would any self-respecting trout fisher want to use a large tube fly with a treble for a hook, which surely you think cannot be a sporting way to catch trout. Of course the answer is that they are used only when in pursuit of the large salmon-sized trout of the biggest reservoirs and natural waters.

I (Bob) clearly remember Brian Bates taking the first double figure brownie from Grafham back in 1975. It weighed a staggering 11lb 5½oz and took an Esmond Drury tube 3in (7.6cm) long. After this capture many anglers who preferred to fish the deep style big fish or nothing tactics, started to experiment with the tubes and similar lures.

At the start plain tubes in either plastic, aluminium or brass were used, anything from 2–3in (5–7.6cm) long. Usually the dressing consisted of a silver or gold mylar body and a coloured hairwing. Black and gold, white and silver and so on through the known colour combinations. At the tail end of the tube a short rubber sleeve was pushed on and this had an important role to play. Once the leader nylon was threaded through and the treble tied on, the shank of the treble was pushed back into the rubber sleeve which held it securely in position making for good hooking.

After a few years, Dick Shrive developed an idea of using very short pieces of tube something like 3/8in (9.5mm) long. These he dressed heavily with fur and feathers making up a 3in (7.6cm) long lure. The idea being that when the treble was tied on and pulled back into the thick dressing it was completely hidden.

I was sent a batch of another kind of tube fly named by its inventor as the Cranston Vaned Tube. These were similar to an ordinary Tube except that they sported a concaved lip which in theory would make them dive and wobble. I had some success when trying out a silver-bodied blue and white hairwing version taking browns to 4¾lb from Rutland. The only drawback with this particular tube was that it had a tendency to spin on the retrieve kinking the leader. This became too much bother and I dropped the idea.

In my opinion the best idea of all for added life-like vibrations was the disc head addition. This was a circular concave disc slid on to the tube at the head and secured with tying silk before forming the normal dressing on the tube. When this particular pattern is retrieved it sets up tremendous vibrations caused by water pressure entering the concaved head and then being forced out like a fountain. A gold body and a multi yellow and black wing has been a highly successful dressing for this tube.

Finally I must complete the set by mentioning a flat shoe horn shaped plastic device which I have seen in use at Rutland. The line is threaded through a hole at the head and rear and a treble is attached. The shovel headed flat plastic body is dressed as normal of course. Its action on the retrieve is to dive deep and to wobble violently from side to side. This action is similar to an American plug known as the Lazy Ike. I have also seen hair slides used to obtain the correct plastic shape. That they work there is no doubt, but as to their legality there is more than a little doubt.

All these Tube Flies can only be fished effectively from a drifting boat and with a fast sinking fly line when the boat needs to be moving bow first down the wind preferably on rudder or perhaps on stern positioned drogue. Each angler casts out from different sides of the boat allowing their lures to swing and run deep.

5 Tandems and Multi-hook Rigs

The idea of big lure, big fish, is about right if you study the big trout returns and for most of the time tandems or any of the other multi-hook rigs are used in conjunction with some form of high density line, usually a very fast sinker or lead core.

This assumption that big trout stay deep close to the bottom for most of the time seems pretty well proven. It is also well known that a fast moving large lure will tempt many a big wary fish to make a mistake if it is running along the bottom.

Normally the styles of fishing used are, to anchor up over a known hotspot or to drift fast downwind on the rudder, skimming the lure along the bottom. At some big reservoirs like Grafham and Rutland, a special deep area of the water allows for trolling. This means that you can trail your lure on a fast sinking line behind the boat as long as you are rowing as motoring is not allowed. This method may not be the most exciting but it certainly can produce a few real big trout.

To rig up a standard tandem lure mount you need two longshank hooks in either Size 6 or 8 and a few inches of 30lb breaking strain nylon. Fix the first hook in the vice and run in a length of silk from the eye down to the bend and back up again. This forms a strong bed which helps the nylon to grip. Next take a pair of pliers and with them crimp one end of the nylon length for approximately 2in (5cm). This crimping roughens the nylon's otherwise smooth surface helping the silk to hold it secure.

When this has been done, hold the nylon over the hook shank so that the bulk projects over the eye and 1in (25mm) of crimped nylon is left hanging over the bend. Then, with the tying silk, bind the nylon firmly to the shank in tight, touching turns. To complete the near hook rig, simply bend the inch of crimped nylon back towards the eye and bind that down giving a five turn whip finish at the eye. Incidentally this doubling back of the nylon prevents it pulling out when a fish is hooked.

To finish the rig off place the second hook in the vice. Start the silk off in the same way and crimp the nylon. Make sure that the gap between the two hooks is only about ¼in (6mm). Any more than this and the two hooks will tend to tangle with each other during casting.

There are a few more very useful rigs. A three hook rig can produce a very long lure up to 6in (15cm) and this type has caught many big fish from the Queen Mother Reservoir coupled with deep fishing tactics. Then there is a rig which Stuart Billam calls his sting in the tail. This comprises a longshank Size 6 hook and a small Size 14 treble on a link which is hidden by the wing feather. A white and silver lure or a red and gold one similar to the Nailer Fly have both proved killing colour combinations at Rutland.

The well known big fish man at Rutland, Fred Wagstaffe, devised a rig for deep fishing which had a wobble movement on its rear hook. He used two double salmon hooks in tandem or Size 4. Instead of making the join traditionally with a single strand of heavy nylon his was a large loop of 30lb flat nylon which allowed the rear dressed hook to develop a distinct wiggle and so enticed more fish to take.

The successful dressing was a huge white deer hair head with white chenille bodies on both front and rear hooks, an orange hackle fibre tail and throat on each hook and long strand white goat hair for the wings.

It is uncanny though how the addition of another material can turn a good lure into a real killer and so it was proved true yet again during the back end of the 1981 season. Duncan Currie my regular partner and I (Peter) had been catching some fine bags of trout on a tandem white and silver lure given to us by a Rutland bailiff. We were quite happy taking browns up to 5lb when I happened to chat to my local tackle dealer and friend Martin Blakeston.

He had been given a length of fine iridescent material by a salesman and asked for my opinion.

The thread-like material resembled very fine lurex which while being basically green, sparkled blue, red and pink. Martin told me that it was the most expensive non-metallic yarn ever produced and was used for ladies' evening wear. Whether this was true I know not but it certainly took the fancy of both browns and rainbows.

On our next trip Duncan and I used the material on some of our lures, including the tandem white and silver. We laid it on along the wing as we thought that this would give it the action necessary to make it sparkle. It took only a couple of trips to realise we were on to a real winner.

At the time the fishing was good but our new material soon changed that and it proved successful right through the following season too. This was highlighted on one particular day when the trout were feeding on perch fry. It was a rough overcast day and as soon as we climbed aboard we motored straight for our favourite spot in the South Arm. There is little point going into detail except to say that we had a superb day. We fished mostly at anchor and from the word go we were into fish.

Towards the evening we had virtually taken double limits of big trout topped by browns of 4, 5 and 6lb in addition to rainbows up to 3½lb. We assumed that everyone else was catching well too but when we later talked to a few boats we discovered that most had done poorly. Even Fred Wagstaffe drifted past asking if we had given up. Fred had not done all that well on this occasion and when we held up some of our fish he was astounded.

Since that time the lure's success has continued. Bob has also taken some good bags of better than average trout on a couple of the lures which I tied for him and can vouch for its superiority over normal dressings.

An outstanding morning's catch for Bob Church taken while deep fishing with a lead core line and tandem white lure.

6 Buoyant Lures

It is thought by some that lures can only be fished deep and fast and whilst this method does catch fish it is by no means the only one. Neither is it always the most effective. Some patterns work best when fished right on the surface to drift like a dry fly or nymph and, though this may sound a little strange, it does have a reason behind it.

As a small fish becomes close to death it loses all sense of balance and often floats to the surface where it kicks around sending out the tell-tale vibrations which the trout home in on. The first time I (Peter) witnessed this litle life and death drama was at Grafham. There had been a high mortality rate in that year's perch fry population and in Savages Creek they were dying off in their thousands.

Although the trout were taking these dying perch they still were not that easy to catch as they were reluctant to chase the usual large lures preferring instead to take the crippled fish from the surface as they drifted slowly along. We tried all sorts of patterns with varying degrees of success before coming up with a buoyant ethafoam perch fry imitation coloured with waterproof pens. These buoyant lures were allowed to simply drift towards a weed bed where the trout lay in wait. There would be an almighty swirl and the lure would disappear down the maw of a great trout.

Although I didn't know it at the time, Dave Barker of Cambridge was also developing his own buoyant perch fry imitations. His though were fashioned from white deer hair which did prove a more natural and effective material. Whilst my lure caught some nice fish his Spondoolie as it was later christened, caught some monsters. It was fished just the same but rode in the surface film more naturally and fooled more of the big, wily trout. It was only a few years later when I was first shown one of Dave's superb imitations that I realised what I was doing wrong.

Luckily, at that time Rutland was experiencing a boom in the perch population, and like Grafham, the fry were dying in huge numbers. The trout took swift advantage of this and soon virtually every fish caught was full of perch. Going back to Dave's pattern I tied up a few myself though I dressed mine to look even more life-like. After a good deal of work perfecting the lure it was true that my dressing did look more like a perch to a human eye but Dave's anaemic pattern still worked just as well if not better.

I still caught good fish though amongst them some large browns, the best being a 6lb taken in the Sailing Club Bay. This pattern, like other buoyant fry imitations, should be fished on a Size 9 or 10 floating shooting head. You need such a heavy line because these lures are large and air resistant and take some casting. You also need a strong leader, remember you are after big fish which may have to be stopped from bolting into weed. Perch are not the only small fish that the trout eat. Roach are also high on the menu and when they die, they too float to the surface. At Rutland Water during the 1980 and 1981 seasons they caused us a few problems, before we finally found a solution.

The trout had been feeding hard on roach fry throughout the whole of September and into October. Whitwell Creek was full of both fry and trout though I didn't know it at the time. Trout were rising every now and again along a very large weed bed. They were not making much of a disturbance when taking so I concluded they were on midge pupae or something similar. Pupae patterns drew a complete blank, so I went through the box but still to no avail. I decided to watch the water for clues and noticed every now and again a small roach would float to the surface and drift along on its side. I watched one slowly drift towards the weed bed until all of a sudden it disappeared in a swirl. The penny had finally dropped. At the time I had no buoyant fry patterns with me but still caught fish by using a Size 6 Baby Doll fished slowly under the surface. Returning home I tied up a few roach fry imitations using plain white ethafoam for the body similar to those used by bailiff John Clarkson. This simple lure consists of a body of white ethafoam with a thicker strip of the same material tied along the back in Baby Doll style. It worked extremely well and up until the end of the season we took some really good bags on it.

While bank fishing, my top bag included two browns of 4lb and 4lb 11 oz, a rainbow of 4lb and five other nice fish up to 3½lb and all fell to the Ethafoam Doll. We weren't the only ones to crack the fry puzzle and soon Whitwell Creek became so popular that you had to arrive very early in the morning to be sure of a spot.

Since then we have developed the original idea to make it even more life-like and now cover the white ethafoam with silver Mylar piping to give a superb scale effect. We also backed the pattern with olive green raffene to imitate the fish's darker back and have added painted eyes. This was not the only alteration. When a small fish dies it tends to float on its side rather than on an even keel. Because of this the new fry is dressed sideways on, using the bend of the hook like a keel to keep it floating flat on the surface. When allowed to drift along with the breeze it looks extremely life-like and does sort out the bigger, more cautious fish.

Fry are not the only food items to be imitated by buoyant patterns. John Goddard's Suspender Buzzer has a ball of plastic foam at the head to keep it floating on the surface. The buoyant Corixa, like the floating Baby Doll is tied with an ethafoam body. Unlike the Baby Doll, the Corixa's body is formed from a block rather than a strip of ethafoam.

If fished correctly this pattern catches well and, because it floats, it should be used on a fast sinking line and a leader no longer than two feet or so. The sinking line is allowed to settle on the bottom when the buoyant Corixa will tend to float towards the surface until it is stopped by the weight of the line. When you begin the retrieve, the Corixa will be pulled down towards the bottom and when you stop, it will float up again imitating well the action of the natural creature. The dressing is quite simple having a body of ethafoam plus a back and paddles of cock pheasant tail fibres. Tying the body is the only tricky part and this is done by cutting a small block of foam to the right size and then splitting down the middle for half its depth. It can then be glued to the hook shank and trimmed to the correct oval shape but make sure the bulk of the foam lays on the top side of the shank. If you don't your buoyant Corixa will fish upside down.

7 The Palmers

Palmered flies have become increasingly popular with the growing interest in competition boat fishing which has followed in the wake of the dramatic increase in the number of anglers taking up stillwater trout fishing. The many clubs which have sprung up hold social fishing days and the more serious eliminators for entry to the international teams. In practically all cases, these competitions are fished to international rules which restricts the size of the flies to a maximum Size 10.

The technique is to fish a team of wet flies in traditional loch style in front of a drifting boat. In a good ripple through to a strong wind a palmered top dropper is certain to be needed. As the angler retrieves his flies close to the boat, he slows up then dibbles, or merely daps the easily seen bushy fly. It often happens that trout which have followed the palmer will only take it when it is bobbed. On other occasions they will follow until it is stopped before turning to take either the centre dropper or the point fly on the way down.

All palmers are hackled from hook bend to eye with heavier turns made at the head. This bushy appearance makes the fly highly visible in the waves that all loch style fishers pray for.

Perhaps the best known of all the palmer style patterns is the Soldier Palmer and this simple fly must account for thousands of trout each summer. Very simply this pattern has a bright red wool or seal's fur body ribbed with gold oval thread and palmered with medium brown hackle feathers. I (Bob) have also had success with yellow, green and brown body versions. Certainly, these are a must for your fly box.

A few seasons back I came across an American pattern which I liked the look of, and decided to give it a try in a very important competition.

This fly was called Queen of the Water, the big event the annual event when the so-called professionals fish against the English International Fly Fishing Association. It was a hot, bright day with very little wind but spotted rippling water around the central reservoir where the aeration boils were working. Because the water temperatures were rising during this mid-June day, I decided on an orange based fly. I ended up with eleven good rainbows to win the individual spot and nearly all fell to this

orange bobfly. Since that lucky first outing, I have placed great faith in this fly and it has scored well so many times at so many different waters.

The dressing
Hook-size 14, 12, 10.
Tail bright red cock hackle fibres.
Body orange floss or a single strand of wool. Palmer body with a medium brown hackle.
Hackle medium brown.
Wing silver mallard.
Head black varnish.

London trout fisher Brian Gent not only ties a very neat fly but he is a loch style enthusiast and he and friend Micky Miller have devised a whole collection of these palmer bodied bobflies. Some were a help to Micky and I during the 1983 season when we successfully eliminated for the England team. My personal favourite is a palmered Wingless Wickham with a red tag tail. Also in their collection is a fluorescent lime green tail and bodied fly which has a ginger palmered body with similarly coloured, but heavier hackle at the head. This one works well in high temperatures and algae stained water.

One of the most famous Irish palmers which has travelled well and certainly catches its share of English trout is the Bibio. I first came across this fly when fishing on Lough Mask where it scores well with the wild browns during the early season. It is used when the small black Chironomid is on the water in April and which the Irish call Duck Flies. I must mention one other very good Irish bobfly The Gosling devised on Lough Melvin.

Down in the West Country at Chew Valley Lake their top palmer is the Grenadier. This is basically an orange bodied, ginger hackled fly and is deadly for rainbows at all the major reservoirs. Another very good mainly orange fly is Old Nick, the brainchild of Nick Nicholson which again was devised to take rainbows in hot weather. It caught limit after limit at Grafham, Pitsford and Rutland in the 1982 and 1983 seasons.

Dressing the Old Nick
Hooks 14, 12, 10.
Body silver lure palmered with a hot orange hackle.
Wing a pinch of hot orange deer hair.
Hackle three or four turns of hot orange hackle.
Head black varnish.

Now you know a little about some top bobfly patterns it helps if you can use them to the best advantage. I gave the basics of the style earlier on, but there are times when experimenting can pay off. For instance when fishing in high waves it is well worth using palmered patterns on both droppers and the point. Brian Gent took a great catch on such a day fishing three Soldier Palmers which he fished very fast through the waves. He told me of its success and I remembered this the next time I was out on a high wave.

The opposite applies of course in a two-inch ripple. Under these calmer conditions the palmer Fly should be a Size 14 with lightly dressed flies of the same size on both the point and centre dropper.

The ideal leader that I often use has two metres of 6lb nylon between the fly line and the top dropper, then a metre of the same nylon to the centre dropper, and finally a further metre to the point. Each join is made by tying a Water Knot. In clear water I go as low as 4lb nylon.

What of the future? These are the first stillwater salmon to be caught from the Ross Fishery. We feel this idea will spread.

8 Specials from America

It was some twenty-five years ago when I (Bob) first started taking the American fishing magazines. These included *Field and Stream*, which I take to this day. I learned such a lot from my reading and I became fascinated with the patterns which they called streamers. Using some of the American ideas I began to tie some patterns of my own, lures that I hoped would be more suited to our reservoirs.

First came the Church Fry, then a Badger and Black, and a bright yellow and silver design. Instead of calling them streamer flies we started calling them lures. Many fabulous patterns from America have proved deadly at catching our trout, the most famous of these being the Muddler Minnow which Tom Saville of Nottingham first introduced at Grafham in the mid-1960s.

In 1973 I was given some popping bug mounts made

with cork bodies and a concaved head. When fixed on the hook and dressed in the favoured colours they certainly looked very impressive. Poppers float of course and each time you twitch retrieve them they create a smacking sound and a stream of bubbles filters away. This crazy action causes fish to investigate, particularly super fit summer rainbows.

In the main, these bugs were used in America for their Small and Large Mouthed Bass and enjoy names such as Marm Minnow, Bullet Bug. After a decade, their use is now widespread over here especially on the large waters where it follows that black, white and orange versions work the best. The Bullet Minnow is a very clever but simple style of fly dressing and the end result looks so realistic that when fish are fry feeding the lure stands the inspection of the wariest trout. It not only looks simple to tie, it is simple. To dress one all you need is a Size 8 longshank hook and some brown and white bucktail. The bucktail is tied on so that it projects over the eye with the brown hair on top of the hook shank and the white below to imitate the pale belly of a small fish. The next step is to simply pull all the hair back along the hook shank like a normal wing making sure that the two colours of hair do not merge.

Using red floss or silk you can then bind the hair down close to the eye to form a pronounced bullet head and a flowing wing. To complete the lure you simply add a couple of coats of varnish to the head along with a pair of eyes to make it even more minnow like.

During the 1983 season we were given some superb American small fish imitations. These were miniatures of their game fish and included dressings for baby brown trout, brook trout and shad. We immediately assumed because they looked so life-like these too would work well in our waters where fry abound. At the time of writing our experiments show that our initial reactions are proving to be well founded.

Of course there is no end to the possibilities now that we have mastered the lure's basic construction. Sometimes we wonder though whether or not this is more like model making than fly tying. Surely if our trout will take the American originals, then the new imitations of our native species are certain to prove effective.

The beauty of these American fry patterns is the way the body is flattened into the exact profile of the natural fry. We decided to use acetate floss as an underbody. If nail varnish remover is painted onto the floss it melts allowing it to be moulded to a fish shape. When it has set a tail of marabou is added and the floss underbody covered with mylar piping. The whole lot is then painted to the correct colours, the eyes added and finally all is treated to a few coats of varnish.

The final new American pattern I must mention is John Witwer's Chamois Leather Lure which has a wonderful wriggly worm-like tail action. I am sure we will be hearing much more about this fly over here in the future. That it works on our trout there is no doubt. All it needs is developing and we are working on it.

The tail is the most interesting part as it gives the fly its action. It is formed by taking a rectangular piece of chamois leather and cutting it into a spiral shape similar to that made when peeling an apple. It is also tapered, the fine end being tied in at the bend. The body is quite simple and can be made of either wool or seal's fur in varying colours. Eyes in the form of metal bath chain beads can also be used and being weighted, they make the lure nose heavy. This results in a Dog Nobbler type action which as we already know is very deadly.

As you pull, the spiralled tail straightens, but when you stop it curls up again giving a superb effect. From what we can see this action is the most natural ever devised and must be a sure-fire killer.

MAJOR STILLWATERS

1 Blagdon Reservoir

It was at the turn of the century that Blagdon reservoir became the first stillwater in Britain to be stocked with rainbow trout. Little could anyone visualise then what a major part this species would play in the quite dramatic growth of stillwater fly fishing. Those American immigrants were the pioneers of all that has followed.

In those early Blagdon years the capture of great fish weighing up to 9lb and averaging around 5lb drew the attention of the serious river fly fishers. Many came to try their hand at this new type of trout fishing bringing with them large salmon flies to try and tempt these salmon-sized rainbows. They worked too, and surely these flies must be termed as the early lure patterns.

To enter Blagdon's fishing lodge is to take a step back into history as stillwater trout fishing heritage looks down from the walls sporting many fine cased specimens. Everything that has followed since stemmed from the need to master catching rainbow trout, the mainstay of today's stillwater fly fisher.

Blagdon at 440 acres may have appeared as a large lake in the early days, but now there are several giant reservoirs which could swallow it up many times over. It is a

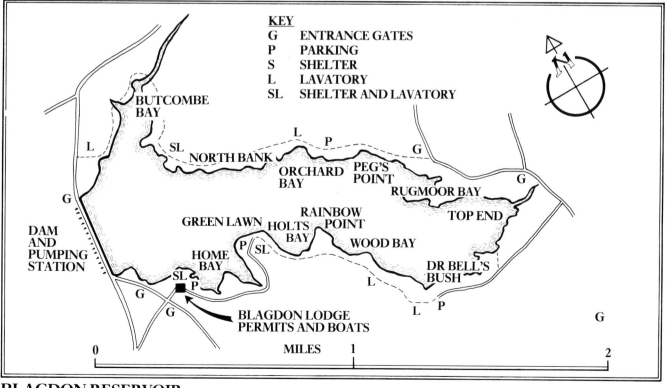

BLAGDON RESERVOIR

Playing a fish from the boat which has drifted on to the shallow at the far end of Blagdon Reservoir.

very pretty place nestling among rolling hills and is known by many as the Jewel of the Mendips. Somehow this, our oldest water, seems to have escaped the rush and bustle often seen at some of the larger, newer waters. I hardly dare tempt fate by admitting that I have never had a bad day there, but it's true.

Before talking about the fishing, I must point out that the stock fish introduced into Blagdon today are the finest I have seen. Full tailed and silver coated, fish of two pounds and above are common right from the season's off.

A previous fishery manager Mr Kennedy Brown was the man to master the secret of bringing the fish into such immaculate condition in early spring. His undeniable success and ideas have remained the fishery's general rearing policy ever since. I have often wondered why this obviously successful scheme has not been copied by other water authorities.

For any experienced and well-read fly dresser the name that instantly comes to mind when Blagdon is mentioned is the legendary Dr Bell. A quiet man, he was really responsible for nymph fishing as we know it today. Carrying on from where he left off has been a matter of simple evolution. As far as I know, he was the first man to dress chironomid pupae in what we now call buzzer style. His Amber Nymph was also a complete breakaway from the sedge imitations which had gone before. It proved a most effective pattern in those pre-war days and still is

today. Another of his many killing patterns is the aptly named Blagdon Green Midge.

Still one of the most favoured bank fishing spots at Blagdon is Dr Bell's Bush which is now more a tree than a shrub. This lies at the shallower end of the lake on the south shore. Because of the shallow, weedy nature of this area very good fly hatches occur more regularly. So it follows that patient bank fishing with a floating fly line and a team of nymphs is the best approach there throughout the season.

The point of Holts Bay is a great spot for intercepting cruising rainbow shoals as they move out of the bay feeding up wind. Of course it is the wind's direction that helps to make many a hotspot and this is as true of Blagdon as it is elsewhere.

During early season when an east wind is blowing, the vast shallows at the western end of the reservoir are nearly always the best fishing area on the water. When boat fishing, a good tactic is to put a drogue out from a central stern position allowing the boat to drift bow first down the wind. Each angler casts out from different sides of the boat using medium speed sinkers such as a Wet Cel II shooting head.

Limit bags of eight fine fish have come my way several times during that first month using this tactic coupled with a Black Chenille lure. Another drift to try is from Peg's Point to Rainbow Point, a good holding area because the depth of water averages no more than 15ft

(4.5m). When a strong north westerly blows, anchoring the boat about 80yd (73m) out from the dam and 150yd (137m) from the south shore is an excellent spot.

I can well remember one mid-summer day on Blagdon my boat partner Peter Dobbs took the first fish of the day, a handsome 3½lb rainbow. This had been taken right off the bottom so we decided to spoon the fish to see what it was feeding on. The stomach of this fish was chock-full of Damsel Fly nymphs and a change to the artificial worked the oracle.

As the weather warms from late May onwards, loch style drifting is the most enjoyable, and often the most prolific boat tactic. Two other, less obvious methods I have used during summer have been to fish a team of three Corixa imitations in the shallows and a number 14 Black and Peacock Spider from which I first trimmed away all the hackle then greased up to fish in that surface film. It pays to be observant at Blagdon so make sure you always take a sinking as well as a floating fly line with you.

My most killing patterns for Blagdon have been the Missionary, Black Buzzer, Leprechaun, Olive Quill,

A superb 4lb 2oz rainbow caught by Jim Collins on a Black Chenille Lure at Blagdon Lake.

Zulu and Muddler Minnow. It is wise to remember that the boats are oar powered only and you need to take your own drogue and anchor.

2 Rutland Water

This 3,300-acre show-piece reservoir is justifiably acclaimed to be the best fly fishing in the whole of Europe. With ten fish weighing over 10lb caught in the 1982 and 1983 seasons, do we need to say more? These fish had grown on from small stock fish which makes them an impressive prize. Fred Wagstaffe really got it right one day when his first three fish all weighed over 9lb. His eight fish limit weighed a staggering 48½lb.

Rutland consists of a main body of water with depths up to 110ft (34m), and twin arms both larger than many reservoirs. It is at the far end of each arm that vast rich shallows are found. There must be over 600 acres or so in the South Arm well below 20ft (6m) in depth and this is where trout are found to be feeding for much of the season. The same applies to the North Arm but the area is not quite as large.

There is always the nagging question when visiting an unfamiliar water of whether to plump for the bank or boat. Here we must stress that a boat does give you a very great advantage. It is only from the end of September onwards that the bank can outfish the boats. A point worth making is that it is advisable to book your boat well in advance of your fishing day because Rutland is very popular. But where to go once you leave the boat jetty is the thing that baffles most fishermen on this inland sea.

Actually it is not as difficult as you may think because trout at Rutland certainly favour different areas under different conditions. The far ends of each shallow arm have been mentioned already and these two zones are great favourites with the regulars.

Let's look at the South Arm first in more detail. As you motor down into it there is a little bay on the far side of the

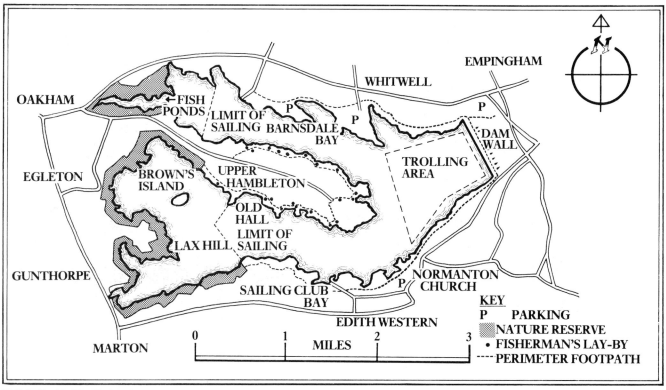

RUTLAND WATER

Yacht Club which is always worth a few drifts to see if anything is doing.

If that spot fails, continuing down the arm you will notice two small spinneys on the left-hand bank known as Berrybuts. The whole area from about 150yd (137m) out from the bank and into it is a good holding spot for both rainbows and browns.

Moving down the arm further, to your right you will see a fine old stone house close to the water's edge. This is known as the Old Hall. There is a bay either side of it and both are good catching areas. One of the most favoured spots of them all is the area known as Brown's Island. This lies approximately halfway across the arm in a line from the Old Hall to a bird hide on the far south bank.

For most of the time at normal level the island is submerged out of sight but even then it is only about seven feet down. The drop-offs around the island encourage trout to stay in its sanctuary where they live and feed for much of the time. This is a very good fishing area for taking fish off the top or deep. The South Arm eventually splits into two other arms from the shallow point known as Lax Hill and for the whole of the summer period, this whole area is alive with trout.

The North Arm has its characteristics too with the whole of the left-hand side being good for brown trout. Then on the right is Barnsdale Bay, which is again very

good for browns. As you continue to motor down the Arm you will see a tower out in the centre. This is a good landmark to try some deep fishing. Take a bearing to drift in a straight line in the direction of the other tower which is in the main body of the reservoir. Down on the bottom there is a pipeline built up on pillars from the lake bed and many big fish gather along it. Naturally this is an area to try the deep specialised techniques with lead core lines and large tandem lures and you can expect to catch trout of 3lb and upwards.

As you continue down the Arm it gets shallower all the time. Right towards the end there is an area known as the Burleigh Fish Ponds. These are submerged ponds of considerable size which were there prior to the flooding of the reservoir.

This is perhaps the best known holding spot in the North Arm as fish move in and out of these deeper holes to rest or feed. It is best fished at anchor. The main body of the reservoir fishes well once the westerly winds of summer blow towards the dam wall. Unlike other reservoirs, the water close to the dam is quite shallow and the bottom shelves only very gradually. This of course gives the dam great strength needed to hold back so much water. The westerly wind pushes great blooms of daphnia towards the direction of the dam and the rainbows follow it like grazing sheep. A great drift is from the Normanton

Rutland's brown trout are big and wild. This 4½lb fish was caught by Rick Nunn and was taken on lead core line and lure while fishing at the bottom of the South Arm.

Peter Gathercole displays his heaviest brown trout of 8lb 15oz, it came from Rutland Water.

Sometimes the big Rutland browns leave the bottom and take a small fly off the top. This 4½lb fish did just that, it fell to the rod of Dave Allen.

Church at about 150yd (137m) out continuing down to the valve tower.

When the summer begins to warm up, a series of aerators are switched on. These are worked from the lake bed and shoot up great whirlpools of oxygenated bubbles from depths of up to 80ft (24m). Naturally trout collect here and mostly they stay very high in the water. It is a good idea to drift the boat into the visible froth and scum lanes that surround these boils. Drift in the down wind tail as the scum lanes join as rainbows just love to nose their way up these slicks. Here a floating line and three traditional wet flies is the best method.

Perhaps the great attraction of Rutland is the great scope for the many styles and methods. The boats have inboard engines and possess built-in rudders which allows for a bow first drift. When sinking lines and lures are used it is possible to hug the bottom by drifting along with the wind at around 100–150yd (91–137m) from the shore. When the westerly wind prevails, you can complete drifts of over 5 miles (8km). As you can imagine a lot of trout are covered at such favourable times.

Big browns or rainbows, Rutland holds them both in plenty. Bob Church displays a fine brace which any visiting angler may catch when spending a day there.

With the growth in popularity of competitive fly fishing Rutland has been used for all the major events. It does of course lend itself beautifully to traditional wet fly fishing. This short line, team of three wet flies method can be quite deadly whether you are in a competition or not. We would highly recommend it on any cloudy or dull day when a strong breeze is blowing.

Some of our favourite wet flies for Rutland include the Invicta, Soldier Palmer, Queen of the Water, Dunkeld, Fiery Brown, Claret and Mallard, Murroughs, the Greenwell's Glory which works well in a buzzer rise, the Silver Invicta, Wickham's Fancy and Old Nick.

For the lures we suggest the Goldie, Christmas Tree, Black Chenille, Concorde, Jack Frost, Badger Matuka, Squirrel and Silver, Appetizer, Muddler Minnow, Orange and White Muddlers, and the controversial Dog and Frog Nobblers and the Waggy Lures.

For nymphs include the Spring Favourite, the various buzzer pupae colours, Pheasant Tails, Damsel Fly Nymph, Black Leech, Shrimp, Corixa and Hatching Sedge.

Dry flies can be useful and the Daddy Longlegs, G & H Sedge and floating snail, floating Suspender Buzzer and floating fry are a must. The range of Unsinkable Rats Tails dry flies work very well here.

3 Grafham Water

On 1 June 1966 a mere forty fly fishers waited at the Grafham lodge to buy a ticket to try out the new water's trout fishing. As they casually chatted away, little did they realise what was in store.

Nobody seemed in much of a hurry to start but one angler ventured down to the water and with his first cast hooked a fish which he eventually landed. It was an immaculate rainbow of nearly 5lb.

It aroused the rest and soon all were fishing. Much to everyone's surprise that was not just an odd big fish, but only a little above the average for all the trout in the new fishery.

The news spread fast with rave reports in the press and just as Blagdon started it all, Grafham must go down in the history books as the water that sparked off the trouting boom for the masses.

The results captured the imagination not only of every trout fly fisher, and there were far fewer of us then, but also of the coarse fisherman who bought fly fishing gear and came to try their luck. Most did well and a new generation of fly fishers was born which has continued to multiply.

The quality and fast growth of Grafham trout has continued over the years and although I (Bob) have caught many rainbows and browns of specimen size none has quite reached 6lb. That said from 1980 onwards the growth rate of the rainbows has been poor when comparing it with all of the 1970s.

This situation has given rise to many theories by the regulars who fish there. First we all knew that it was the prolific daphnia blooms which provided rainbows with the high protein diet responsible for the fast growth rate. For example, a one-pound stock fish in April reached 3lb by mid-August. That is some growth rate for wild fish.

Since 1980 there appears to be less Daphnia and it was rumoured that the Authority needed to treat the water to kill of the algae as it was becoming excessive and was blocking the water draw-off filters. Remember that it is the algae that Daphnia feeds on and so the food chain was broken. However, the Authority denied any such treatment.

In the mid-1970s Grafham began to receive more attention from boat fishers who virtually always fished on the top and the fishery became the most used venue for club competitions and the eliminators for the English National which is another reason why the fish size dropped. A survey proved that fish taken by surface fishing tactics averaged less than half the size of those

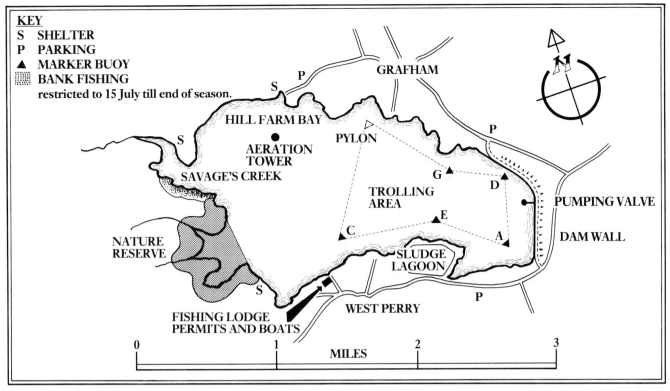

KEY
S SHELTER
P PARKING
▲ MARKER BUOY
▦ BANK FISHING
restricted to 15 July till end of season.

GRAFHAM

HILL FARM BAY

PYLON

AERATION
TOWER

SAVAGE'S CREEK

TROLLING
AREA

G

D

E

C

A

PUMPING VALVE

DAM WALL

NATURE
RESERVE

SLUDGE
LAGOON

WEST PERRY

FISHING LODGE
PERMITS AND BOATS

0   1   2   3
MILES

GRAFHAM WATER

Grafham bailiff Terry Kaye fires the gun which starts an important
competition. In this case, the final Midland Eliminator for the English
National.

caught deep on sinking fly lines.

A method which accounted for many very big fish at Grafham was to drift point first down-wind with the aid of a portable rudder. This Dick Shrive innovation proved popular until it was banned in the mid-1970s. It allowed for a searching technique with fast sinking lines and lures which was the downfall of many large specimen brown trout and the larger rainbows which also tend to live and feed close to the bottom in deep water.

Grafham has produced three double figure browns with the heaviest coming from the bank, or should I say dam wall. It fell to early morning angler Brian Capener who caught a 12lb 6oz fish on a Black Buzzer nymph. The best rainbow ever caught is one of 9lb 2oz.

The thing that we both like about Grafham is that it has a list of predictable hotspots which all fish well at different times of the year. For general loch style drift fishing there are always plenty of fish to catch up to around 2lb which rise throughout the main summer months. This style of fishing is so enjoyable that the quarry do not need to be monsters.

Let's now take you fishing to some of our favourite

A 3lb Grafham rainbow for Arthur Cove, taken close to the valve tower at the dam.

Many boats head straight for the Dam while fishing at Grafham.

Grafham hotspots and go through the best ways of exploiting them. First and perhaps best known is the Aeration Tower in Hill Farm Bay on the north shore. This tower stands in 30ft (9m) of water when the reservoir is at top level. It is the ideal anchoring spot for deep fishing with lures and sinking shooting head lines. The area around the tower harbours all sorts of coarse fish fry in their millions and so provides a natural larder for trout especially the larger specimens. It is the bigger fish that tend to feed most on fry for much of the season.

Anchor by the bows some 35–40yd (32–37m) upwind of the tower and then cast your lure towards it. If you can hit the stonework and then allow it to sink into the depths right up against the tower you are in with a good chance of attracting one of the big fry chasers.

On a west wind there is an excellent drift from the corner of the Sludge Lagoon and down towards the right-hand corner of the dam by marker buoy A. There are always plenty of surface feeding fish here and the same applies opposite on the north bank by marker buoy G.

Exactly halfway across the reservoir between these points is the pumping in valve. It is here that water enters the reservoir from the Great Ouse. At this point the water is 50ft (15m) deep. When the pumps are on, a great boil of water mushrooms on the surface and many trout are attracted to it. Drifting down beyond the boil in the wake of its twin tail the scum lanes produce very good sport to

A 5lb brown trout caught by Bob Church from Grafham at the end of the season was showing a dark colour as it neared spawning time. Bob quickly returned the fish alive.

floating and slow sink line tactics.

Towards the back end of the season the shallow weedy areas around Savages Creek begin to fish really well for big browns and rainbows. This is the spot where fish seem to gather in a sort of shoaling courtship prior to going through the motions of spawning. At this time they fry-feed and take a fish imitating lure very well. Again fishing at anchor or from the bank gives the best results.

4 Lough Mask and Lough Carra

The wildest, most exciting and even dangerous trout water we have ever fished just has to be the 22,000-acre Lough Mask in Co. Mayo in the west of Ireland. Mask is a nightmare jumble of giant limestone boulders with jagged edges as sharp as razors. These are easily seen and avoided by the fishing boats when the lough is in one of its calmer moods. Even on a gentle swell you can see the occasional rock resembling something like a church steeple just inches from the surface as the waves swell and

subside.

Mask can change from a placid inland sea into something rivalling the North Atlantic in a very short space of time. Storms creep in on a westerly wind and sweep down over the rugged Connemara mountains. So the first thing to advise for your holiday visit is to fish with one of the many professional ghillies that make their living as boatmen on the lough. Only after several trips out with a ghillie is it safe to go out alone, and even then great care

101

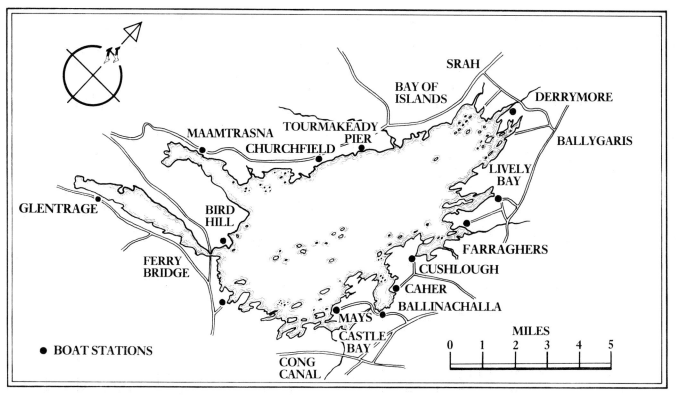

LOUGH MASK FISHERY

must always be taken.

You would never believe how much fly fishing enjoyment you are missing until you have spent the day afloat with an Irish ghillie. The first lesson most people learn, as we did, is that life can be enjoyed much more if the pace of things is slowed down. The catching of wild brown trout in a lough over seven times as large as Rutland is naturally very pleasant, but equally enjoyable is the company.

When your sides are not aching with laughter at your ghillie's never ending tales he will be singing you some pleasant Irish folk song. He will make you stop fishing at lunch-time no matter if sport has just improved. You then motor to the nearest island, where he produces an old black kettle for a proper brew-up on a driftwood fire. When early evening comes and everything looks perfect for the rise to begin, he will say, 'Righto lads, let's be going in now for dinner and a few jars'. Yes, there's more to trout fishing than catching fish in Ireland.

On each of our visits we have based ourselves at the little town of Ballinrobe close to Cushlough Bay, where many of the boats are moored. We usually stay at the guest house of Nan and Robbie O'Grady. The food is excellent and Robbie, an ex-Irish international, has four boats on Mask and one on Carra, which is a few miles away.

This magnificent huge 17¾lb brown trout was caught by Des Elliott from Dublin on Ireland's impressive Lough Mask. It fell to a 2½in trolled spoon.

102

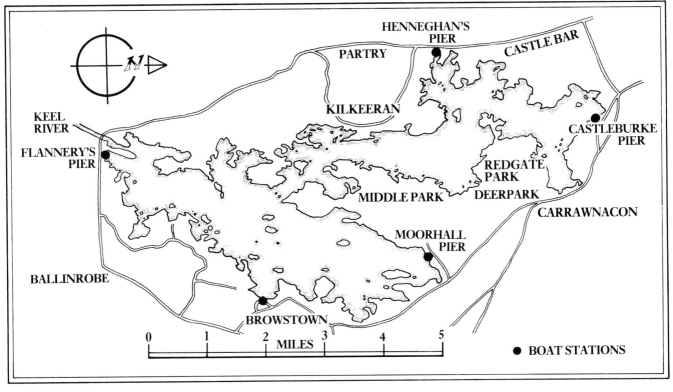

LOUGH CARRA FISHERY

My first ever trip was in early May and I (Bob) partnered up with experienced wet fly fisherman Frank Cutler, with Robbie as our ghillie. The weather was very unkind as we suffered very strong squally cold winds all week which set some really big, frightening waves roaring down the lough. With the safety angle of prime importance we needed to fish in the sheltered waters around the rocky islands and bays. Nevertheless, these shallower areas are good fish holding spots and we were soon rising and catching a few nice brownies.

One of the largest of these islands is called Devenish which boasts a herd of wild goats on it. Frank and I fished traditional wet fly tactics with long rods of 11ft (3.35m), floating lines and three fly casts. Even in such a blow there were a few olives hatching and the early small black chironomid which the Irish call the Duck Fly. Our very first drift produced three trout, I had one of around 2½lb; which Robbie called a Gillaroo. He pointed out the double bulge in its stomach; apparently they have developed two stomachs over thousands of years of evolution. It looked like a fatter, more spotted brown trout to me.

Although we were too early for the Mayfly hatch, there were quite a lot of small dark sedges flying with the Olives and chironomids. These we imitated with a favourite Irish tying called the Sooty Olive.

Teal and Black, Claret and Mallard, Golden Olive and Invicta were all very good. But as Frank discovered, in the largest waves it was a Soldier Palmer on the top dropper which made the fish rise up from nowhere – even if they often took one of the other flies. Even in these poor conditions we found Mask trout to be free risers but we were only hooking about one-third of the fish that came to the fly. When hooked they fought and jumped more times than a Grafham rainbow. Their average size is about 1½lb but the fly takes them to 6lb. Deep trolling with spoons has taken them to 20lb and the mind boggles at such fish.

We caught plenty of fish during the week, mostly on traditional wet fly. However, I did experiment with the nymph and caught several fish on a Black Buzzer pupae. Alan Pearson, who was also in the party, fished from the bank of one of the islands one day and he caught on a leaded Dick Walker Mayfly Nymph. So there is scope for experiment amongst the tradition. On a couple of later trips Peter came along, one in mid-June when the Mayfly was just past its peak but was still quite good. Then we caught nearly all our fish on yellow Mayflies.

Two more trips in August saw yet another change and this time the great red sedge was the dominant fly. These are called Murroughs by the Irish and we favoured body colours of claret, brown and grey, with the wing tied

Peter Gathercole and Steven Church fish loch style in perfect conditions for Lough Mask.

rolled. Other flies that worked quite well were Connemara Black, Bibio, Green Peter, Green Mayfly, all of them traditional Irish Flies. Our English Zulu and Black Pennell and even a small Muddler Minnow all caught fish well.

Lough Carra is joined to Mask by a river which runs out of the lough. My first impression of this eight-mile long lough was that it was more like looking at a coral reef. All of the shore lines were packed with white snail shells and the water is crystal clear.

It is a very shallow lough never going much over 15ft (4.5m) deep. The pure white bottom can be seen at all times even when drifting far out in the boat. Naturally the very alkalinity grows some very good brown trout as we found out.

With no rocks or boulders to worry about we fished short line drift tactics until 1.30 a.m. for one evening rise simply because that's when it ended! This activity was to small sedges and very interesting it all was as we normally stop fishing several hours earlier in England even in high summer.

Because of the unique white calcified bottom and a near full moon we could see quite well and it proved a point that trout feed well at night and on the surface. The best flies for Carra were Golden Olive, Olive Quill, Small Brown Sedge and Black Pennell.

One big lesson I did learn from the ghillies was how

Ace ghillie Robbie O'Grady displays a 'Gillaroo' brown trout caught by Bob Church on an Invicta.

incredibly effective dapping was at catching these cautious brown trout. The tackle is simple. Although you can manage with a trout rod of 11ft (3.35m) or more, better still is a 13ft (4m) coarse rod. The line is very inexpensive at about £2 a spool. It is called either blow line or dapping floss and is a special synthetic fibre and is very light. To the end of the floss you tie a short nylon leader and fine wire hook which is usually a Size 10 or 12.

Hold the rod nearly vertical and then feed out line with the wind. While the rod is held high the natural or artificial fly if there is sufficient wind, will blow out over the surface. Now lower the rod point and the fly will drop naturally onto the water. Leave it there for a second or two then lift and repeat. Make sure that your line does not touch the water or it will become saturated and too heavy to be lifted by the wind. As the boat drifts down-wind, new water is covered all the time. Jigging the rod top can help, for this makes the fly skitter across the surface in a series of little skips and jumps, an action you cannot achieve with a normal fly line.

On Mask and Carra the favourite naturals to dap with are Mayflies, large Sedges, Daddy Longlegs and the best of them all, grasshoppers which are best kept in narrow-necked plastic bottles. This makes it easy to select one or two baits at a time without them all flying or jumping away.

The fishing on both loughs is free, all you need to do is book your boats and ghillies, the prices of which will vary.

5 Chew Valley Lake

Prior to Grafham's opening, the 1,200-acre Chew Valley Lake was always considered the Mecca for any keen trout man. It opened in 1956 and although there were always plenty of big trout to be caught there were not the number of fly fishers about then and the national angling press did not cover the sport as well as it does today.

Like Blagdon, Chew has the best possible stock fish. You will not see better at any of the big reservoir fisheries. Both bank and boat fishing is good and the moorings at Woodford fishing lodge hold approximately 30 boats all with Seagull engines.

I (Bob) always found it best to fish from the bank with a lure in the early morning and then to switch to nymph tactics around mid-morning. Two well known spots for bigger than average trout are the deep water marks on the Woodford and Wally banks.

It is quite possible to cast from the bank into over 25ft (8m) of water which is something you cannot do very often on any stillwater fishery. By mid-summer huge shoals of roach and perch fry gather here.

A dawn start using fry imitations like the Appetizer, Missionary or White Muddler pay off, particularly when coupled with a slow-sinking shooting head line. Another favourite bank spot is Nunnery Point and down into Herons Green Bay. This area is noted for its tremendous buzzer hatches. I would consider this one of the best spots for evening fishing with a floating line and a team of nymphs. Over the 10 miles (16km) of bank space, access is no problem as many little roads lead to suitable car parking and toilet facilities.

These days when I travel down to Chew I always make it a day or two's boat fishing with a good companion. A boat has so much to offer as for much of the season trout are quite free rising.

. One of my favourite drifts is the same as many of Chew's regulars, being right across the Roman Shallows. This area fishes best on a dull day with grey rolling clouds and a moderate westerly wind.

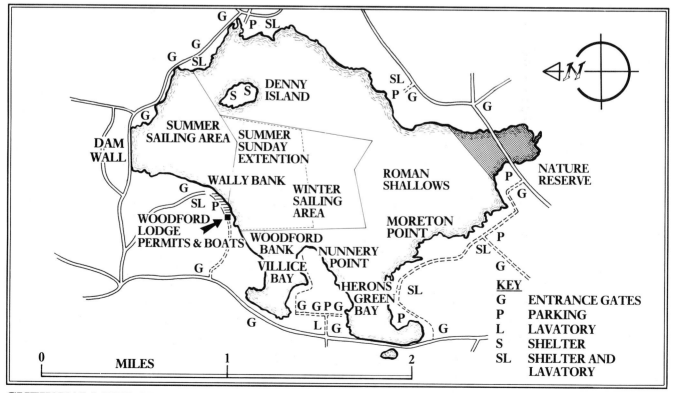

CHEW VALLEY LAKE

Peter Dobbs brings a fine quality rainbow trout to net at Chew Valley Lake.

My favourite wet fly pattern for Chew is the Olive Quill and I have caught well with this when buzzer are about. A Ginger Quill is also worth having on the cast and these two imitative patterns work well on Size 12 hooks without any need for the normal bob fly top dropper of the bushy type. Just fish them slowly back with figure of eight retrieve using a drogue from the broadside position to keep a steady speed of drift.

During mid-summer with the sedges about, drifting remains a winning method and the flies to use now are Invicta, Wickham's Fancy, Grenadier and Soldier Palmer. However, my most killing method at this time has been fishing a standard Muddler Minnow on a floating line. Casting as far as possible downwind then stripping the flies back with long fast pulls against the waves has an irresistible effect on the super fit rainbows, some of which will be over 3lb.

On the poorer days when you are cursed with a bright sun, or barely a breeze, anchoring up and nymph fishing will produce the best results. The shallower spots such as Villice Bay, Moretons Bank off Denny Island are ideal places for this technique. Here my good friend Frank Cutler caught an 8lb brown trout a few years ago. Herons Green Bay and the road end of the nature reserve are other worthwhile places.

Two natural insects prolific on Chew are the Damsel Fly and the Corixa, so it is a good idea to imitate these when fishing at anchor. That said a Black Chenille lure and the Stick Fly both have impressive records when fished slow and deep at Chew, so these must be given a try if nothing reacts to the small fly approach.

Sometimes Chew can be spoiled by a thick green algae in late August and this can stifle sport. It is a proven fact that trout go off their feed when the bloom is at its worst, but even if they are feeding, the chances of them seeing our flies in this pea soup are slight. I have found sinking lines and lures to be a complete waste of time in these conditions. Better to wait until evening when if you drop your fly near the odd rise you may induce a take. If the algae bloom looks like reducing the oxygen level too much the aeration pumps are switched on. These are situated close to the main dam in the deep water. You can

Frank Cutler shows the size of rainbow trout that he and Bob Church caught at Chew Valley Lake when they were feeding on fry.

only get close to the area from a boat but it's well worth fishing under these adverse conditions.

Frank Cutler and I arrived at Chew to fish for a couple of days late in August. Another visiting angler advised us to fish by the dam where three pumps were aerating the water. But he warned us that it was like a cod war out there with boats forever jockeying for a favourable position.

Four other boats were in the fishing area when we motored as close as we dare to the erupting water. The oxygen being pumped in to combat the algae bloom had attracted huge shoals of small roach, which were at their thickest in the whirlpools. The reservoir was virtually flat calm except for the splashes of good-sized rainbow trout as they viciously attacked the fry. When trout are in this mood they can often become just as preoccupied as they can when feeding on the tiniest of flies. It is important to find the right pattern of lure, which on this day proved to be a pure White Muddler with silver body and the old favourite Baby Doll.

Covering an explosive rise was not difficult. There were enough to have caught 100 fish but of course it was not as easy as that. Frank and I caught a couple of trout on a white Baby Doll fished on a floating shooting head. Then I tried a Size 6 White Muddler on a very slow-sink shooting head. This brought me three good fish in three casts including one at 4lb. I thought I had found the answer but as so often happens sport went quiet soon afterwards.

Fishing nearby were two friends from Staffordshire, Tony Ward and Bill Birnie. As we drifted closer, I noticed they were catching fish fairly consistently by using three white lures on a floating line. Normally I would always use a single lure, but this time the three lure method was working well. Presumably the rainbows mistook the lures for part of a fleeing shoal of fry.

While casting out, I watched the trout herding the fry together before bulldozing into the attack. As we know, trout do this to stun the fry before moving in to mop up the injured fish. At one stage after quickly changing up to the three lure tactic, I hooked a 2lb plus rainbow and a 2lb brown on the same cast – an exciting moment indeed. Bill Birnie went one better when he hooked a 2½lb brown and two 2½lb perch all at the same time. Certainly it had become an all action day when all predatory species were gorging the fry. Both our boats finished with double limits.

The second day started in similar fashion until a fleet of yachts broke up the feeding fish. When the fry re-formed the trout proved far more difficult to tempt until Frank eventually changed to a team of three, Size 10 Dunkelds complete with flashing jungle cock eyes.

Again we finished with double limits for both boats using traditional drifting tactics, casting down the wind to the fish. I have recalled these very productive two days so you will remember what to do if ever you see aerators working at any of the big reservoirs in high summer. Fish close to them for there are bound to be some feeding trout close by.

Chew Valley Lake is located south of Bristol in the Mendip Hills. The fishery has produced rainbows and browns of 10lb 14oz and 10lb 12oz respectively.

6 Loch Watten and the Hill Lochs

Do you fancy a trip to the most northerly part of Scotland where fly fishing for wild brown trout can be found in no less than 110 lochs? Then make for Caithness. When it comes to catching completely wild fish from scenic places it doesn't matter if the trout are not as large as those from the lowland England reservoirs.

At around 1,000 acres, Loch Watten is by far the largest water in Caithness and at first glance I knew it was my kind of water. It has an average depth of about 12ft (3.65m) and the water is spring fed and crystal clear, rather than being peat stained as many lochs can be.

My first trip to Watten, where fishing is free save the hiring of a boat, was blessed with a perfect wave and rolling grey clouds, no better conditions could be asked for.

Thurso tackle dealer Sandy Harper had arranged the boat and was to partner me for the day. As we began our first drift, it was noticeable that our tackle varied considerably. Sandy had set up the traditional Scottish outfit of a 9½ft (2.9m) Sharpes Scottie split cane rod and a

number 6 double taper sinking fly line. He had a team of three flies, all variations of the famous Orkney pattern called the Ke-He. In contrast I fished with my 11ft (3.35m) carbon loch style rod, a number 7 weight forward matt finish floating line and some tried and trusted English reservoir patterns, an Olive Quill on the point, a Zulu in the centre and a Soldier Palmer on the top dropper.

Fortunately I had taken my drogue along for it was needed straight away to slow the boat down. My optimism was quickly fulfilled I quickly took four immaculate browns that looked for all the world like sea trout. Every positive take came to the Soldier Palmer with its tiny fluorescent red tail and couldn't be missed. I was casting about 18yd (16m), certainly no more, then retrieving a few pulls before lifting the long rod to bob my top dropper. Most of the fish took on the actual retrieve rather like reservoir rainbows would.

Meanwhile Sandy fished a very short line and although he was using a sinking line at such short range he used it

Storm clouds gather and come in low on a typical Scottish loch.

Thurso tackle dealer Sandy Harper nets a Loch Watten wild brown trout.

mainly to stop the wind blowing the bob fly about giving him perfect control. It wasn't until we drifted onto a shallow weedy area that he took his first fish, but at 1½lb it was the heaviest so far.

Fish started to come regularly now and I had two more, this time to the Zulu. I chopped and changed my point fly several times to no avail. I was impressed by the size of these brownies which were around the pound mark. On most other Scottish lochs when such numbers of trout were being caught they were always smaller. I spooned some to find mostly black shrimps but Sandy's bigger fish from the weedy area was full of sticklebacks which was something I didn't expect to find so far north.

Sandy started to rise a lot of fish which boiled at the fly without taking, but by mid-afternoon he had taken three more fish. The wind had increased, to around Force 4 and the odd wave broke over the gunwale.

Takes slowed down so I delved into my fly box with the idea of offering a fly they couldn't miss seeing and out went a Size 8 Wickham's Fancy which was deliberately overdressed. It worked like a dream and soon four more browns fell to this fly, and again all came to the retrieve through the now big wave.

A few more fish were caught but gradually they went off as tea-time approached and we called it a day. Sandy told me how impressed he was with the performance of my weight forward fly line and admitted that he didn't

know of anyone in the locality who used one. That trip to Loch Watten proved that there is a great advantage in using the new approach to loch style drifting and casting a much longer line. This gives you the chance of attracting extra takes on the retrieve as well as the bob or dibble of the top dropper. Certainly England's most famous competitive boat fisher Bob Draper uses the long casting technique regularly, and I recommend you do too.

There are many lochs to choose from if you visit this beautiful part of Scotland. Loch St John's is known for its large fish and is more for the experienced fly fisher who loves a challenge to catch bigger than average trout. Browns to 4lb and more are certainly a possibility. Permits to fish come from the Northern Sands Hotel.

It would be to miss a golden opportunity to forgo spending a day or two on one or more of the remote Caithness hill lochs. These are places of complete solitude and where the silence is so intense it's deafening.

Sandy and I had a few drinks one evening and I quizzed him about these lochs. He agreed to take me to his favourite. The drive through the remote tracks of Lord Thurso's estate to Loch Caol was quite stunning. The heather was alive with grouse and rabbits, some pure black. I saw a peregrine diving on a six-strong flock of geese. A moment to remember indeed.

We passed a number of small lochs until we came to the end of the narrow track. It was time to start walking.

Bob Church tackles up on Loch Caol, the little hill loch way out on Lord Thurso's estate.

And what a perfect little loch it was, spring fed clear water with a hard stone bottom and at a guess about fifty acres or so.

Sandy looked out on the water nostalgically and I had to admit I had never fished anywhere like this. The first sound to be heard was a splashy rise from a trout as it took a Heather Fly off the top. This sound broke my hypnotic stare across the pollution-free paradise where there was not another person for miles and miles.

Lord Thurso has provided a modern fibre glass boat on all of his better trout lochs. He is also a very keen conservationist and all his waters are fly only fisheries. No re-stocking with imported hatchery fish has ever taken place and never will. But occasionally Lord Thurso has arranged to give nature a helping hand by transferring browns to the loch from the river and small burns. He puts them into larger sporting lochs where the otherwise stunted fish treble their size.

Our fishing turned out to be difficult as the sun shone and only a light ripple broke the surface. Most of the trout caught were much smaller than Watten's and were released. My best fish was 13½in (34cm) long and just broke the pound. The main food for the trout was masses of pink daphnia, sedges and Heather flies. As we sat in the fishing hut towards tea-time Sandy warned that without a breeze the midges would eat us alive. The walls were pitted with names carved by some of the visitors to

A fine Loch Caol wild brown trout.

this beautiful place. I just had to add mine before I left, so if you ever get to Caol, look my name up carved into the wood.

7 Pitsford Water

This is one reservoir that has improved with time since it first opened in 1963. At 800 acres it is quite sizeable and provides the visiting fisherman with plenty of choice as to what tactics to employ.

Pitsford has the reputation of enjoying the most prolific fly hatches of any reservoir, making it a must if you enjoy imitative fishing where matching the hatch is so important. I (Bob) usually concentrate on Pitsford from late May onwards as then the fly life is building up to a peak in July.

Most certainly no other water offers such fine hatches of Olives which can be seen daily from late May. Chironomids and sedges are plentiful, so too is the Caenis, Phantom Midge, Damsel Fly and a great variety of bugs, crustaceans and fry. From all this you can see if you don't like lure fishing Pitsford is the place to go.

The reservoir has its fishing lodge adjacent to the Holcot Arm where the boats are moored. Close to this point the road which joins the Kettering Road to the

Market Harborough Road at Brixworth crosses the reservoir over a long causeway. The fishing lodge side of the causeway is the shallowest and has three little feeder streams entering at the top of the Holcot, Walgrave and Scaldwell Arms. A number of brown trout spawn successfully in these streams as the bailiffs have laid extra gravel where the flow is greatest. This experiment has helped Nature a little and we often encounter immaculate four-inch browns with beautiful red spots in the reservoir.

Pitsford must be classed as a late developer, for in its early days it was absolutely plagued with perch which ate much the same diet as the trout and so kept the growth rate down. Perch were also a menace because they took the flies, nymphs or lures far more readily than the trout three at a time.

Fortunately in 1969 along came a perch disease which swept the country and this killed the lot. Millions of them

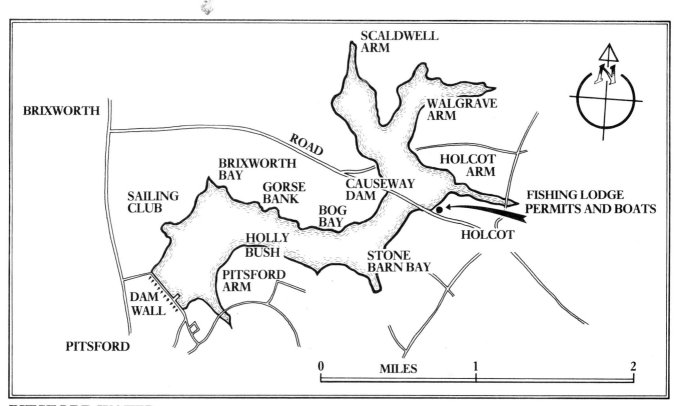

PITSFORD WATER

Launching a boat from Pitsford's Boat jetty.

Nymph fishing in a quiet sheltered corner at Pitsford.

littered the banks. Without the competition of perch Pitsford's trout have been growing at a much faster rate making it comparable with the best reservoirs.

What I enjoy most about Pitsford is that it allows me to experiment more with my own imitative patterns. Because of its prolific hatches of fly I have also been able to develop certain techniques which have stood me in good stead on other fisheries. I well remember one particular rise to buzzer in the early 1970s when fish were moving well taking the pupae about six inches (15cm) down. A normal team of three Size 12 buzzers was providing little response. The nymphs were retrieved at varying depths, I greased up and fished virtually on the top and still no response. Other anglers close by were suffering too and I decided it must be our presentation that was wrong. How could I get my nymphs to stay at six inches below the surface? I then hit on the idea of putting a buoyant Size 10 Black Muddler on the point and tied on two six-inch droppers further up the leader. I sprayed the Muddler to ensure it would stay floating, as a controller for the two brown buzzer pupae and rubbed the whole of my leader down with mud. This rig ensured that I could present the nymphs just six inches down and that they would stay at that depth no matter if I was retrieving or merely drifting round with the wave action of the wind.

I settled for the drifting technique and as my nymphs passed close to a rise takes became regular and I soon had my limit of eight fine fish. My fishing companion that day was Nick Nicholson and when he changed to the same tactics he too caught his limit transforming his cursing and moaning to a satisfied grin. The double limit consisted of a three to one in favour of browns and three were over 3lb and I lost one at the net of 5lb plus.

Log this interesting method and use it at the appropriate time when the trout want the nymph just sub-surface. I am sure you will be pleasantly surprised. It works at sedge time just as well.

Pitsford seems to have more than its fair share of olive or green hatching flies. As well as the Pond Olive, the chironomids too are often light olive. The normal standard patterns do catch fish but after much experiment I devised a pattern which consistently outfished all of them.

From my observations, when fish were rising in a light breeze during a June evening and when the olive buzzer was hatching, many trout were taking the adult fly as it sat momentarily on the surface. The Greenwell's Glory or Olive Quill dressed on a Size 14 or 12 were my usual choice and they caught a few fish. I worked on a new pattern using a similar base and profile of these two flies but enhanced the new dressing by taking a gold lurex tag right round the bend of the hook. Aptly I christened the new pattern June Fly and it has worked very effectively since its first outing. Now I wouldn't fish at Pitsford without it. The dressing is described in the chapter on Olives.

At present the Anglian Water is working on providing better access and more car parks for anglers at Pitsford. In the past, long walks have always been needed. The fishing at the deeper end of the reservoir by the main dam is good from bank or boat for most of the season. The water at this point is shared by a yacht club but the two sports seem to work together without any serious disagreements.

The car park at Pitsford village allows fishing close to the dam and also along the favoured stretches known as the Pines and the Hollybush. In the past it has entailed a long walk from the causeway to get to Brixworth Bay on the far side of the reservoir and I assume this will be one of the new access points.

My favourite bank spot is on the area known as Gorse Bank where the shallows drop away quickly into the deep water. Two other spots that often fish well for the bank man are Bog Bay and Stone Barn Bay.

Boat fishing at Pitsford is of course a joy and I know a number of very good fly fishers who refuse to go any-where else whether they prefer drifting traditionally with three wet flies, anchoring up in a quiet shallow bay to nymph fish or drifting on the rudder down the centre of the lake with a sunken lure. Pitsford responds to all

tactics. I might add a single dry fly is sometimes the deadliest method of the lot.

Flies that work well at Pitsford are the various buzzer pupae, the Pheasant Tail, Tiger Nymph, Phantom Midge, Sedge Pupae (green and amber) and Damsel Fly. Good wet flies are the June Fly, Olive Quill, Greenwell's Glory, Claret and Mallard, Queen of the Water, Red Spider, Teal and Orange, Invicta, Soldier Palmer, Grenadier and Brown Sedge. Worthwhile lures include the Baby Doll, Jersey Herd, Black Chenille, Muddler Minnow, Poly Butcher, Sweeney Todd and Appetizer. Good dry Flies include Rats Tails, Bi-Visible Sedge, Daddy Longlegs and Pond Olive.

Loch style fishing when the olives are up gives this kind of sport at Pitsford.

A nice brownie in the net which took a June Fly during an olive rise at Pitsford.

8 Queen Mother Reservoir

Fishing a concrete saucer-shaped reservoir may not be everyone's idea of a day's sport, but for those who become depressed with this thought, I suggest you think again.

I have fished a number of these concrete bowl reser-voirs including Toft Newton in Lincolnshire, Farmoor I

and II near Oxford, Barn Elms and Walthamstow in London, but by far the most appealing is the 600-acre Queen Mother Reservoir at Datchet.

Fishing this large expanse of water can be a noisy business with jets either taking off or landing at the

Anglers are seen here fishing off the specially built casting platform at
Queen Mother Reservoir. They are casting into very deep water.

nearby Heathrow Airport. However, the quality and size of the trout in the reservoir keeps your interest on the excellent fishing as opposed to plane spotting.

Because of the steeply shelving dam walls, the fishing was always boat only when run by the Thames Water Authority. This always proved very good but it limited the numbers of fishermen.

When Roger Haynes was given the opportunity to take the water on as a private enterprise in 1982 the stocking ratio improved. Then, for the beginning of the 1983 season half the reservoir's perimeter was fitted with sturdy casting platforms spread out at reasonable distances.

I have always found hotspots on the slipways at this reservoir and the one on the Windsor Castle side is my favourite. It has been such a lucky fishing position for me as the feature change in the concrete creates differing currents and this certainly attracts big trout to the area. I took browns to 5lb and rainbows to 6lb 10oz using fry lure tactics, on a lead impregnated shooting head fly line.

In past seasons tactics have all been boat fishing. Because there was no bank fishing and therefore no disturbance, the fish would very often be in close. I would drift my boat either on drogue or rudder parallel along the bank, about 35yd (32m) out.

The tactic was to cast my single lure so as to land on the smooth concrete of the dam and then slowly retrieve as it slid, or should I say swam down into the depths. These tactics will remain very good now where no casting platforms have been erected. In the past the Appetizer and pure White Muddler have been my most effective patterns.

Queen Mother is one of those very deep reservoirs where even the local experts become preoccupied with its mysteries. So far three double figure wild rainbows have been caught there, a feat even the mighty Grafham and Rutland cannot match.

Nearest to the first 10lb plus brown trout is a fine 9lb 6oz fish which fell to local expert Mike Peters. Mike specialises in deep lure fishing from a boat and he has a slogan which is 'the deeper, the bigger, the fewer' and how right he is.

Apart from the slipways on the far side there are two more close to the fishing lodge and boat jetty. Usually the prevailing wind is blowing in here and as my good friend and regular expert Brian Gent will tell you it is where the big fish are to be found for much of the time. Brian should know as his personal best is a 10¼lb rainbow from this spot.

He favours fluorescent green in his lure patterns as it attracts big rainbows from very deep down. These are depths of 40ft (12m) and more where there is plenty of natural food like shrimp, stickleback and snails.

The two other main features at Queen Mother are the valve tower with its bridge supported by several concrete pillars and a second tower out in the centre. There depths of around 80ft (24m) can be found. Mike Peters has mastered the art of fishing these depths with lead core line. He has taken many big fish on his special seven-inch lures tied on three hook rigs.

I have fished the reservoir in mid-summer when a good wave has been on using the traditional loch style drifting tactics over some very deep water. On this sort of day rainbows are invariably up in the water and they rise up from nowhere to take small wet flies. Certainly it would be a mistake to think that just because the water is very deep you in turn must fish likewise. If there is a grey sky, a good wave and a warm westerly blow, always start off on the top if you're boat fishing.

With all these platforms available, bank fishing is popular, and bear in mind there are not many waters where a 25yd (23m) cast drops you into 40ft (12m) of water. Because of these depths trout regularly are in close.

If a strong wind is blowing into you the trout come in right into the margins, so use a medium sinking line and fish a small lure or Dog Nobbler, trying to retrieve at different depths. Usually I follow the code of early season black based lures, mid-summer and high temperatures orange based lures and autumn white based lures. These are good general rules to follow.

If you are unfortunate enough to arrive at the reservoir in bright sun and flat calm conditions it will be more difficult but not impossible. You could try very long casting with a lead impregnated shooting head and inch retrieve a small lure or similar size nymph such as a Black Leech, Stick Fly, Damsel Fly or Brer Rabbit. Alternatively, use a floating line or sink-tip shooting head of the home-made type. Then set up a five-metre leader of 5lb breaking strain nylon carrying two droppers. A good set-up would be a weighted Shrimp or Corixa on the point, a buzzer or Pheasant Tail Nymph in the middle and a Hatching Sedge pattern on the top.

Fished patiently and very slowly with figure of eight retrieving you would save the day and catch some trout. Remember this tip when fishing in this style; the less you do, the more takes you get. Often the mistake is to get over-anxious and be forever pulling in and casting.

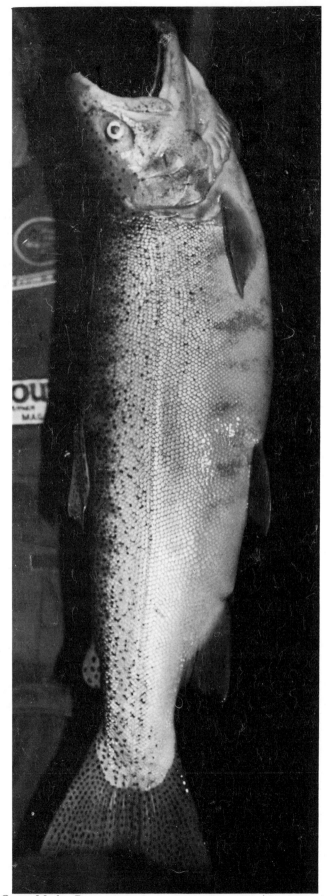

Queen Mother Reservoir produces some really excellent fish. Just look at this magnificent 'wild' rainbow caught by Bob Church while it was fry feeding.

9 Tittesworth Reservoir

Nestling beneath the Pennine Range in a completely unspoilt part of England lies the 200-acre Tittesworth reservoir. It is the closest one can get to an Irish lough or a Scottish loch for its rugged appearance. For those who must have the surroundings right as well as the trout, this is the place for you.

I (Bob) have fished Tittesworth on a number of occasions, and each time sport was excellent and held my attention with its great variety. Although Tittesworth is a good bank fishing water, after driving a fair distance I like to treat myself to a boat and there are several good reasons for using a boat here as I quickly found out.

Similar to the Scottish lochs, the bottom feed is not all that good, so the trout become free risers and lend themselves perfectly to the traditional loch style short line fished from a broadside drifting boat. A great many interesting areas close into the bank are steep sloping and very deep. This provides virgin fishing as thick undergrowth and woodland make any bank casting impossible.

A boat therefore is the only means of approaching these fish holding spots, either by drifting or anchoring up.

Tittesworth holds a good head of browns both stocked and high proportion of wild fish. These fish breed in the main feeder stream the Churnet which rises as a spring at Middle Hills on the edge of the Pennines. Most of the big browns live a sulky existence in Tittesworth deeps and have never seen a lure. They could be the perfect target for any deep water lure specialist who likes to fish exclusively for big browns. The months of May, September or October would be best to try for them. That they exist there is in no doubt, the best landed so far being one of 9lb 5oz caught in September. Ken Scragg, a bailiff at Tittesworth, once pulled out a huge brown from the margins which was in its death throes. This double figure fish had choked to death after eating two stock rainbow trout.

There is one massive brown estimated at about 16lb which regularly shows itself close to the lodge area. It

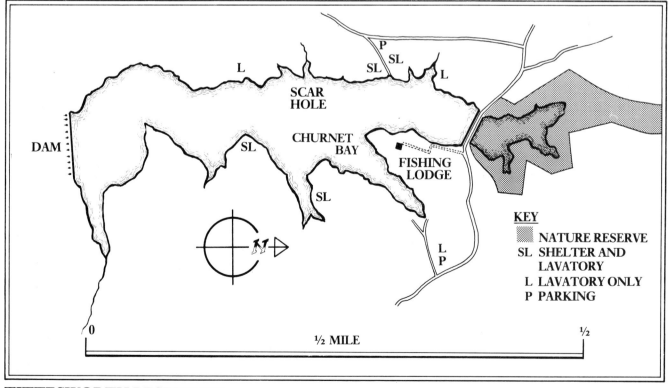

TITTESWORTH RESERVOIR

Looking down towards the main dam from the approach road at Tittesworth Reservoir.

patrols a beat into Churnet Bay and lives on stockies and coarse fish. Need I say more?

Tittesworth Fly Fishing Club chairman is Selwyn Hughes the ex-Welsh international fly fisher who is a classic exponent of the delicate art of short lining. Selwyn catches most of his fish off the top by fishing a team of three small flies on a floating fly line and an 11ft (3.35m) rod. A real sportsman, Selwyn returns far more trout than he ever kills but one day when I was fishing at the reservoir he had killed a small 6in (15cm) rainbow to show me. He wanted a second opinion on his belief that this was a self-bred wild rainbow, which as you will appreciate is a very rare occurrence for any stillwater in Britain.

Back at the lodge I inspected the fish which was bright silver and quite perfect with every fin intact. The little fish was hardy looking and solid fleshed and I had no hesitation in giving my opinion that it was a wild fish. That Churnet stream must be very pure and ideal not only for successful breeding of a batch of browns each year but also a few rainbows.

The very first trout I ever caught from Tittesworth was a fine brown of 2½lb and that came from Churnet Bay. It had twice as many red spots as black and I am sure it had grown on from stream bred stock. It was cold early April with the water gin clear, I fished deep with a 10ft (3m) powerful rod and a number 9 shooting head to obtain maximum casting distance. My lure was a single pure White Muddler. I could not help but be impressed with

the place as my second fish was a 3¼lb silver hen rainbow which took a Jack Frost. The day ended with my angling companion Keith Robinson and I taking a good limit apiece.

When fishing here later in April I have been lucky enough to fish for trout that were feeding on tiny black Chironomids right in the surface film. On one occasion Geoff Smith and I had tremendous sport while drifting loch style with three small flies. We proved on this day that even in very cold weather trout will come up and feed on the surface if there is fly there to tempt them.

The early black buzzer is quite small almost everywhere about the country, and number 14 hooks were the best on this occasion. It is also very noticeable how trout like to take the fly, or should I say pupae, just as it is about to hatch into a winged adult. This happens about two or three inches below the surface and creates a 'bulge' rise.

Sometimes the feeding trout can be very selective but on this occasion they were bang on once we got the flies right. The best set up was Black Pennell on the point, a March Brown in the centre and a Black and Peacock on the top dropper. It proved to be a fine day's sport as Geoff caught twenty, while I caught eighteen, keeping only the deepest hooked fish for a limit of six each. Even now, a couple of years later, when I see Geoff he asks when we are going back to Tittesworth again.

There is so much to attract keen fly fishers to Tittesworth and perhaps the biggest pull of all is the Mayfly hatches of early June. It is quite rare for an English

Selwyn Hughes is chairman of the Tittesworth Fly Fishers Club. Here
he shows a fine 3½lb rainbow caught on a small fly from the woody
bank area at Scar Hole, Tittesworth.

reservoir to have a regular Mayfly hatch but here it never fails. Again the river Churnet plays a part as this is where the Mayfly originates. After the valley was flooded to form the reservoir early in the 1960s, the Mayfly soon multiplied all over the lake giving great sport with tremendous rises and catches when most other reservoirs struggle to provide sport at all.

If you tie up a few Mayfly dun patterns in readiness for a trip to Tittesworth make sure to dress the bodies in a green shade. The nymphs and Spent Mayfly patterns can have greenish brown bodies. These are a somewhat darker Mayfly than those you see in the south of the country. Just to prove what a really good fishery Tittesworth is becoming the catches in the early weeks of the

1983 season were very impressive. It became apparent that the quality of the stock fish was far better than ever before, this included many fine browns to 3lb, good rainbows to a similar weight and brook trout up to 2lb, although I did witness one of 4¼lb.

After a late mid-morning start I took my best ever limit from the reservoir. Three fish fell to a small Minstrel Muddler on a medium sinking line. Then when they went off that I changed up to a bright yellow chenille Dog Nobbler and I had really good quality browns queuing up to take it. Six browns for near 17lb was the grand total, so as you can see with all this variety Tittesworth should be on your visiting card.

10 Ardleigh Reservoir

Both Peter and I enjoy fishing at the smaller, more personal type of reservoir. Places like Ravensthorpe, Thornton and Sutton Bingham immediately come to mind, but I (Bob) like a trip to Ardleigh Reservoir near Colchester, Essex, best of all.

At only 130 acres the reservoir's long irregular shape with its many bays gives the impression of a much larger water. The fishery usually averages an annual catch of around 25,000 trout with both browns and rainbows topping the 6lb mark. Some years ago I did see a 9lb 11oz brown caught from the bank on a Missionary lure in a shallow bay some 300 yards down from the boat moorings. This is still a record for the reservoir.

Ardleigh is managed privately by Richard Connell, a very professional Scotsman, who understands trout rearing and breeding inside out. Living right beside the fishery he can dictate his put and take stocking policies to perfection.

There are twenty clinker built wooden rowing boats and in true Scottish style they have their oars permanently fixed on a peg rather than a normal rowlock. This is a much better system and makes life easier for the oarsman. These boats are better than the fibreglass types for loch style drifting as they sit much steadier in the water.

On overcast windy days from May onwards the short line method is the best. Favourite wet flies for Ardleigh are the Greenwell Spider, Partridge and Orange, Dunkeld with jungle cock eyes, Black Pennell, Woodcock and Yellow and the Jersey Herd. I have noticed many times that size of fly is so important and can remember two separate occasions when changing from a Size 10 to a Size 14 of the same pattern turned dismal results into quick limits, the patterns in question being Jersey Herd and Black Pennell.

Ardleigh also offers good lure fishing from the boats. During the early season colder water, it is best to anchor up and I find that about 60yd (55m) off the shore onto which the wind is blowing into is best. My old reliable standby the Black Chenille lure has caught me many fish at Ardleigh as has the white Baby Doll. Keep to the smaller sizes (10 and 8 for the best results) as most of the trout average around the pound mark.

Richard Connell does allow the use of a portable

Steven Church brings a trout to hand from the brown trout only water at Ardleigh.

rudder and as you can imagine on such a long reasonably shallow water this allows for some very good drifts. It was while fishing in this way, each angler casting from different sides of the boat with fast sinking fly lines and Black and Silver Tandem Lures that I caught my best Ardleigh trout, a brown of 3lb 11oz.

Sometimes in summer the fishing may have been poor all day, but don't pack up and head for home too early. Often a tremendous rise will occur very late, far too late in fact for the boats to be out. Usually it is the buzzer or sedge hatching on the point of darkness that causes this situation. It is fortunate that Richard Connell is also an understanding fly fisher as well as a fishery manager, and on such days he usually allows you to fish on into darkness from the bank.

It is now I must mention nymphs for this late evening sport as they are invaluable. The Ardleigh Nymph is the reservoir favourite and since being introduced to it I have caught fish at many other waters as well. My Spring Favourite works well so does the black buzzer. Regular local expert Cyril Francis and I spent a day together and he uses a single, lightly leaded Pheasant Tail Nymph for most of his fishing. These are the tips he passed on to me which give him great consistency at Ardleigh.

One of his favourite spots is the wooded area for he has found that he can catch large browns from the bank here, his best reaching 5½lb. He waits for the early season hustle and bustle to die down, then concentrates on fishing under the trees. He stresses the need to keep still. It is best to keep as concealed as possible, wearing drab clothing, and to fish the margins as you would a river.

He mostly fishes along the bottom with a floating fly line, a 12ft (3.65m) leader and a single leaded Pheasant Tail Nymph. This careful and very slow approach is the only way Cyril has found to outwit the larger browns. A final point Cyril made was that he sometimes hears anglers moaning about the number of small trout in Ardleigh. He would agree the place is full of fish, but that there are also enough big ones to make it a very interesting challenge.

On my last trip to Ardleigh I spent the day fishing the latest section to be opened. This is just eight acres situated where the Wick Road crosses the reservoir, cutting off this very attractive creek. Richard Connell loves his brown trout and so he made this all brown stocking like a wild little Scottish loch.

This natural looking water appealed to me as it would to any discerning fly fisher who can at times get a little fed

Ardleigh expert Cyril Francis shows two brace of early season rainbows on his Pheasant Tail Nymph tactics.

up with rainbows. In fact I don't know of many managed brown trout only waters in the whole of England, and what makes it especially nice is that no more than five anglers a day are allowed to fish in the new section. The day I chose saw the heavens open and the continuous pouring rain this April day was, to say the least, off-putting. But, even under such terrible conditions, from lunch-time onwards there was a steady rise to a hatch of pale olive buzzers in the calm water out of the wind and the fish were taking the nymph as they struggled to emerge in the surface film. I put up with the rain and enjoyed excellent sport using a Size 14 Black Pennell. This I fished singly on a 4lb leader and floating line. I also greased the leader nylon every so often by rubbing my fingers across my forehead to keep the fly close to the surface.

I found that by retrieving slightly faster, the hooking ratio increased even though takes became fewer. The limit for this water is six fish which I easily managed. The limit is eight fish in the main reservoir.

Here is the dressing for Richard Connell's Ardleigh Nymph for it is not widely known.

Hooks 16–14–12–10 medium shank, bronze.
Tying silk black.
Tail natural Greenwell hackle fibres.
Body Pheasant tail fibres ribbed with gold wire.
Thorax Peacock herl.
Hackle Small hen Greenwells.
Head black varnish.

11 Draycote Reservoir

Having fished Draycote since it first opened in 1971, I (Bob) have witnessed its very good seasons, its disasters and latterly a return to good form and management.

Back in 1972 and 1973 Draycote provided me with the most consistent brown trout fishing I have ever had, with thousands of fish in the reservoir in the 2lb to 5lb weight class. At first they were not that easy to catch, as often they would be out in the deep water well away from the bank. This led me to develop the lead core shooting head and the special powerful rod needed to handle it. At the same time I was the first person to use chenille which provided the body for my Black Chenille Lure. In the past decade this pattern has probably caught more and larger trout than any other lure or fly pattern.

We soon found that Draycote's bottom contours varied quite a lot and had a number of large areas of shallows surrounded by sharp drop-offs, into much deeper water. So, to be continuously successful it meant taking to the boats and then using them with a little more imagination than had been done by strictly traditional trout fly fishers of the past. Special drogues and portable rudders were developed and depth sounders were used for the first time to help pinpoint the bank edges. Word spread and soon all the regular Draycote rods were taking consistent catches of browns. In the July of 1973 came the first major sedge hatches and this provided evening surface fishing on the top *par excellence.*

It was about this time that we first noticed some of the larger browns were showing signs of being out of condition. It transpired that a tapeworm stomach parasite had started to affect the good stock of big browns in epidemic numbers. It was terrible to watch as the fishery deteriorated for seemingly nothing could be done to help. Eventually the disease ran its course and slowly Draycote sparked back into life. For example, in the first four weeks of the 1983 season, over 13,000 trout were caught from Draycote which meant that the fishery was well and truly back on song.

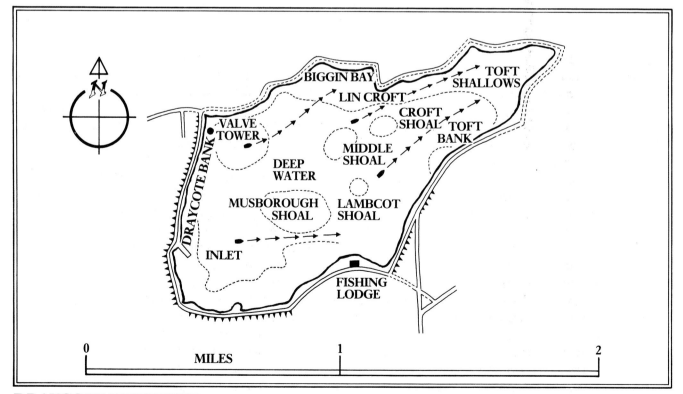

DRAYCOTE RESERVOIR

Fishing off one of Draycote's rocky dam walls needs a careful step, but it produces good catches.

I can well remember when new fishery officer Keith Causer took control at Draycote prior to the 1982 season. He told me that with such a highly populated area to draw from, he was determined that Draycote would be a success for both anglers and the Severn and Trent Authority. So far he has more than kept to his word.

Included in his policy alterations is the stocking of better quality and bigger trout. The reservoir is now more of a rainbow water but even so in the last two seasons browns to 9lb 6oz and rainbows to 8lb 7oz have been taken by bank anglers. It is this dramatic general improvement in the bank fishing that has influenced the great Draycote revival. One of my old experienced fly fishing friends is John Snelson who has always been the top rod at Draycote fishing there five or six times a week.

John confirmed that where we always relied on boats for big catches it is now the turn of the bank to produce the best sport. The methods have changed as well with John catching most of his trout on small flies. He told me that his most effective patterns which were currently accounting for hundreds of Draycote trout were simple spider flies similar to a Black Pennell. His favourite is a simple medium brown silk thread body with a fuse wire ribbing with a couple of turns of ordinary brown hen hackle at the head. This is a very good tip from one of the country's most successful trout catchers.

The most prolific of Draycote's hotspots is the creek-like area known as Toft Shallows which lies at the north-east end of the reservoir close to the M45. Other favoured bank spots of mine are Toft Bank, Biggin Bay, Lin Croft Point and the main dam bank.

From the boat I will give you four excellent drifts for fishing either sinking or floating fly lines according to the prevailing conditions. The first is on a south-west wind from the valve tower right down into Biggin Bay. On the same wind travel from the Middle Shoal through the channel of Croft Shoal and Lin Croft point at around 150yd (137m) from the shore, continuing right down into Toft Shallows.

A similar drift can be found on the far side of the reservoir from Lambcot Shoal passing Toft Bank at 100yd (91m) out and continuing down into Toft Bay and Shallows. Finally there is the drift from in front of the Inlet stream going back towards the fishing lodge. On this one you pass the large Musborough Shoal and either concentrate on the channel between it and the shore or drift over the shallower water across this submerged island.

Bank fishing methods differ according to the time of year and also the areas you are fishing. Normally at the season's outset in April, I would use a medium sinking shooting head outfit. The early fish always lay deep or on the bottom, but of course this can be in fairly shallow water. A small dark Size 10 lure is usually a consistent way of taking fish if it is retrieved steadily and slowly along the bottom. Remember there will be no weed about so your hook will not keep fouling up as it would in summer. At this time the trout are often feeding on tiny chironomid larvae.

Towards the end of April and into May the small black chironomid is prolific which keeps the trout on the move at varying depths. A floating line, or in some cases the home-made sink-tip shooting head is a great help when wanting to fish a nymph deep down. I have found so many times at Draycote that the less you retrieve when fishing the buzzer the better your chances. My favourite nymphs for the water include the Tiger Nymph, a standard Black buzzer pupae, a few up in exaggerated sizes up to Size 8, the Mole Nymph, and Pheasant Tail nymphs both in the standard and hackled versions.

Of the wet fly patterns, the Blae and Black, Black and Peacock Spider, and Greenwell's Glory work well early on as do the Cinnamon and Gold, Silver March Brown, Ginger Quill, Wickham's Fancy, Invicta and small Muddler Minnows in mid-summer. Occasionally a dry sedge can work wonders in flat calm high summer conditions.

Lures that do well are the Black Chenille, Black and Silver Hairwing, Ace of Spades, Sweeney Todd in both normal and green variants, Muddler Minnow, White Muddler, Black Muddler, Whisky Fly and the Missionary.

Draycote has a perimeter road running all round its 600 acres so bank hopping is a simple matter if you have a pair of car roof holders. There are 30 boats on Draycote, approximately half motor, half rowing.

Fishing a bow anchored boat in a big wind and high wave. The spot is off Lin Croft Point at Draycote Reservoir, here Ron Kyte unhooks a good brown.

Bev Perkins with a 6lb 10oz brown trout taken from the Tofts Shallows while boat fishing with a lead core line and lure.

12 Eyebrook Reservoir

The late trout maestro Cyril Inwood could never understand why I bothered with early season trouting. Great angler though he was he was against the trend to make our seasons longer and longer.

When Eyebrook opened its season on 1 April even this was too early for Cyril. I first fished Eyebrook over twenty years ago and I have to agree that my records over this period prove Cyril to be correct. Like Pitsford, Eyebrook is an imitative fly fisherman's dream water having prolific hatches of various fly life, plus a good back-up of bugs and bottom food the season through. Eyebrook's 400 acres are perfect on the eye, so all in all it is a very pleasant place to spend a day.

As far as I can see the only thing that has changed in twenty years is that in the early days the stock fish were all 12–13in (30–33cm) and equal browns and rainbows. Now there are more fish stocked and more fish caught (around 22,500 average). However, the size and quality of the stock fish is not as good as it was and of course we have mainly rainbows.

We must not dwell on the past too much because where this reservoir is concerned the pleasure of the actual fishing techniques is more important than catching specimen trout. Even so there are enough two pounders around to make it interesting. By May the fly life has had a chance to become very active and it is now that conditions are perfect for nymph fishing. That great dedicated nymph fisherman Arthur Cove perfected many of his successful tactics at Eyebrook at this time of year. Arthur's version of the Pheasant Tail Nymph has proved to be a top all round imitation.

A Pheasant Tail Nymph can suggest so many different aquatic life forms when fished slowly and carefully with figure of eight retrieve on a long leader and floating fly line. The trout at Eyebrook may ignore all types of lure offerings only to fall for a well presented nymph on the first cast.

It is a good idea to take your car right to the far end of

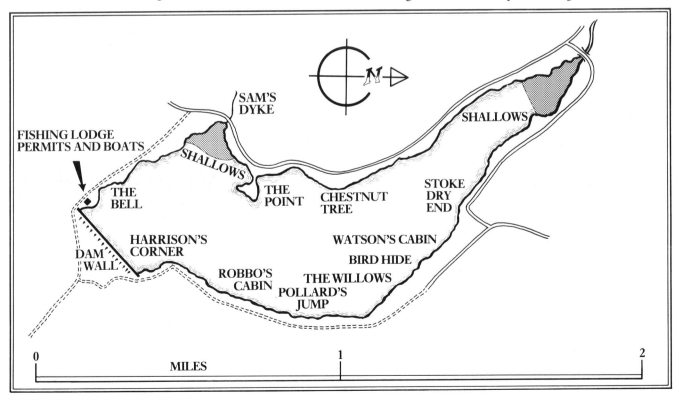

EYEBROOK RESERVOIR

Early season and a full house attendance at Eyebrook Reservoir.

the wooded bank at Stoke Dry End which is opposite the fishing lodge. When tackling up, travel light so you can keep on the move. A 9½ft (2.9m) rod carrying a number 7 or number 8 floating line is as good a travelling outfit as any. Have a couple of spools of nylon, a marrow spoon priest and a fly wallet full of your favourite nymphs in your pocket. Finally attach a flick up landing net to a D ring on your waistcoat, on the non-casting side and you are now ready to fish and move at will without forever bending down and carrying excessive and unwanted extra tackle.

There are times at Eyebrook when plenty of buzzers are hatching and fish are rising to them, or so it would seem. A more careful examination has often revealed that the trout are ignoring the buzzers (equivalent to number 12 hook size) and are taking a tiny light brown greyish hatching insect too tiny to imitate but hatches off in millions. I suspect this is yet another member of the chironomid family.

I can well remember casting to a number of rising fish with various nymph changes, all of which were ignored. I eventually put on a 3lb leader and a Size 16 Pheasant Tail. I then took two brace of good residual fish in the next hour while everyone else failed. Such satisfying moments are to be had at Eyebrook.

The tip here is, don't be misled by what you first see. Make sure you determine what the fish are feeding on

before trying for them. I like to cast across the wind and bring the nymphs round nice and slowly. I deliberately allow a limited bow to form in the floating line as it drifts with the wind or breeze which helps for good secure hooking. Keep moving along the bank and trying new spots but only wade if you have to.

Pheasant Tail Nymphs with varying coloured thorax are killing patterns at Eyebrook as the season wears on. For example at sedge time from late June onwards, a green amber or yellow is good. These imitate the bottom crawling caddis grub and the ascending sedge pupae.

In July when the daphnia blooms try a Pheasant Tail with red or orange thorax. July also witnesses the arrival of an abundance of new food at Eyebrook with the appearance in the marginal weed beds of teeming thousands of tiny fry. These are the newly hatched off-spring of the recently spawned roach. They are a delicacy that trout like and the Eyebrook fish are quick to realise there are some easy pickings to be had.

There are several lure imitations with which we match these pin-heads. One of the best is certainly a Size 10 or 8 white thorax Pheasant Tail on a longshank hook. Tie a few up on nickel-plated hooks which can help. Fish this singly keeping to the floating fly line and long leader. When drawing in close, you will notice many of the pin-heads shoal round the artificial and follow it in. This

126

is an added attraction for a feeding trout. As he moves in for the kill, the shoal panics and scatters into the weeds, leaving just the artificial to be taken.

When tying your Pheasant Tails, the easiest way of making the varying colour thorax is to dub onto the tying silk either seal's fur, Superla dubbing mix or wool, all are ideal for the job. Build a ball shape, but leave a few stray fibres. Cover these with a sparse throat hackle of light brown cock fibres and a normal shell back finish of feather fibre.

The whole of the wooded shoreline is productive. Known hotspot landmarks to look out for include Watson's Cabin, the Bird Hide, the Willows, Pollard's Jump, Robbo's Cabin and Harrison's Corner which is close to the dam. My best ever bank catches have come from the point which protrudes way out into the reservoir, this is on the opposite side of the water. Fish often feed upwind, coming out of the bay into which runs Sam's Dyke. Shallow wading off the tip of the point is a great vantage point and many fish can be covered. During the early April weeks Sam's Dyke itself is a holding spot and I have taken browns to 3lb by casting along the channel and fishing the bottom.

The only two other spots I favour from the bank are The Bell, which is not far from the lodge. The Chestnut Tree which lies at the far end well past the point is worth an hour or two. All these places are accessible by road and the car can be left just a very short walk from the water.

Favourite flies for Eyebrook include Invicta, Silver Invicta, Wickham's Fancy, Greenwell's Glory, Blae and Black, Black Pennell, Butcher, Ginger Quill and small Brown Sedge.

Nymphs include the Pheasant Tail variants, Hare's Ear, Buzzers in standard, suspender and marabou bodied forms, Amber Nymph, Caddis Grub, Damsel Fly, Brer Rabbit, Green Midge and Bloodworm.

Dry flies of the sedge type and Daddy Longlegs work well during their seasons. For lures, all the popular patterns and even the latest types work well early and late in the season, but keep the hook size down to a longshank 10 or at maximum a Size 8.

There are plenty of boats at Eyebrook. All are rowing boats but electric battery engines of your own can be used with permission. There is a no limit rule and although I personally do not agree with this it shows the fishery officer has great faith in his put-and-take stocking policy. Eyebrook Reservoir is situated not far from Corby at Caldecott and is overlooked by the famous Rockingham Castle.

13 The Gravel Pit Fisheries

A whole new group of medium-sized trout fisheries has sprung up throughout the country during the past decade, most being developed from old gravel pit workings. These crystal clear, gravel-filtered waters are as productive as any allowing plenty of sunlight to penetrate deep down encouraging the growth of many different types of water plants. These help the food chain along and provide cover for the trout.

The fly life is often far more varied than on the other kinds of trout water which is a big bonus. As well as regular hatches of buzzer, Pond Olives are common. In recent seasons this type of water has encouraged Mayfly to become re-established in areas where it has not been seen for years. It is the sedge though that thrives best of all and at some gravel pit fisheries I (Bob) go to, the hatch at dusk needs to be seen to be believed.

Because of the high alkalinity these waters abound with plenty of crustaceans and the various bugs. As you can see, the trout's natural larder is fairly complete. To tell you something about the fishing at these gravel pits, I have chosen three well known ones that I fish reasonably often. They are Ringstead Grange in Northamptonshire, Horseshoe Lake in Gloucestershire and the Lechlade Trout Fishery in the Cotswolds.

Ringstead Grange

This 36-acre water lays adjacent to the middle reaches of the River Nene in a picturesque valley and has become a firm favourite with many regular Midland trout fishers. The water is run by local farmer Harold Foster who has perfected a stocking policy which gives every visitor an equal chance no matter what time of the season you go to fish.

There is a six fish limit but catch and release is allowed provided the trout are not handled and lifted from the water. At all such fisheries where these rules apply we advise that the angler either file away the barb from his fly or at least compress it flat with a pair of forceps.

The thing that pleases me most about Ringstead is the mixture of species. You never really know what you will hook into next. It holds a good stock of smallish browns and rainbows, with a back-up of fish in the 2lb class. Certainly it is fairly normal to have a 3lb or 4lb fish figuring among a limit bag. Six-pound plus fish turn up virtually every week throughout the season. Both Peter and I have the distinction of holding the fishery record, albeit for a short period. The best rainbow for the water is 14¼lb and the best brown scales over 8lb although a 14lb brown was found dead in the margins. The best brook trout ever taken weighed 4½lb.

The master at work. England Fly Fishing Team Captain Bob Draper hooks a fish while loch style drifting at Ringstead Grange.

Bob nets it safely aboard.

Apart from the straightforward early season small lure and sinking lines tactics, the floating line lure fishing also takes a lot of good trout. The best method has been to fish a single Dog Nobbler on a floating line. This head weighted lure dives deep and is retrieved in a series of jerky pulls. It also sometimes helps to work the rod tip in true sink and draw bait style.

In the 1983 season I had even more success on the more streamlined and delicate Frog Nobblers dressed on a small normal shank Size 10 hook. When the water is clear, these lures can be fished on much finer nylon which helps to fool the fish and also allows the lure to move more seductively.

General nymph fishing tactics from the bank take some beating and the methods we have referred to at other waters work well here. On many evenings you will see

nymph expert Arthur Cove at Ringstead and he doesn't waste his time where the fishing is not up to scratch.

There are seven boats on Ringstead and I do enjoy fishing here using traditional drifting loch style with a team of small wet flies. There may not be a sign of a fish rising anywhere but, because the water is fairly clear and shallowish, you can easily induce fish to rise to the artificial fly. Most anglers who use the boats will anchor up and fish either nymphs or lures but my advice is to be more versatile.

There is one very deep bay at Ringstead situated in the top left-hand corner close to the river. Here the depth is as much as 18ft (5.5m) and it is a very good holding spot for the daytime fishing when temperatures are high in mid-summer.

Horseshoe Lake

This is a superb place to spend a day fishing no matter what time of the season. Although I (Bob) need to drive 85 miles down the old Fosse Way to get to Horseshoe Lake, I have never had a bad day there and the fish have been of the highest quality.

A long peninsula extends out into the aptly named lake to provide lots of bank fishing space. I usually make for a favourite spot in the top left-hand corner of the lake where an inlet pipe pushes a good flow of water in from an adjoining pit. The depth here is quite good and you can cast into 15ft (4.6m) of water and as trout are always attracted to running water it is safe to say there are plenty of fish around this spot.

My other favoured place is the deep hole (over 30 feet) which starts at the tip of the right arm of the horseshoe shape and extends a third of the way along the arm. The best casting position is from off the peninsula and if you use a sinking shooting head and can punch out 30yd (27m) or more, your fly will drop into the deep water where many big trout live.

During early season when the wind is blowing into the tips of the arms both are well worth fishing. I took my best Horseshoe fish, a 6lb 10oz rainbow half-way along the left arm. My tactics that day were to fish a home-made sink-tip shooting head with a number 12 Jack Frost on the point and a buzzer pupae imitation on a dropper.

There was a strong wind blowing so I merely cast out dropping my flies approximately in the middle of the arm, and let the wind do the rest. The take was a classic as I watched the bow in the line straightening out.

The Mayfly hatch is very good and lasts for about three weeks, with the peak coming usually the second week in June. At this time both nymph fishing with Dick Walker's famous leaded pattern or using a static dry fly with a spent pattern will both take a lot of fish.

Horseshoe Lake is owned and managed by Jerry and Alison Kemp of Gerrards Cross Fish Farms which turns up to 20,000 fish loose into the lake each season. Fishery records give the best rainbow at 13lb 5oz and the best brown at 6lb 2oz. Horseshoe Lake holds plenty of brook trout to 2½lb and a few large Tiger Trout. It is also expected that the new trend towards salmon stocking will be tried in the future.

The fishery lies close to the village of South Cerney off Wildmoor Lane. Telephone Cirencester 861034.

Horseshoe Lake's record double limit bag fell to Syd Brock of Oxford. The smallest rainbow went 6lb 2oz and the largest 12lb 5oz. This record will take some beating.

Bob Church with a really great fish from Horseshoe Lake, this 6lb 10oz specimen rainbow took a No. 10 Jack Frost Lure fished on a floating line.

129

Alan Pearson plays a hard fighting rainbow trout on his new boron fly rod. He is fishing the top lake at Lechlade Trout Fishery in the Cotswolds.

Lechlade Trout Fishery

Try a journey through the scenic Cotswold villages and arrive at our third gravel pit fishery along the Burford to Lechlade Road. I must admit I (Bob) knew nothing about this water until 1983 when I made three trips there. Everyone produced excellent catches with rainbows of over 4lb on each occasion.

Two very carefully landscaped lakes have been created from the old gravel workings to give about 10 acres of water. Much care was taken by the excavators to leave the surrounding woodland and adjacent River Leach in their original state. The work was completed in 1979 and now the lakes give the impression of natural waters.

Owner John Taylor plans to make the lakes the finest of their type in Britain. He certainly offers better than average-sized trout because his fish farm is just a stone's throw away. As I saw for myself he rears a large stock of fine fish of all sizes including big ones into double figures. I checked the record returns book at the lodge and found the best brown was 10½lb and the best rainbow 7½lb.

As I tackled up for my first session at Lechlade I saw one angler take a brace of rainbows in five minutes weighing 4½lb and 3½lb. No wonder I mis-threaded a ring in my haste to get fishing. By the way this hectic sport happened in the middle of a sunny flat calm day when things should have been quiet.

I noticed a few Damsels and Mayfly coming off, and chose to use a lightly leaded Damsel Fly Nymph. Again the water was very clear but depths up to 15 feet or so were apparent, so I fished my nymph on a neutral density fly line.

By tea-time I had deceived two brace of bright silver rainbows, the smallest weighing 2½lb and the best 4½lb. Pretty impressive size and quality you must admit and they fought hard too having been reared in the fast flowing River Leach, a Thames main tributary which runs alongside the fishery. As evening approached I changed my tactics and tied on a Size 8 Black Dog Nobbler. I cast out towards the island on the top lake, allowed the lure to sink to the bottom and began to retrieve in a series of jerks. As I drew the lure into the margins I became aware of a fish following, a very big one too which set my heart pounding. At the last second the fish, a brownie into double figures, realised all was not well and retreated. He was just a whisker away from taking, so once again I must wait if ever I am to achieve my final trout fishing ambition of taking a double figure brownie on a fly.

To give you some idea of the fishery's potential, the next two trips were even better. The heaviest fish I saw landed was 6¼lb and four pounders were common.

14 Natural Trout Lakes

Many fine landscaped lakes of the once large estates designed by Capability Brown have been turned into trout fisheries during the past twenty years. The dramatic growth in the number of anglers has made such waters an attractive business proposition. These lakes don't have the water clarity of the gravel pits and usually this makes the trout a little easier to catch.

Once again to get you into the atmosphere of this type of water it will be a good idea if I (Bob) take you on a trip to three of my favourites – Leominstead Lake in the heart of the New Forest, Bayham Lake in Kent and Westward Park Lake near Droitwich in Worcestershire.

Leominstead Lake

This secluded beauty spot is hidden deep in the New Forest close to Emery Down near Lyndhurst. I have met a few interesting characters in the world of trout fishing but the owner and builder of this fishery, Leo Jarmal, takes some beating.

Leominstead has a 300-year-old history and when Leo first took over in the 1960s it was a coarse fishery for carp and tench. Leo removed the coarse fish to another lake in the forest and then began to create his picture postcard trout water. He preserved all the surrounding trees and much of the lake's eight acres is bordered by rhododendrons.

Leo built a series of casting platforms which stretch well out into the lake, enabling the angler to cast along the margins under the trees where fish like to lay or well out into the lake without fear of getting hooked up a tree.

Leo holds great pride in his reputation of producing top quality fish. The average size is very high with one day producing two rainbows over 8lb, a seven pounder and two more over 6lb. My best brace on that eventful day went 5lb and 4¼lb with all the general back-up fish scaling between 2lb and 2½lb.

Because you cannot see the fish in the peaty water, it can be a problem sorting out the bigger ones before

Looking down the lake at Leominstead.

catching a limit of two pounders. The most successful method of all being a medium sinking fly line and a single nymph or small lure. By the way Leominstead has a one-inch limit to fly size.

Early in the season during April it is best to let your lure sink well down to the bottom before retrieving very slowly for a few pulls. If nothing happens allow the lure to sink back to the bottom before re commencing the slow retrieve. Takes often come during the second pull following the pause and are usually the bigger fish. It happens enough to prove it as a method which must be remembered for trial elsewhere.

My favourite spot at Leominstead is the corner close to the weighing-in hut. The water gets shallower as you approach the top end of the lake and here floating line and Dog or Frog Nobblers on Size 10 hooks work well. In the dark coloured water, yellow has proved to be a good colour.

The stream that runs through the lake is a River Test tributary and at times of heavy rain a few sea trout get over the sluice and into the lake. Towards autumn the browns, which don't show themselves all that regularly, usually feed with more confidence and I had some great sport with these during late September. They range from a pound to 3lb and have yellow gold bellies rather than silver.

There is an air of friendliness at Leominstead created by Leo and his wife Rosie. Leo has built a summer house for the use of his customers, most of which finish up as friends.

The fishery records are topped by a 13lb rainbow and brown trout to 6lb 9oz.

Bayham Lake

This 16-acre lake lies between Tunbridge Wells and Lamberhurst in Kent. Set in the grounds of Bayham Abbey, one whole side of the lake has thick rhododendrons growing right down to the water, a quite marvellous sight when the blossom is at its peak.

Bayham is fed by little River Teise, which unfortunately turns very coloured after heavy rain and this spoils the fishing for a time. The outflow of the lake produces a series of cascade pools as the level of the river drops. These are well stocked and provide an attractive alternative to the lake. You are restricted to nymph or dry fly on the pools.

The top trout catching fly here is Dick Walker's Mayfly Nymph followed by the Black Chenille and Viva lures. When the sedge are about in numbers the Invicta and Soldier Palmer are the pick of local patterns.

On my visits to Bayham I have found three major hotspots. The first is from the boat jetty to the corner of the dam, the second is on the far side of the dam by the outflow. The most productive area, especially when the weather is very warm, is right up into the channel of the Teise feeder stream where it enters the lake.

I have good reason to remember this spot well for during the TV South Pro-Celebrity fly fishing competition it played a big part in the final result. During the morning session local expert Brian Harris had been drawn to partner Leonard Parkin whilst Jack Charlton and I were drawn together.

In blazing sun and an algae coloured lake, Jack and I struggled for no reward in the two-hour morning session. Meanwhile Brian and Leonard came in with twenty-two fish topped by a six pounder way ahead of the rest. It didn't take us long to figure out their tactic, which was to anchor the boat in the mouth of the feeder stream and to cast their flies up into the channel close to the mesh of the barrier put there to stop fish from escaping up into the stream. It was now obvious that lots of fish were shoaled up there to get away from the thick suspended algae. Naturally the oxygen content was higher where the stream came in.

Jack, as ever the perfect competitor, gave me a little team talk during the break, and made sure that our boat would be first there at the stream entrance for the second half. Somehow we managed to sneak in before Roger Daltrey and Taff Price secured the plum position.

As often happens the fish had gone off in the heat of the midday sun. Eventually, Jack caught one on a Black Chenille lure and a sinking fly line. I changed up to a floating line, put on a leader of 4lb nylon and tied on a Size 10 Superla Brown Nymph with an orange hackle and light leading.

The method was to cast out into the channel and to wait until the nymph hit bottom. Then with the slowest of slow figure of eight retrieves I began to inch the nymph

A view looking up the picturesque Bayham Lake, Kent.

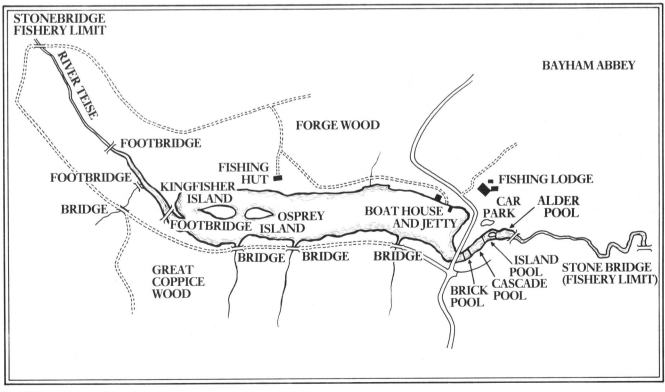

STONEBRIDGE FISHERY LIMIT

RIVER TEISE

BAYHAM ABBEY

FORGE WOOD

FOOTBRIDGE

FOOTBRIDGE

FISHING HUT

KINGFISHER ISLAND

FISHING LODGE

BRIDGE

FOOTBRIDGE

OSPREY ISLAND

BOAT HOUSE AND JETTY

CAR PARK

ALDER POOL

GREAT COPPICE WOOD

BRIDGE

BRIDGE

BRIDGE

BRICK POOL

CASCADE POOL

ISLAND POOL

STONE BRIDGE (FISHERY LIMIT)

BAYHAM LAKE

133

along. At first I had one or two tiny plucks that I missed. Then I started to watch just the end of my floating line. As soon as it moved even an inch I struck and nine times out of ten hooked a good trout. In the end I had sixteen rainbows to 4¼lb, and Jack finished with four to give us a team weight for twenty fish of nearly 40lb gaining us a comfortable second position in the match.

Westwood Park Lake

At 60 acres this is one of the largest of the natural trout lakes. During the past forty years it has changed from trout to coarse fishing, then in 1981 back to trout. Now in the ownership of Reg Treble, the water has developed into a first-class trout fishery.

Although some bank fishing is possible this water is best fished from a boat and there are forty good-sized fibreglass punts provided. During the cold water of early or late season, anchoring is certainly the favoured method and produces good catches.

However, in summer this lake does have some marvellous fly hatches. The buzzers are large and to imitate them you need a Size 10 hook which is about right for the sedges are very plentiful. I once shared a boat here with Gareth Edwards of Welsh rugby fame, and on that occasion we needed to change from lures to small flies when a tremendous hatch started.

Fishing at anchor can of course be a bit of a hit and miss affair and you will not always drop straight onto the fish. I remember having to move five or six times before taking my first fish on one trip, but when it came it was a bright silver 3lb rainbow.

A spot I favour is at the far corner of the dam by the old black hut. A weed bed extends out from the shallows with a reed-fringed bank running away from the dam. This little bay where the shallows drop into deeper water always holds good fish.

Fish imitating lures work very well simply because the lake holds a big head of roach. A fair proportion of trout feed on fry throughout the season and not just at the back end as happens at some waters. Lures such as the Appetizer, Jack Frost, Baby Doll and Missionary all work well, as do white Dog and Frog Nobblers.

The deepest water I have found at Westwood lies out from the dam, but even then it is no more than 12ft (3.65m) at the most. For this reason fast sinking fly lines

Remember these spots when you visit Bayham and keep this slow nymph method in mind if the water is cloudy, as it often can be. It is a fact that if you retrieve your fly or lure too fast in coloured water the trout just don't have a chance to see it. Bayham's records include a rainbow of 12lb 3oz and a brown of 4lb 6oz.

Gareth Edwards and Bob Church shared this fabulous all rainbow catch at Westwood Park.

are a waste of time and a slow to medium sink rated line is all you require for the deepest fishing.

On such a large shallow water it is a good idea to take full advantage of the boats, for many anglers never bother to give traditional drifting a try unless they are on a reservoir or loch. Westwood lends itself perfectly to short line fishing with a team of wet flies and I would go as far as saying it can be the deadliest way of taking trout there. The conditions you need are an overcast day and warm strong breeze. You will need to take your own boat drogue to steady the drift and the style entails a fair amount of rowing back up the wind, but I guarantee you will catch a lot more trout than you would at anchor.

Flies for drifting here include the Claret and Mallard, Invicta, Fiery Brown, Golden Olive, Greenwell's Glory, Olive and Ginger Quills, Soldier Palmer, Hackled Wickham and Grenadier. Also try a Butcher or a Dunkeld on the point with a fairly fast retrieve.

The lake lies a short distance from the M5 motorway near Droitwich and is the largest water in Worcestershire.

15 The Small Fisheries

Apart from the big reservoirs, small fisheries as they are termed have made good trout fishing available in areas where previously there was none at all. These waters, which can be anything from a quarter of an acre up to a chain of small pools consisting of 30 acres and more have sprung up throughout the country. They have certainly helped recruit many new fly fishers who have later developed into fly fishers who appreciate all the different types of water.

The one great asset of the small fisheries is that in comparison to the larger waters, their stocking policies are more easily managed. What usually happens is that stocking is done prior to the fishery opening in the morning which is usually at the civilised time of 9 a.m. If, for example, a total catch for the particular pool on the previous day was forty fish, then forty new fish will be stocked. This way each visitor has an equal chance.

The main attraction at many of the small fisheries is the chance of hooking a large specimen in excess of 5lb. Some waters have built up a reputation for producing these huge specimens with Avington in Hampshire leading the way. If you are to avoid the smaller stock fish a specialised approach is needed.

Avington is a must, so too are Nythe Lake, which again is in Hampshire and Church Hill Farm at Mursley in Buckinghamshire.

Avington

Just as we have a Division I in football with clubs of the calibre of Liverpool leading the way, we have a similar situation in trout fishing. Without any doubt Avington has led the way since the early 1970s in the big trout stakes. For double figure specimens no other fishery comes near to touching it.

The British Record rainbow trout at 19½lb caught by Alan Pearson was an Avington giant as was an even larger fish of 20lb 5oz which he discounted as it was foul hooked in the cheek. My best from Avington was 16¾lb, followed by one of 15½lb and a few lesser doubles. If this is not enough to wet a fisher's appetite there have been browns to 13½lb, the biggest ever cheetah trout at 9lb 14oz, and the American brook trout record of 5lb 8oz, which again fell to Alan Pearson. This big fish reputation is expected to continue thanks to Sam Holland who is ably supported by his manager Roy Ward.

There are three pools at Avington which total nearly seven acres. Avington has an annual turnover of 9,000 trout with a minimum weight of 2lb. A day ticket allows for a four fish limit, the record such catch is 48½lb. Because such large trout are to be expected it is no good fishing here with delicate tackle. A fairly powerful rod between 9¼–10½ft (2.8–3.2m) is fine. I like a number 8 weight forward fly line which helps when casting the leaded nymphs, which are an absolute must. I would

135

A view of Avington's top lake.

never go below a 6lb breaking strain leader and three metres of nylon direct from the spool. A fishing waistcoat with a marrow spoon priest goes in one pocket, a wallet full of my favourite leaded nymphs and a hook sharpener in another, a few spools of nylon, a fishing hat, my Polaroids and a large framed deep mesh landing net completes the outfit. Now I am ready to go big fish hunting without being over-burdened with tackle.

The great thrill of fishing at Avington is that for most of the time the water is gin clear and the fish can be seen and stalked. Because the margins are quite deep the leaded nymph floating line combination catches a lot of trout. The whole secret of success is to cast and to bring the nymph quickly close to the fish's vision and at the exact depth he is cruising at. The 'jiggle jiggle' retrieve should be in the same direction as the fish is swimming.

It doesn't pay when visual fishing to wait for arm-stopping takes because very often these fish take the nymph into their mouths and then eject it without anything being registered on the retrieving hand. If, however, you keep a careful eye on your nymph and then watch the trout actually take it into its mouth, an immediate reaction strike sets the hook home. Exciting fishing indeed.

The three pools have one thing in common, a deep hole at each end. Unquestionably these are the hotspots of each pool and should be given a fair trial before moving on. On the far side of the middle pool there is a long deep bank and the whole length is perhaps the most productive on the fishery.

Do these big fish fight well? I must admit this varies considerably. A 15½-pounder in the middle lake took my full fly line and twenty-five yards of backing in seconds. It certainly was a fine fish and put up a great fight. A 12½lb rainbow fought similarly and so did a 9¾lb fish. I can also remember though the rather disappointing fight of my heaviest, the 16¾lb fish.

While host to a party of American tourist anglers some good fish were being landed and I had taken a perfect silver 6¼lb rainbow. Just before midday I saw a fish cruising along the weeds of the far bank in the top lake. I pitched my Westward Bug to land three yards in front of it, watched the bug sink and saw the trout take. I had hooked one of the big cheetah trout and for ten minutes I could do nothing with it but hope he would soon tire. Eventually I landed a prime 7½lb cheetah, the fifth largest ever caught.

A second visit of note was a day spent with Alan

Pearson making a television film. We were late arriving and the fishery was lined with anglers. I remember Alan losing a big fish soon after starting. When he moved I stayed and fished on. With the cameras rolling, I managed an 8½lb rainbow then another of 9¾lb, this last one performing well for the cameras. Alan and I walked to the end of the top lake, and by now most anglers were resting and having their sandwiches. As we reached the top corner of the lake we both spotted a good fish at the same time. The fish was lying close to the overflow and high in the water facing the flow of water which sped up before running out of the lake. Pesumably food items were being washed his way and he was picking them off as they passed by.

My first cast was poor but I didn't frighten him. My second attempt was spot on landing just a yard beyond his nose. I drew the bug across his nose quite fast and had an immediate solid take. After a spirited fight on tackle meant for larger fish, I landed a fine brook trout. This was back in 1978 when the record for this species was only just over 3lb. Alan was more aware of the situation than I was and made me go back to the lodge to weigh the fish properly which was sound advice as the fish turned out to be the new English brook trout record at 3lb 4½oz.

My favourite leaded nymphs for Avington include Walker's Mayfly, Damselfly, Green Beast, Black Wonderbug, the Nettie Superla Bug, Wilshaw's Wobbling Corixa, and my own invention, the Westward Bug which caught my best rainbow, brook and cheetah. For those who tie their own leaded nymphs, don't overdo the lead so as to make them uncastable.

The Westward Bug dressing:
Hook Size 8 longshank bronze.
Tying silk brown or black.
Weighted underbody of lead foil from a wine bottle top.
Body dubbed on marabou brown feather fibre and ribbed with orange floss.
Shellback brown feather fibre.
Hackle Honey coloured cock hackle fibres, beard only.

Nythe Lake

The rich alkaline chalky soil of Hampshire is a superb base for trout rearing and trout fisheries. Dave Riley is in the position of having both in a lovely spot situated at the source of the River Arle, a tributary of the world famous River Itchen. Nythe Lake is springfed and stocked with large rainbows, some big browns and of late, some very big tiger trout. The tiger trout, being a brown and brook trout cross breed, looks impressive, but it is not too easy to catch inheriting its behaviour from its wily brown ancestors.

Nythe is a special place with only four anglers a day being allowed to fish and so costs a little more to fish than other waters. I have fished Nythe when it has been gin clear and then Avington style tactics should be adopted. In warm weather algae sometimes colours the water, and then different methods pay off.

I fished on such a day with Dave Allen and soon we realised that some sort of sinking line was needed. The answer we thought was to fish our lures deep over the clear gravel bottom but after spending a fair time with the well known lure patterns we were failing miserably. It finally dawned that perhaps they had seen them all before and were too suspicious to take. We searched through the fly boxes and sorted out a couple of those creations you sometimes tie and then think what a waste of time that was. Mine was a brown chenille body with a big yellow and brown long fibred hackle at the head. Dave's was a horrid multi-coloured job. You would never have believed the change of fortunes, it was quite incredible. We landed eight rainbows with none under 3½lb in the next hour.

The well-travelled angler Trevor Housby fishes Nythe quite regularly and he assures me it's the best of the lot, which is testimony enough. I am not sure of the exact top weights for the water but they are high, including tigers over 5lb, which is something unheard of elsewhere.

Peter Stone playing a fish in Jubilee Lake at Church Hill Farm.

Church Hill Farm

Church Hill Farm comprises two lakes; Dogleg at 2¾ acres and Jubilee at 8 acres. Both have islands in the centre and are set in scenic Buckinghamshire farmland. The lakes were purpose-built trout waters created by constructing dams across a stream-fed valley. This was the brainchild of owners Tim Daniels and Don Griggs who took their idea a stage further by converting an old barn into a clubhouse serving hot lunches.

Approximately 9,000 fish are stocked annually on a put-and-take basis at an average size of 2lb. Seventy-five per cent are rainbows, twenty per cent browns with brook trout, tiger trout and golden rainbow trout making up the numbers. Apparently this strain came about through a pigment failing. By selecting the most colourful parents a rare and continuing strain has been developed.

There are no coarse fish in the lakes to trouble fly fishers, but there are plenty of stickleback which provide good food for the trout and for the angler to imitate with his lures.

Church Hill is a water where I either do very well or fail completely. My best fish are a 7¼lb rainbow and browns to 4½lb, both of which fell to my Black Chenille lure fished in a different way.

The method now is to fish a floating fly line, a four-yard 6lb leader and a single, Size 8 Black Chenille lure, with a small, soft shot pinched on close to the eye. There needs to be colour in the water and a good wind blowing for the method to work, a situation common during the early part of the season. It is a case of just casting across the wind and letting the wave action do the rest. It's amazing how many more trout you can catch by fishing

deep with this set-up rather than by simply casting and retrieving with a sinking fly line. Surprisingly the best results of all come when the lakes are well attended and are receiving a lot of fishing pressure.

I suppose my favourite spots are fishing out from the dams into the deepest water and long casting with sinking shooting heads and lures does take some very good bags. You need a medium sinker for the small Dogleg lake and a lead coated line for the larger Jubilee lake where there are depths up to 35ft (10.7m).

As the summer wears on, many of the good fish which have been in the water awhile become difficult to tempt. Even so, they still sometimes show themselves in the now very clear water. The Avington style leaded nymph approach can be used, or perhaps best of all, traditional nymph fishing.

It is a time now to risk lighter leaders and nymphs as small as Size 14s and 12s. There are plenty of buzzers and sedges hatching for most of the summer, and the better class of resident trout feed on these regularly. It therefore follows that a nymph presented at the right depth will give you more chance during the general fishing hours.

A final tip, do fish a large White Muddler on a fast sinking head right on dusk straight out from the overflow on the main dam on Jubilee lake. In the past I've found it tempts some good browns which only come onto feed just before dark.

Fishery records for Church Hill are rainbows to 15¾lb, golden rainbows to 10½lb, brown trout to 9lb, a brook trout of 3¼lb and a tiger trout of 2lb 2oz.

Appendix 1
Fly tyings

CORIXA

Buoyant Corixa
Hook: 10–12.
Silk: brown.
Body: plasterzote glued and shaped.
Shell back: pheasant tail feather fibre.
Legs: pheasant tail two or three fibres each side.
Varnish: clear.

Leggy Corixa
Hook: 10–12–14.
Silk: brown.
Body: white wool ribbed silver wire.
Shell back: pheasant tail feather fibre.
Legs: Pheasant tail fibres prominent.
Varnish: clear.

Goose Biot Corixa
Hook: 10–12.
Silk: brown.
Body: silver lurex wound over floss underbody, ribbed silver wire.
Shell back: cock pheasant tail fibres.
Legs: two dyed brown goose biots.
Varnish: clear.

Yellow Bodied Corixa
Hook: 10–12–14.
Silk: brown.
Body: yellow floss or wool, ribbed silver wire.
Shell back: pheasant tail feather fibre.
Hackle: (throat) honey cock fibres.
Varnish: clear.

CHIRONOMIDS

Copydex Bloodworm
Hook: 10–12–14.
Silk: red.
Tail: red copydex.
Body: red floss silk, ribbed silver wire.
Hackle: red.
Varnish: clear.

Green Larvae
Hook: 10–12–14.
Silk: green.
Body: pale green floss, ribbed fine copper wire.
Hackle: light green two turns.
Varnish: clear.

Blae and Black
Hook: 10–12–14.
Silk: black.
Tail: golden pheasant tippet.
Body: black floss, ribbed silver wire.
Hackle: black cock fibres.
Wing: grey starling primary.
Varnish: black.

Black Pennell
Hook: 6–10–12.
Silk: black.
Tail: golden pheasant tippet.
Body: black floss, ribbed silver wire.
Hackle: two or three turns of black cock.
Varnish: black.

Black Midge Pupa (known as Buzzer Nymph)
Hook: 8–10–12–14.
Silk: black.
Tail: white hackle fibres.
Body: black floss, ribbed fine silver wire.
Thorax: peacock herl topped with white hackle fibres.
Varnish: black.

Suspender Buzzer (Goddard)

Hook: 10–12–14.
Silk: black.
Tail: white hackle tips trimmed.
Body: vary colours (floss, wool or seal's fur), ribbed, finest wire.
Thorax: peacock herl or grey rabbit.
Head: ball of polystyrene trapped in white stocking material.
Varnish: black.

Brown Marabou Buzzer

Hook: 10–12–14.
Silk: black.
Tail: white marabou trimmed.
Thorax and body: brown marabou dubbed on, fine silver wire ribbing.
Wing cases: white feather fibre.
Head: white marabou fibres.
Varnish: black.

Peter's Emerging Midge

Hook: 10–12–14.
Silk: black.
Body: detached, of heavy nylon.
Thorax and body: peacock herl tied in with clear varnish.
Hackle: medium brown cock two turns.
Varnish: black.

True to Life Midge Pupa

Hook: 10–12–14.
Silk: black.
Tail: white marabou trimmed.
Body: dyed and red feather fibres, ribbed, fine polythene strip.
Thorax: grey rabbit.
Wing cases: brown feather fibre.
Wings: brown goose biots trimmed.
Head: filaments of white marabou.
Varnish: black.

Adult Midge

Hook: 10–12–14.
Silk: brown.
Abdomen: grey brown feather fibre, ribbed stripped hackle stalk.
Thorax: brown marabou.
Wing cases: brown feather fibre.
Hackle: natural red cock.
Varnish: clear.

DAPHNIA

Black Chenille

Hook: 6–8–10 longshank.
Silk: black.
Tail: black cock hackle fibres.
Body: black chenille, ribbed silver tinsel.
Hackle: throat only, black.
Wing: four black cock hackles.
Varnish: black.

Old Nick

Hook: 10–12–14.
Silk: black.
Tail: hot orange hackle fibres.
Body: silver tinsel plamered hot orange hackle.
Hackle: three full turns of hot orange hackle.
Varnish: black.

Whisky Fly

Hook: 6–8–10 longshank.
Silk: red.
Body: silver tinsel, ribbed red silk.
Hackle: hot orange hackle fibres.
Wing: hot orange goat hair.
Varnish: clear.

Mickey Finn

Hook: 6–8–10 longshank.
Silk: black.
Body: silver tinsel.
Hackle: optional mixed red and yellow hackle fibres.
Wing: red goat hair topped with yellow goat hair.
Varnish: black.

Leprechaun

Hook: 6–8–10 longshank.
Silk: black.
Body: fluorescent lime green chenille, ribbed silver tinsel.
Tail: green hackle fibres.
Body: fluorescent lime green chenille, ribbed silver tinsel.
Hackle: green hackle fibres.
Wing: fluorescent green squirrel tail hair.
Varnish: black.

Grenadier

Hook: 10–12–14.
Silk: black.

Body: orange seal's fur ribbed with palmered light brown hackle.
Hackle: two or three extra turns.
Varnish: black.

Teal and Orange

Hook: 10–12–14.
Silk: black.
Tail: orange hackle fibres.
Body: orange seal's fur, ribbed gold wire.
Hackle: orange hackle fibres.
Wing: teal.
Varnish: black.

Orange Muddler

Hook: 6–8–10 longshank.
Silk: black.
Body: gold tinsel.
Wing: orange goat hair or orange marabou.
Head: ball shaped deer hair.
Varnish: black.

Dunkeld

Hook: 8–10–12–14.
Silk: black.
Tail: orange hackle fibres.
Body: gold tinsel palmered with orange hackle.
Hackle: two further turns orange hackle.
Wing: bronze mallard.
Varnish: black.

THE OLIVES

Olive Quill

Hook: 10 to 16.
Silk: olive.
Tail: olive dyed hackle fibres.
Body: stripped peacock eye quill.
Hackle: olive cock.
Wing: starling primary.
Varnish: clear.

June Fly

Hook: 10 to 14.
Silk: olive.
Tag: gold lurex, tied well round the bend.
Body: pastel olive green wool.

Hackle: well marked badger or furnace.
Wing: starling primary.
Varnish: clear.

Greenwell's Glory

Hook: 10 to 16.
Silk: primrose well waxed.
Ribbing: fine round gold tinsel.
Body: same as silk.
Hackle: light furnace.
Wing: starling primary.
Varnish: clear.

Pheasant Tail Nymph

Hook: 10 to 16.
Silk: brown.
Tail: fibres of cock pheasant tail.
Body: same.
Ribbing: copper wire.
Thorax and wing cases: fibres of cock pheasant tail.
Varnish: clear.

Spring Favourite

Hook: 10 to 14.
Silk: black.
Tail: white cock hackle fibres.
Ribbing: fine gold wire.
Body: olive marabou dubbed on.
Thorax: built up olive marabou, then grey mallard feather fibre to form shell back.
Hackle: throat only yellow cock hackle fibres.
Varnish: black.

Peter's Olive

Hook: 12 to 14.
Silk: olive.
Tail: olive hackle fibres.
Body: mixed brown and olive dubbing.
Ribbing: stripped hackle stalk.
Wing: starling primary tied upright.
Hackle: olive cock.
Varnish: clear.

Apricot Poly Spinner

Hook: 12 to 14.
Silk: brown.
Tail: grey mallard flank fibres.
Body: apricot feather fibre.

Ribbing: fine copper wire.
Wing: polypropylene floss.
Thorax: brown dubbing.
Varnish: clear.

CRANE FLY

Crane Fly Dapping Pattern
Hook: 10 longshank.
Silk: brown.
Body: brown feather fibre, ribbed copper wire.
Legs: knotted pheasant tail fibres.
Hackle: natural brown cock long fibres.
Varnish: clear.

Standard Crane Fly
Hook: 10 longshank.
Silk: brown.
Body: brown feather fibre.
Legs: knotted pheasant tail fibres.
Hackle: cree cock.
Wing: Plymouth rock hackle points.
Varnish: clear.

Latex Bodied Crane Fly
Hook: 10 longshank.
Silk: brown.
Under body: section fine feather quill.
Over body: clear latex.
Legs: knotted pheasant tail fibres.
Hackle: blue dun.
Wing: Plymouth rock hackle points.
Varnish: clear.

FRY

Missionary
Hook: 6–8–10–12 longshank.
Silk: black.
Tail: crimson cock hackle fibres.
Body: white chenille, ribbed silver oval thread.
Hackle: throat only, crimson cock.
Wing: silver mallard tied whole.
Varnish: black.

Appetizer
Hook: 6–8–10–12 longshank.
Silk: black.
Tail: mixed orange, green and silver mallard fibres.
Body: white chenille, ribbed silver oval thread.
Hackle: throat only, mixed orange, green and silver mallard fibres.
Under Wing: white marabou.
Over Wing: natural grey squirrel tail hair.
Varnish: black.

Jersey Herd
Hook: 6–8–10 longshank.
Silk: black.
Body: copper or gold tinsel, ribbed similar wire.
Tail and Back: bronze peacock herl.
Hackle: hot orange, occasionally yellow.
Head: peacock herl.
Varnish: black.

Baby Doll Variant
Hook: 6–8–10 longshank.
Silk: black.
Tail and Back: white nylon baby wool.
Body: white chenille.
Hackle: hot orange.
Varnish: black.

Muddler Minnow
Hook: 6–8–10 longshank.
Silk: black.
Tail: oak turkey.
Body: gold tinsel, ribbed gold wire.
Wing: oak turkey.
Head: natural deer hair clipped.
Varnish: clear.

White Marabou Tandem Muddler
Hook: tandem mount on 6–4 longshank.
Silk: black.
Tail: white hackle fibres.
Body: white chenille, ribbed silver oval thread.
Under Wing: white marabou.
Over Wing: blue and black goat hair sparse.
Head: white deer hair clipped.
Varnish: clear.

White Muddler
Hook: 6–8–10 longshank.
Silk: black.
Tail: white swan or goose.
Body: silver tinsel.
Wing: white swan or goose.
Head: white deer hair spun on and clipped.
Varnish: clear.

Squirrel and Silver
Hook: 6–8–10 longshank.
Silk: black.
Tail: crimson wool.
Body: silver candle-lite, ribbed silver wire.
Hackle: silver mallard fibres.
Wing: natural squirrel tail hair.
Varnish: black.

Badger Matuka
Hook: 6–8–10 longshank.
Silk: black.
Tail and Wing: white chenille, one turn orange at throat, ribbed silver oval thread.
Hackle: hot orange.
Varnish: black.

Sinfoil's Fry
Hook: 6–8–10 longshank.
Silk: black.
Under Body: dash of red wool at throat.
Body: clear polythene stretched on.
Wing: silver mallard.
Head: large black varnish with eye painted on.

Jack Frost
Hook: 6–8–10 longshank.
Silk: black.
Tail: crimson wool.
Under Body: white nylon wool.
Over Body: clear polythene stretched on.
Wing: white marabou.
Hackle: three turns white cock, one turn crimson.
Varnish: black.

Mylar Bodied Fry
Hook: 6–8.
Silk: black.
Under Body: floss.
Over Body: silver mylar.
Tail and Back: brown synthetic raffine.
Hackle: crimson fibres.
Head: black varnish with eye painted on.

SHRIMPS & HOGLOUSE

Walker's Shrimp
Hook: 10–12, leaded.
Silk: brown.
Body: mixed green, buff and pink wool.
Hackle: buff cock trimmed.
Shell back: clear varnish, three coats.
Varnish: clear.

Seal's Fur Shrimp
Hook: 10–12.
Silk: brown.
Body: brown seal's fur, ribbed silver wire.
Shell back: thick polythene strip.
Varnish: clear.

True to Life Shrimp
Hook: 10–12.
Silk: brown.
Body: olive and brown marabou.
Shell back: strip thick polythene, ribbed silver wire.
Legs: olive feather fibre.
Varnish: clear.

True to Life Hoglouse
Hook: 10–12.
Silk: brown.
Body: natural hare's fur dubbed on.
Hackle: short brown partridge laid over back.
Rib: gold wire.
Back and Tail: grey mottled feather fibre.
Varnish: clear.

DRAGON & DAMSEL FLIES

Dragonfly Nymph
Hook: 6–8 longshank.
Silk: olive.
Tail: three dyed brown goose biots.
Body: dark olive seal's fur, ribbed gold wire.

Thorax: dark olive seal's fur.
Wing cases: olive feather fibre.
Head: brown partridge.
Eyes: melted 30lb breaking strain nylon.
Varnish: clear.

Leaded Damsel Nymph

Hook: 8–10 longshank.
Silk: brown.
Tail: olive feather fibre.
Body: mixed green, blue and orange wool dubbed on, ribbed brown tying silk.
Hackle: brown partridge.
Varnish: clear.

Dry Blue Adult Damsel Fly

Hook: 8.
Silk: black.
Abdomen: blue lurex wound over 30lb breaking strain nylon.
Thorax: blue feather fibre with black feather fibre shell back.
Wings: two tips of blue dun cock hackle.
Hackle: Plymouth rock.
Eyes: melted 30lb breaking strain nylon.
Varnish: black.

Traditional Damsel Nymph

Hook: 8–10.
Silk: green or brown.
Tail: olive hackle fibres.
Body: olive floss.
Body hackle: olive cock palmered and trimmed.
Thorax: olive floss.
Hackle: olive hen.
Varnish: clear.

Marabou Bodied Damsel Nymph

Hook: 8–10 longshank.
Silk: green.
Tail: olive hackle fibres.
Body: olive marabou dubbed on.
Thorax: dark olive marabou.
Wing cases: light green feather.
Eyes: optional.
Varnish: clear.

Bob's Damsel Nymph

Hook: 8–10 longshank.
Silk: olive.

Tail: two light olive hen hackle tips.
Body: dark olive seal's fur, ribbed fine silver wire.
Thorax: dark olive seal's fur with brown feather shellback.
Hackle: grey partridge.
Varnish: clear.

THE SEDGES

Stick Fly

Hook: 8–10 longshank.
Silk: brown.
Body: peacock herl, ribbed copper wire.
Thorax: yellow wool.
Hackle: honey cock.
Varnish: clear.

Brown and Yellow Nymph

Hook: 8–10 longshank.
Silk: brown.
Tail: pheasant tail fibres.
Body: rear portion brown seal's fur, front half yellow seal's fur, ribbed gold wire.
Hackle: yellow cock.
Varnish: clear.

True to Life Sedge Pupa

Hook: 10–12.
Silk: brown.
Body: yellow angora wool, ribbed stripped cock hackle stalk.
Varnish: clear.

Amber Nymph

Hook: 10–12–14.
Silk: brown.
Body: amber seal's fur.
Thorax: brown seal's fur.
Shell back: grey feather fibre.
Hackle: white cock.
Varnish: clear.

Inwood's Ginger Palmer

Hook: 10–12–14.
Silk: brown.
Body: gold tinsel.
Hackle: ginger or light brown, palmered.
Varnish: clear.

Superla Sedge
Hook: 10–12–14.
Silk: brown.
Body: brown superla dubbing, ribbed gold wire.
Hackle: dark brown.
Wing: brown feather fibre.
Varnish: clear.

Latex Grub
Hook: 10–12–14.
Silk: brown.
Body: clear latex.
Thorax: brown ostrich.
Hackle: light yellow cock.
Varnish: clear.

Murrough
Hook: 8–10–12 longshank.
Silk: brown.
Body: brown or claret seal's fur, ribbed gold wire.
Hackle: brown cock prominent.
Wing: rolled brown feather fibre.
Antenna: hackle stalks.
Varnish: clear.

Wickham's Fancy
Hook: 10–12–14.
Silk: brown.
Body: gold tinsel.
Hackle: light brown palmered.
Wing: starling.
Varnish: clear.

Mini Muddler
Hook: 10–12.
Silk: black.
Tail: oak turkey.
Body: gold tinsel, ribbed gold wire.
Wing: oak turkey.
Head: spun natural deer hair.
Varnish: clear.

Invicta
Hook: 10–12–14.
Silk: brown.
Tail: gold pheasant crest.
Body: yellow seal's fur, ribbed gold wire.
Hackle: brown palmered.

Throat Hackle: blue jay.
Wing: hen pheasant.
Varnish: clear.

PHANTOM MIDGE

Phantom Larva
Hook: 12–14 longshank nickel.
Silk: brown.
Body: stretched clear polythene.
Hackle: white hen.
Varnish: clear.

Glennon's Phantom Nymph
Hook: 12–14.
Silk: brown.
Body: white ostrich or suede chenille.
Shell back: pastel lightest green feather fibres.
Varnish: clear.

Phantom Pupa
Hook: 12–14.
Silk: brown.
Body: white fluorescent floss, ribbed silver wire.
Thorax: yellow and orange seal's fur.
Breathing filaments: white feather fibre.
Wing cases: brown feather fibre.
Varnish: clear.

LEECHES

Black Leech
Hook: 8–10 longshank.
Silk: black.
Underbody: leaded carrot shape.
Tail: black marabou.
Body: black suede chenille.
Varnish: black.

Olive and Brown Leech
Hook: 8–10 longshank.
Silk: brown.
Tail: olive and brown marabou.
Body: grey rabbit dubbed on.
Thorax: grey rabbit.
Shellback: grey feather over thorax.

Hackle: ginger sparse.
Varnish: clear.

CAENIS

Caenis Silver Nymph
Hook: 16.
Silk: brown.
Body: silver lurex.
Thorax: white fur or wool dubbed on.
Shell back and Antenna: teal feather.
Varnish: clear.

Caenis Nymph
Hook: 16.
Silk: brown.
Body: dubbed white wool or fur.
Thorax: peacock herl.
Hackle: white hen.
Varnish: clear.

Poly Winged Caenis
Hook: 16.
Silk: brown.
Tail: white cock hackle fibres.
Body: white wool, ribbed silver wire.
Thorax: peacock herl.
Wing: poly floss.
Varnish: clear.

No Hackle Caenis
Hook: 16.
Silk: brown.
Tail: white cock hackle tips.
Body: white wool or ostrich.
Thorax: peacock herl.
Wing: white swan or goose.
Varnish: clear.

Caenis Cluster
Hook: 12 longshank nickel.
Silk: brown.
Tail: white cock hackle fibres.
Body: white wool or rabbit fur dubbed on.
Hackle: white cock four equal sections.
Varnish: clear.

Grey Duster
Hook: 16.
Silk: brown.
Tail: cream hackle tips.
Body: grey rabbit fur dubbed on.
Hackle: well marked badger.
Varnish: clear.

Tups Indispensable
Hook: 16.
Silk: black.
Tail: grey cock hackle fibres.
Body: yellow mohair or floss.
Thorax: mixed cream and crimson seal's fur.
Hackle: grey cock.
Varnish: black.

SNAIL

Black Floating Snail
Hook: 10–12–14.
Silk: black.
Body: spun on black deer hair trimmed to shape.
Varnish: black.

Natural Deer Hair Snail
Hook: 10–12.
Silk: brown.
Body: natural deer hair spun on and trimmed to shape.
Varnish: black.

Black and Peacock Spider
Hook: 10–12–14.
Silk: black.
Body: bronze peacock herl, ribbed silver wire.
Hackle: three turns of long fibred black hen.
Varnish: black.

Clarkson's Deer Hair Snail
Hook: 10–12.
Silk: brown.
Body: natural deer hair spun on and trimmed.
Underbody: brown raffine.
Varnish: clear.

Grafham Snail
Hook: 10–12–14.
Silk: black.
Body: black suede chenille, ribbed silver wire.
Shell back: black feather fibre.
Hackle: black cock.
Varnish: black.

MAYFLY

Straddle Bug Mayfly
Hook: 8–10 longshank.
Silk: brown.
Tail: pheasant tail feather fibre.
Body: yellow or green floss, ribbed silver oval thread.
Hackle: mallard breast feather dyed olive or yellow, highlight with a touch of orange hackle.
Varnish: clear.

Mask Mayfly
Hook: 8–10 longshank.
Silk: brown.
Tail: pheasant tail feather fibre.
Body: yellow floss or wool, ribbed with copper wire.
Hackle: mallard feather dyed yellow.
Varnish: clear.

Bob's Spent Mayfly
Hook: 8–10 longshank fine wire.
Silk: brown.
Tail: pheasant tail feather fibres.
Body: cream floss, ribbed silver wire.
Wings: two pairs dark olive hackles tied spent.
Hackle: green cock.
Varnish: clear.

Hamill's Killer Mayfly
Hook: 8–10 longshank.
Silk: black.
Tail: black squirrel hair and golden pheasant tippet.
Body: bright yellow chenille.
Wing: silver mallard.
Varnish: black.

Deer Hair Static Spent Mayfly
Hook: 8–10 longshank.
Silk: brown.

Tail: pheasant tail feather fibre.
Body: cream floss, ribbed tying silk.
Wing: natural dark brown deer hair.
Varnish: clear.

Palmered Mayfly Nobbler
Hook: 8–10 longshank. Small lead shot pinched on and stuck at eye.
Silk: black.
Tail: cream angora marabou.
Body: cream angora chenille.
Hackle: Plymouth rock palmered.
Head: black varnish shot and paint on eye.

Walker's Mayfly Nymph
Hook: 8 longshank. Leaded underbody.
Silk: brown.
Tail: pheasant tail feather fibre.
Body: angora wool, ribbed tying silk.
Shell back: pheasant tail feather fibre.
Legs: pheasant tail feather fibre.
Varnish: clear.

Wulff Mayfly
Hook: 8–10 longshank.
Silk: brown.
Tail: natural squirrel tail hair.
Body: cream wool, ribbed silver wire.
Wings: natural squirrel tail hair tied spent and forward.
Hackle: light badger.
Varnish: clear.

MISCELLANEOUS

Flying Black Ant
Hook: 12–14.
Silk: black.
Body and Thorax: black tying silk formed and varnished.
Wing: white cock hackle tips.
Hackle: black cock.
Varnish: black.

Drone Fly
Hook: 10–12–14.
Silk: brown.
Body: yellow suede chenille, ribbed tying silk.
Wing: grey cock hackle tips.

Hackle: grey cock edged bright crimson ostrich.
Varnish: clear.

Coch-y-Bonddhu
Hook: 10–12–14.
Silk: brown.
Tag: gold lurex.
Body: bronze peacock herl.
Hackle: medium brown hen.
Varnish: clear.

Hawthorn Fly
Hook: 10–12–14.
Silk: black.
Body: black seal's fur, ribbed clear polythene.
Thorax: black seal's fur.
Hackle: black hen.
Legs: strand of black feather fibre.
Wing: white cock hackle tips.
Varnish: black.

RECENT DEVELOPMENTS

Rat's Tail
Hook: 10–12–14.
Silk: brown.
Tail and Body: orange deer hair laid flat and ribbed with tying silk.
Hackle: dark brown cock.
Varnish: clear.

Disc Head Tube Fly
Hook: tube 2in to 3in.
Silk: black.
Disc Head: plastic cut from lid of 35mm film case.
Body: silver or gold tinsel.
Wing: orange but various colours.
Varnish: black.

Original Flectolite Lure
Hook: 4–6 with a size 14 treble on link at tail.
Silk: yellow.
Tail: elastic band covered in self-adhesive gold flectolite with a flat end to give wobble.
Cheeks: gold flectolite.
Wing: natural squirrel tail hair.

Head: yellow deer hair clipped to ball shape.
Varnish: clear.

Waggy Lure
Hook: salmon double in 6–8.
Silk: black.
Tail: white rubber sand eel section.
Body: silver mylar.
Hackle: hot orange.
Wing: white marabou.
Head: white suede chenille.
Eyes: metal beads from bath plug chain.
Varnish: black.

Frog Nobbler
Hook: 10 medium or longshank.
Silk: black.
Tail: black and white marabou.
Body: gold lurex.
Varnish: black.
(Try many colour variations.)

Dog Nobbler
Hook: 6–8.
Silk: black.
Tail: orange marabou.
Body: orange chenille, ribbed silver wire.
Head: peacock herl.
Varnish: black.
(Try many colour variations.)

Standard Tube Fly
Hook: tube 2in to 4in.
Silk: black.
Body: silver mylar.
Wing: black goat or skunk.
Varnish: black.

White Tandem with Fluorescent
Hook: tandem mount on 6 longshank.
Silk: black.
Body: silver mylar.
Wing: four white cock hackles with green fluorescent material worked in.
Hackle: crimson.
Varnish: black.

Three Hook Lure
Hook: three mounted on size 8 longshank.
Silk: black.
Tail: yellow cock fibres.
Body: silver tinsel.
Wing: four large yellow cock hackles.
Hackle: yellow cock.
Varnish: black.

Sideways Fry
Hook: 6–8.
Silk: black.
Under Body: ethafoam.
Over Body: silver mylar and green raffine.
Head: black varnish with eyes.

Deer Hair Perch Fry
Hook: 4–6 longshank.
Silk: brown.
Tail: crimson hackle fibres.
Body: natural deer hair clipped to shape, coloured with water-proof pens.
Varnish: clear.
(See chapter for details.)

Buoyant Baby Doll
Hook: 4–6–8.
Silk: black.
Body: white ethafoam strip.
Tail and Back: white ethafoam.
Varnish: black.

Sting-in-the-Tail Nailer
Hook: 6 with size 16 treble.
Silk: black.
Body: copper lurex, ribbed copper wire.
Under Wing: crimson goat hair.
Over Wing: brown goat hair.
Hackle: crimson cock.
Varnish: black.

American Mylar Fry Brown Trout
Hook: 6–8 longshank.
Silk: black.
Tail: marabou.
Under Body: acetate floss (special application, see chapter).
Over Body: mylar, painted and varnished.

American Mylar Fry Brook Trout
Hook: 6–8 longshank.
As above with different markings painted on.

American Mylar Fry Shad
Hook: 6–8 longshank.
As above with different markings painted on.

Bullet Minnow
Hook: 6–8 longshank.
Silk: black.
Body:
    Top layer: brown calf tail hair.
    Bottom layer: white calf tail hair tied in and swept back.
Clear varnish over head part and all eyes.

Chamois Leather Leech
Hook: 6–8 longshank.
Silk: brown.
Tail: chamois leather cut circular.
Body: brown dubbing mixture.
Hackle: brown cock.
Eyes: metal bath plug chain beads.
Varnish: clear.

Soldier Palmer
Hook: 10–12–14.
Silk: brown.
Tail and Body: red wool.
Hackle: palmered light brown cock with an extra turn at head.
Varnish: clear.

Red Tailed Wickhams
Hook: 10–12–14.
Silk: brown.
Tail: red floss fluorescent.
Body: gold lurex.
Hackle: palmered light brown cock with an extra turn at the head.
Varnish: clear.

Brian Gent's Bob Fly
Hook: 10–12–14.
Silk: green.
Tail and Body: fluorescent lime green wool.
Hackle: palmered light brown with an extra turn at the head.
Varnish: clear.

Goldie

Hook: 6–8–10 longshank.
Silk: black.
Tail: yellow cock hackle fibres.
Body: gold tinsel, ribbed gold wire.
Hackle: yellow cock.
Under Wing: yellow goat hair.
Over Wing: black goat hair.
Varnish: black.

Green Beast

Hook: 6–8 longshank, leaded.
Silk: brown.
Tail: green feather fibre.
Body: green floss, ribbed silver wire.
Hackle: light partridge.
Varnish: clear.

Brer Rabbit Nymph

Hook: 6–8 longshank, leaded.
Silk: brown.
Tail: brown feather fibre.
Body: brown seal's fur.
Thorax: grey rabbit.
Hackle: partridge.
Varnish: clear.

Westward Bug

Hook: 6–8 longshank, leaded.
Silk: brown.
Body: brown marabou, ribbed orange floss.
Hackle: honey.
Shell Back: grey or brown feather fibre.
Varnish: clear.

Appendix 2

List of reservoirs

Blagdon, Somerset.
Tickets available from the Bristol Waterworks Company, Chew Stoke, Bristol. Telephone Chew Magna (027589) 2339.

Rutland Water, Nr Oakham.
The fishing lodge is at Whitwell, where permits may be purchased. Telephone Empingham (078086) 770.

Grafham Water, Nr Buckden.
The fishing lodge is at West Perry village.

Lough Mask and Lough Carra.
Fishing free.

Chew Valley Lake, Nr Bristol.
For further details contact the Bristol Waterworks Company, Woodford Lodge, Chew Stoke, Nr Bristol. Telephone Chew Magna (027589) 2339.

Loch Watten, Caithness.
For further information write to the Caithness Tourist Centre, Whitechapel Road, Wick, Caithness.

Pitsford Reservoir, Nr Northampton.
For further details telephone Walgrave St Peters (0604) 826350.

The Queen Mother Reservoir, Nr Datchet.
For bookings contact Roger Haynes, Queen Mother Reservoir, Horton Road, Horton, Slough, Berkshire. Telephone Colnbrook (02812) 3605.

Tittesworth Reservoir, Nr Leek, Staffordshire.
Telephone (0538) 834389.

Ardleigh Reservoir, Nr Colchester, Essex.
For day tickets or boat reservations, contact Richard Connell, Administration Block, Ardleigh Reservoir, Treatment Works, Colchester. Telephone Colchester (0206) 230642.

Draycote Water, Nr Rugby.
Day tickets can be obtained through Kite's Hardwick Filling Station near the main gates on the A426. Telephone Rugby (0788) 812018.

Eyebrook Reservoir, Nr Corby.
For day and boat bookings telephone Rockingham (0536) 770264.

Ringstead Grange, Northamptonshire.
For tickets telephone Wellingborough (0933) 622960.

Horseshoe Lake, Gloucestershire.
Location near the village of South Cerney off Wildmoor Lane. Telephone Cirencester (0285) 861034.

Lechlade Trout Fishery, Nr Lechlade.
For information or tickets telephone John or Elsa Taylor at Faringdon (0367) 52754.

Leominstead Lake, New Forest, Hampshire.
For bookings telephone Leo or Rosie Jarmal on Lyndhurst (042128) 2610.

Bayham Lake, Kent.
Bayham is a day-ticket water. For reservations telephone John Parkman at Tunbridge Wells (0892) 890276.

Westwood Park Lake, Worcestershire.
For reservations telephone Reg Treble at Droitwich (0905) 778904 (daytime), or (0902) 700202 (evenings).

Avington, Nr Itchen Abbas, Hampshire.
For bookings telephone Itchen Abbas (096278) 312.

Nythe Lake, Nr Alresford, Hampshire.
For bookings, telephone Dave Riley at Alresford (096273) 2776.

Church Hill Farm, Mursley, Buckinghamshire.
For bookings telephone Mursley (029672) 524.

Index